عِيدُ الِاسْتِقْلَال
çiidu -l- istiqlaal
Independence Day

ابْن
'ibn
son

فَنُّ الْخَطّ
fan-nu -l- *kh*aṭ-ṭ
calligraphy

قِيثَارَة (غِيتَار)
qii*th*aarah (*gh*iitaar)
guitar

تَلْعَبُ كُرَةَ السَّلَّة
talçabu kurata -s-sal-lah
she plays basketball

لَيْل
layl
night

The free online audio recordings for pronunciation practice may be accessed as follows:

Type the following URL below into your web browser.

https://www.tuttlepublishing.com/arabic-picture-dictionary

For support, email us at info@tuttlepublishing.com

ARABIC PICTURE DICTIONARY

LEARN 1,500 KEY ARABIC WORDS AND PHRASES

Islam Medhat Farag

TUTTLE Publishing

Tokyo | Rutland, Vermont | Singapore

Contents

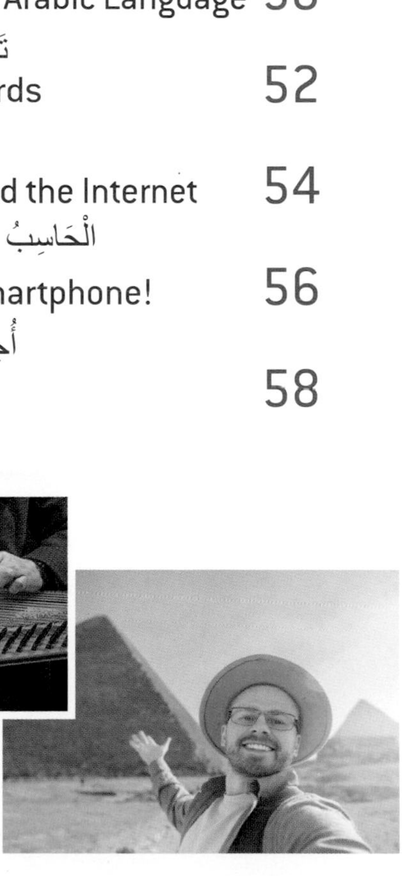

A Basic Introduction to Arabic

This dictionary is an invaluable tool to help you learn and develop your Arabic vocabulary—the key to language proficiency. To help you make the most of this dictionary, the following is a brief overview of the basic features of the Arabic language.

1. Why is learning Arabic worth it?
Arabic is an important language to learn, as it opens up communication with millions of people across the globe and can lead to numerous employment opportunities. With 22 countries officially recognizing Arabic as their first language—including Egypt, the United Arab Emirates, Qatar, Iraq, Saudi Arabia and Morocco—Modern Standard Arabic is spoken by 275 million people, ranking it the fifth most widely spoken language in the world. It is also one of the six official languages of the United Nations. Finally, the US State Department has identified it as a strategically critical language. By improving your knowledge of Arabic vocabulary through this dictionary, you can also gain a deeper understanding of the Arabic world and its culture.

2. Modern Standard Arabic (MSA) and Arabic Dialects
Learning about Arabic dialect variations is essential to effectively communicating with Arabic speakers from different regions and comprehensively understanding the language and culture. There are two main varieties of Arabic: Modern Standard Arabic (MSA), also called **Fuṣḥaa**, and Arabic dialects, called **çam-miy-yah**. MSA is the standard variety. It is mainly used in official documents and writing. People in all Arabic-speaking countries universally understand it—it is the language of media, literature, and formal settings. On the other hand, Arabic dialects are specific to certain regions or countries, reflecting the cultural and social diversity of the Arab world. These dialects are used in daily conversations and informal settings. For example, the Egyptian dialect (**Maṣri**) is spoken in Egypt, whereas the Levantine dialect (***Sh*aamii**) is spoken in Syria, Jordan, Lebanon and Palestine.

This dictionary primarily presents MSA, the standard Arabic language, to facilitate everyday communication so you can be widely understood by Arabic speakers from different regions. Nonetheless, sometimes dialectical synonyms are provided in parentheses. For instance, as shown in the example below, you will find the word "computer" translated into MSA, alongside the dialectal synonym in parenthesis. This way, you can enhance your communication skills and adapt to specific contexts and audiences.

computer حَاسِبٌ آلِيّ **ḥaasibun 'aaliy-y (كُمْبْيُوتَر kumbuyuutar)**

Notes on the Writing System

3. The Arabic Script

وَمَنْ يَتَهَيَّبْ صُعُودَ الْجِبَالْ ** يَعِشْ أَبَدَ الدَّهرِ بَيْنَ الْحُفَرْ

أَبُو الْقَاسِمِ الشَّابِّي **abuu 'alqaasim 'a*sh*-*sh*aa-b-biy-y**

"Whoever fears climbing the mountains, lives forever between ditches"

As shown in the poetic line above, the Arabic writing system has some key features that are different from English. First, the Arabic script is written from right to left. When writing it, one should begin on the right side and move toward the left (except when writing numbers).

The second feature is that Arabic is written with cursive letters that are connected together to form words. Note that each cursive letter has three written shapes depending on its position in a word: 1) initial, 2) middle and 3) full/final shape. The initial shape is used at the beginning of a word, whereas the full or the ending shape is used at the end of a word. Let's take the letter ج (**jiim**) as an example.

The initial shape of the letter ج (**jiim**) is جـ
The middle shape of the letter ج (**jiim**) is ـجـ
The full/final shape of the letter ج (**jiim**) is ج or ـج

To connect the letter ج (**jiim**) with the following or preceding letter, note that linking dashes are used.

Note that not all Arabic letters can be joined to a letter coming after it. They are rule-governed, as indicated in the table below. For example, the letter د (**daal**) cannot be connected to the letter coming after it. As such, this letter's shapes are as follows:

The initial shape of the letter د (**daal**) is د (No linking dash)
The middle shape of the letter د (**daal**) is ـد
The full/final shape of the letter د (**daal**) is ـد (Only a linking dash with the preceding letter)

The Arabic Letters Arranged by Their Shape Similarities

Individual Letters	Names	Initial Shape	Middle Shape	Final Shape (Full shape)
ا	ʻalif	ا	ـا	ـا
ل	laam	لـ	ـلـ	ـل
ك	kaaf	كـ	ـكـ	ـك
ب	baaʻ	بـ	ـبـ	ـب
ت	taaʻ	تـ	ـتـ	ـت
ث	*th*aaʻ	ثـ	ـثـ	ـث
ن	nuun	نـ	ـنـ	ـن
ي	yaaʻ	يـ	ـيـ	ـي
ج	jiim	جـ	ـجـ	ـج
ح	ḥaaʻ	حـ	ـحـ	ـح
خ	*kh*aaʻ	خـ	ـخـ	ـخ
س	siin	سـ	ـسـ	ـس
ش	*sh*iin	شـ	ـشـ	ـش
ص	ṣaad	صـ	ـصـ	ـص
ض	ḍaad	ضـ	ـضـ	ـض
ط	ṭaaʻ	طـ	ـطـ	ـط
ظ	ẓaaʻ	ظـ	ـظـ	ـظ
ع	çayn	عـ	ـعـ	ـع
غ	*gh*ayn	غـ	ـغـ	ـغ
ف	faaʻ	فـ	ـفـ	ـف
ق	qaaf	قـ	ـقـ	ـق
م	miim	مـ	ـمـ	ـم
ه	haaʻ	هـ	ـهـ	ـه // ه
و	waaw	و	ـو	ـو
د	daal	د	ـد	ـد
ذ	*thz*aal	ذ	ـذ	ـذ
ر	raaʻ	ر	ـر	ـر
ز	zay	ز	ـز	ـز

Notes on Pronunciation

4. Pronunciation

The Arabic language is phonetic, meaning that each letter of the alphabet corresponds to one sound that is always pronounced the same way. This makes it easy to pronounce unknown words, but also places great emphasis on the correct pronunciation of the letters. Arabic words are spelled exactly as they are pronounced. As a result, how you pronounce words determines how you write them, and vice versa.

The Arabic alphabet has 28 consonants and 6 vowels (3 short vowels and 3 long vowels). The Arabic letters also have diacritics or tone marks added *above* or *below* them to modify their pronounciation. Three other diacritics—**sukuun**, ***sh*ad-dah** and **tanwiin**—are used to mark no vowel, a geminate, or the addition of the ending sound /**n**/, respectively.

5. Short vowels and sukuun diacritics

The short vowel and **sukuun** diacritics are fundamental to pronouncing the consonants. As a rule of thumb, whenever you pronounce a letter, you utter the first consonant sound of the letter's name, followed by the diacritic sound. Let's go over each one of the diacritics.

5.1. The short vowel **fatḥah** = /**a**/

The short vowel called **fatḥah** is represented by adding a small slanted line ◌َ *above* the letter. The **fatḥah** adds the vowel sound /**a**/ as in c**a**t. For example, if the letter **jiim** ج has a **fatḥah** placed above it (جَ), then it is pronounced /**ja**/. The pronunciation consists of the first consonant sound of the letter **jiim**, which is /**j**/, followed by the **fatḥah** sound, which is /**a**/.

5.2. The short vowel **ḍam-mah** = /**u**/

The second short vowel is called **ḍam-mah**, and is written as a small **waaw** ◌ُ *above* the letter. The **ḍam-mah** adds the vowel sound /**u**/ as in sh**oo**t. Your lips should be rounded when you produce this short vowel. For example, if the letter **jiim** ج has a **ḍam-mah** placed above it (جُ), then it is pronounced /**ju**/.

5.3. The short vowel **kasrah** = /**i**/

The third short vowel is called **kasrah** and is written as a small slanted line ◌ِ *below* the letter. The **kasrah** adds the vowel sound /**i**/ as in s**i**t. For example, if the letter **jiim** ج has a **kasrah** placed under it (جِ), then it is pronounced /**ji**/.

5.4. The **sukuun** (no vowel)

The **sukuun** diacritic is written as a small circle ◌ْ *above* the letter. The **sukuun** tells the reader to pronounce the first consonant sound of the letter's name alone. For example, if the letter **jiim** ج has a **sukuun** placed above it (جْ), then it is pronounced /**j**/ without any vowel added.

Now, let's apply these rules in reading words. Let's take the word جَزَرْ , a carrot, as an example. It is pronounced /**jazar**/ جَزَرْ . Let's chunk it to see how it is pronounced. The word جَزَرْ consists of the letter **jiim** + **fatḥah** = /**ja**/ جَ followed by the letter: **zay** + **fatḥah** = /**za**/ زَ and **raa'** + **sukuun** = /**r**/ رْ. So, putting them altogether makes the word pronounced as /**ja-za-r**/.

6. Long vowels

Arabic has three letters that can serve as both consonants and long vowels. These are **'alif** ا, **waaw** و and **yaa'** ي. When any of these three letters comes after a consonant letter with the same corresponding short diacritic, you extend the pronunciation of the short vowel, turning it into a long vowel. For example, if the letter **jiim + fatḥah /ja/** جَ is followed by **'alif**, then the **fatḥah** is extended to become a long vowel, pronounced as **/jaa/** جَا.

The same applies to the long vowel **waaw** و, which extends the **ḍam-mah** sound **/u/** into **/uu/**. For example, if the letter **jiim + ḍam-mah /ju/** جُ is followed by **waaw**, then the **ḍam-mah** is extended to become a long vowel, pronounced as **/juu/** جُو.

Similarly, **yaa'** as a long vowel is the extension of short vowel **/i/**. For example, if the letter **jiim + kasrah / ji/** جِ is followed by **yaa'**, then the **kasrah** is extended to a become a long vowel, pronounced as **/jii/** جِي.

7. The double consonant symbol *sh*ad-dah

The symbol ***sh*ad-dah** is a small w ّ placed above a consonant. This indicates that the consonant sound is geminated, doubling the sound of the consonant letter. To pronounce a letter with ***sh*ad-dah**, you say the first consonant in a geminated letter with **sukuun** (no short vowel added), then say the second doubled letter along with the designated tone mark. Note that the Arabic ***sh*ad-dah** differs from double consonants in English, where the two consonants are typically pronounced as a single sound. For example, the double [**nn**] in the word co**nn**ect is actually pronounced as one /**n**/, and the double [**rr**] in the word co**rr**ect is pronounced as one /**r**/. But in Arabic, these double consonants are pronounced very distinctly as two separate letters, as if you had to say /**con-nect**/ and /**cor-rect**/ in English, with a pause in between the two consonants.

In transliterating the geminated letter, I used a dash between the doubled letter to make it more noticeable for you. In the following examples, the letter **baa** has a ***sh*ad-dah**, which is represented by doubling the letter **b** with a dash in between, or /**b-b**/

طَبَّاخ is pronounced **ṭab-baa*kh*** (a cook); سَبُّورَة is pronounced **sab-buurah** (a board)

8. Tanwiin /-n/

The **tanwiin** is the last diacritic symbol discussed here. It is written either as a double **fatḥah** ً, double **ḍam-mah** ٌ or double **kasrah** ٍ. It is added at the end of nouns or adverbs. When a word has the **tanwiin** added, it means you add the suffix **-an**, **-un**, or **-in** at the end of the word, depending on the vowel diacritic used. **Tanwiin**, as a pronunciation marker, communicates grammatical information, marking a noun case or a part of speech.

Example: كِتَابٌ kitaab***un*** (a book [in a subjective case]); كِتَابًا kitaab***an*** (a book [in a objective case]); كِتَابٍ kitaab***in*** (a book [in a prepositional phrase])

9. Arabic Grammar

Proper grammar is crucial for constructing sentences. I briefly discuss some basic grammar rules you should be aware of when using the dictionary.

9.1 Gender forms of Arabic Nouns

In Arabic, nouns are divided into masculine (m) and feminine (f) categories. Feminine words are typically marked by a **taa' marbuuṭah** symbol at the end, pronounced as /**-h**/.

Typically, most words related to nature (such as earth and sky) and countries (such as America and Egypt) are feminine by default and do not have any masculine counterparts, so no gender markers can be added to them.

Examples: كُرَّاسَة **kur-rasah** (a notebook); سَيَّارَة **say-yaarah** (a car)

Similarly, some nouns are considered masculine by default and have no equivalent feminine counterparts, so no gender markers can be added.

Examples: كِتَاب **kitab** (book); مَكْتَب **maktab** (a disk)

Some nouns, such as professions and animals, have both masculine and feminine versions. By adding a **taa' marbuuṭah** ة / ـة to the end of a masculine noun, it becomes feminine. This adds /**-h**/ at the end.

Examples: a male teacher is مُدَرِّس **mudar-ris** and a female teacher is مُدَرِّسَة **mudar-risah**
a male dog is كَلْب **kalb** and a female dog is كَلْبَة **kalbah**

9.2 Adjectives must agree with the nouns they modify

Adjectives in Arabic follow the nouns they describe and must match the gender and number of the noun. If a noun is feminine, then the adjective must be feminine. To make an adjective feminine, simple add a **taa' marbuuṭah** ة / ـة to it.

Example: a kind male teacher is مُدَرِّس طَيِّب **mudar-ris ṭay-yib** and a kind female teacher is مُدَرِّسَة طَيِّبَة **mudar-risah ṭay-yibah**

Most adjectives in this dictionary are written in the masculine form. If you need to form the feminine version, simply add a **taa' marbuuṭah** ة / ـة /**-h**/ to the end of the adjective.

9.3 Notes on Verbs and Nouns

Note that in this dictionary, almost all verbs are presented in the present tense stem form as indicated by "to + verb."

Example: to play يَلْعَب **/yalçab/.**

Otherwise, it is noted by the corresponding translation. For example, "she plays" corresponds to "تَلْعَب" **/talçab/**.

Also note that plural nouns are categorized into three types: masculine plural, feminine plural, and broken irregular plural, each has its forming rules. The masculine plural is formed by adding ون **waaw** + **nuun** or ين **yaa** + **nuun** to the noun.

Examples: a teacher is مُعَلِّم **muçal-lim**; teachers is مُعَلِّمُون **muçal-limuun**

The feminine plural of words ending with **taa' marbuuṭah** is formed by removing the **taa' marbuuṭah** and then adding **'alif + taa'**.

Examples: a female teacher is مُعَلِّمَة **muçal-limah**; female teachers is مُعَلِّمَات **muçal-limaat**

It is advisable to memorize the irregular plural forms of nouns (called broken plurals) whenever you encounter them.

When using the dictionary, please keep in mind the following:

1. Words are written in the singular form or otherwise noted.
2. Verbs are written in the present stem form "to+ infinitive" or otherwise noted. Make sure you conjugate the verb properly to correspond with the subject pronoun.
3. Nouns and adjectives are written in the masculine form or otherwise noted.
4. You, a subject pronoun, has many forms. For example, you (addressing a male) **'anta** أَنْتَ, you (addressing a female) **'anti** أَنْتِ, and you (addressing plural males) **'antum** أَنْتُمْ. You (masculine) **'anta** أَنْتَ is commonly used or otherwise noted.

10. Full form

Except for certain noun group such as pronouns and prepositions, diacritics is added to the final letter of content words to provide grammar information, marking their functions within a sentence. For example, a noun's final tone mark can indicate whether it functions as the subject or the object of a sentence.

Example: "The boy" in the following sentence ends with **ḍam-mah /u/** and functions as the subject:

الْوَلَدُ يَأْكُلُ التُّفَّاحَ. **'alwaldu ya'kulu tuf-faaḥ** The boy eats the apples.

In the following sentence, "the boy" functions as the object and thus the last tone mark is **fatḥah /a/**:

الْمُعَلِّمُ يُعَلِّمُ الْوَلَدَ. **'almu'al-limu yu'al-limu 'alwalada** The teacher teaches the boy.

10.1 Pause form

Correctly using the grammatical tone marks is challenging for most Arabic native speakers nowadays. To avoid using the wrong tone mark and messing up the intended meaning, Arabic native speakers commonly end all content words with a **sukuun** (which means no vowel added). You should do the same!

Thus, the majority Arabic speakers use the pause form when speaking, meaning that they make every content word end with **sukuun**, as shown in the example below:

الولَدْ يأكلْ التفاحْ. **'alwald ya'kul 'at-tuf-faaḥ** The boy eats the apples

المعلمْ يعلمْ الولَدْ. **'almuçal-lim yuçal-lim 'alwalad** The teacher teaches the boy.

In this dictionary, sentences and phrases are written in their full form. Nonetheless, feel free to practice the pause form by not pronouncing the last tone mark placed on every content word.

11. Transliteration symbols

Another useful feature of this dictionary is that it provides the pronunciation of every word, phrase, and sentence through the use of transliteration symbols, listed in the table on facing page. Despite the challenge of representing the pronunciation of words and sentences through the transliteration symbols, all words and sentences are transliterated accurately, reflecting as possible the corresponding correct pronunciation. Note that while transliteration is a good tool for learning and practicing how to pronounce words, it is highly recommended to listen to the audio recordings and practice reading Arabic words without looking at the transliteration.

Transliteration Symbols of Arabic Alphabet

Arabic letter	Arabic Name	Symbol	Sound
ء	hamzah	‘	Uh[‘]oh
ب	baa‘	b	**b**at
ت	taa‘	t	sa**t**
ث	*th*aa‘	*th*	**th**ree
ج	jiim	j	**j**ar
ح	ḥaa‘	ḥ	(no English equivalent)
خ	*kh*aa‘	*kh*	*kh*aled
د	daal	d	**dad**
ذ	*thz*aal	*thz*	***th***ere
ر	raa‘	r	**r**at
ز	zay	z	**z**oo
س	siin	s	**s**and
ش	*sh*iin	*sh*	*sh*ip
ص	ṣaad	ṣ	**s**aw
ض	ḍaad	ḍ	(no English equivalent)
ط	ṭaa‘	ṭ	(no English equivalent)
ظ	ẓaa‘	ẓ	(no English equivalent)
ع	çayn	ç	(no English equivalent)
غ	*gh*ayn	*gh*	(no English equivalent)
ف	faa‘	f	**f**at
ق	qaaf	q	**c**ool
ك	kaaf	k	**k**it
ل	laam	l	**l**ion
م	miim	m	**m**oney
ن	nuun	n	**n**ap
ه	haa‘	h	**h**ot
و	waaw	w	**w**o**w**
ي	yaa‘	y	**y**ard

Short vowels vs long vowels

Short and long vowels	Pronunciation	Arabic Name	English example
◌َ	a	fatḥah	C**a**t
◌َ + ا	aa	‘alif + fatḥah	Tab (extend the **a** sound a little more, as if you say t**aaa**b)
◌ُ	u	ḍam-mah	p**oo**l
◌ُ+و	uu	waaw + ḍam-mah	z**oo**
◌ِ	i	kasrah	k**i**t
◌ِ + ي	ii	kasrah	Sh**ee**t

This amazing dictionary could not have been done without the support of many great people whose help is invaluable. Many thanks to the Tuttle Publishing team for showing belief and confidence in my work. To **Robert Goforth**, the Tuttle Publishing editor, and **June Chong**, the editorial supervisor, thank you for your assistance, patience, and guidance. Special thanks go to **Mustafa Hamdoun**, my Arabic mentor, for proofreading and providing expert advice on Arabic language-related issues that came up during the development of this dictionary. Many thanks to my outstanding students: **Brenna Callahan** and **Dallas Mercurio** for the audio recordings. Lastly, my deepest gratitude goes to my parents: **Medhat** and **Fatima**; my brothers: **Kareem**, **Sameh**, and **Omar**; and my wife and kids: **Mona**, **Medhat**, and **Tukka**, for their endless support and encouragement! Thank you all!

تَمَّ بِفَضْلِ اللهِ وَبِحَمْدِهِ

نَسْأَلُ اللهَ (تَعَالَى) التَّوْفِيقَ وَأَنْ يَكُونَ هَذَا الْقَامُوسُ عَوْنًا لِكُلِّ مُتَعَلِّمِي اللُّغَةِ الْعَرَبِيَّةِ

1 تَشَرَّفْتُ بِلِقَائِك
tashar-raftu biliqaa'ik
Honored to Meet You

1 أَهْلًا وَسَهْلًا، كَيْفَ حَالُكَ؟
'ahlan wa sahlan, kayfa ḥaaluka
Hello, how are you (m)?

2 أَنَا بِخَيْر. شُكْرًا!
'ana bi*kh*ayr, *sh*ukran
I am fine, thank you!

3 يُقَابِل
yuqaabil
to meet

8 مَاذَا؟
maa*th*zaa
what?

9 رَاضِي
raaḍii
satisfied

10 سَعِيد
saçiid
happy

11 مَسْرُور
masruur
joyful

4 يَا مِدْحَتُ، قَابِلْ فَاطِمَةَ!
yaa Medḥat, qaabil Faaṭimah
Oh [calling] Medhat, meet Fatima.

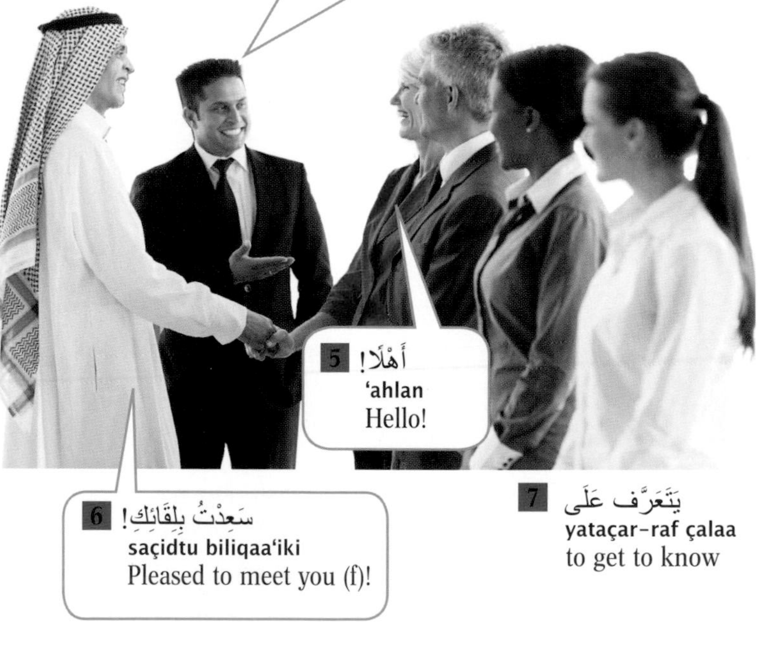

5 أَهْلًا!
'ahlan
Hello!

6 سَعِدْتُ بِلِقَائِكِ!
saçidtu biliqaa'iki
Pleased to meet you (f)!

7 يَتَعَرَّف عَلَى
yataçar-raf çalaa
to get to know

12 يُنَادِي
yunaadii
to call

13 يَتَمَنَّى
yataman-naa
to wish

15 أَهْلًا، اسْمِي مُنَى. مَا اسْمُكَ؟
'ahlan 'ismii Mona. ma smuka
Hi, my name is Mona. What is your name (m) ?

16 اسْمِي مُصْطَفَى حَمْدون. هَذِهِ بِطَاقَتِي.
'ismii muṣṭafaa ḥamduun, haa*thz*ihi biṭaaqatii
My name is Mustafa Hamdoun. Here is my namecard.

14 عَرِّفْ نَفْسَكَ
çar-rif nafsaka
introduce yourself (m)

17 مَعَ السَّلَامَةِ!
maça s-salaamah
Goodbye!

18 اللّه يُسَلِّمُكَ
Allah yusal-limuka (m)
اللّه يُسَلِّمُكِ
Allah yusal-limuki (f)
Response to goodbye.

19 تَجَمُّع
tajam-muç
gathering

Additional Vocabulary

23 اسْم
'ism
name

24 يُقَبِّل
yuqab-bil
to kiss

25 يَبْتَسِم
yabtasim
to smile

26 يَحْضُن
yaḥḍun
to hug

27 يُحَيِّي
yuḥay-yii
to greet

28 يُدَرْدِش
yudardi*sh*
to chat

29 اسْمُ الْعَائِلَة
'ismu -l-çaa'ilah
family name

30 حَضْرَتُكَ
ḥaḍratuka
you (m) polite
حَضْرَتُكِ
ḥaḍratuki
you (f) polite

31 يَعْرِف
yaçrif
to know

32 جِنْسِيَّة
jinsiy-yah
nationality

33 مَا الْأَخْبَار؟
ma-l-'a*kh*baar?
How are things?

34 لِمَاذَا؟
limaa*thz*aa
Why?

35 أَصْدِقَاء
'aṣdiqaa'
friends

36 يُسَلِّمُ بِالْيَدِ
yusal-limu bilyad
to shake hands

37 يُلَوِّحُ بِالْيَدِ
yulaw-wiḥu bilyad
to wave

38 يُرَبِّتُ عَلَى الْكَتِفِ
yurab-bitu çala -l-katif
to pat on the shoulder

39 يَبْدَأُ الْمُحَادَثَةَ
yabda'u-l-muḥaada*th*ah
to start a conversation

40 يُجْرِي مُحَادَثَةً صَغِيرَةً
yujrii muḥaada*th*atan ṣa*gh*iirah
to make a small talk

21 شُكْرًا!
*sh*ukran
Thank you!

22 الْعَفْوُ
'alçafw
You are welcome.

20 زَبُون
zabuun
customer

2 عَائِلَتِي
çaa‘ilatii
My Family

1 ابْن
‘ibn
son

2 ذَكَر
***thz*akar**
male

3 أُنْثَى
‘un*th*aa
female

4 أَطْفَال
‘aṭfaal
children

5 ابْنَة
‘ibnah
daughter

6 وَالِدَان
waalidaan
parents

Additional Vocabulary

25 زَوْجَة
zawjah
wife

26 زَوْج
zawj
husband

27 زَوْجُ الابْنَة
zawju -libnah
son-in-law

28 زَوْجَةُ الابْن
zawjatu -libn
daughter-in-law

29 حَفِيد
ḥafiid
grandson

30 حَفِيدَة
ḥafiidah
granddaughter

31 أَقَارِب
‘aqaarib
relatives

32 نَسِيب
nasiib
brother-in-law

33 نَسِيبَتِي
nasiibatii
my sister-in-law

34 ابْنُ عَمِّي
‘ibnu -çam-mii
my cousin (m)
(paternal side)

35 ابْنَةُ عَمِّي
‘ibnatu -çam-mii
my cousin (f)
(paternal side)

36 ابْنُ خَالِي
‘ibnu-*kh*aalii
my cousin (m)
(maternal side)

37 ابْنَةُ خَالِي
‘ibnatu-*kh*aalii
my cousin (f)
(maternal side)

38 إِخْوَة
‘i*kh*wah
siblings

39 أُسْرَة
‘usrah
family

40 نَفْس
nafs
self

41 صَغِير
ṣa*gh*iir
young (small)

42 مُتَحَمِّس
mutaḥam-mis
enthusiastic

43 يَعْتَقِد
yaçtaqid
to believe

44 جَار
jaar
neighbor

45 كَمْ أَخًا أَوْ أُخْتًا لَدَيْكِ؟
kam ‘a*kh*an ‘aw ‘u*kh*tan ladayki
How many siblings do you (f) have?

46 لَدَيَّ أُخْتٌ وَاحِدَةٌ كَبِيرَة، وَأَخٌ وَاحِدٌ صَغِير.
laday-ya ‘u*kh*tun waaḥidatun kabiirah, wa ‘a*kh*un waaḥidun ṣa*gh*iir
I have one older sister and one younger brother.

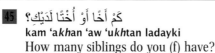

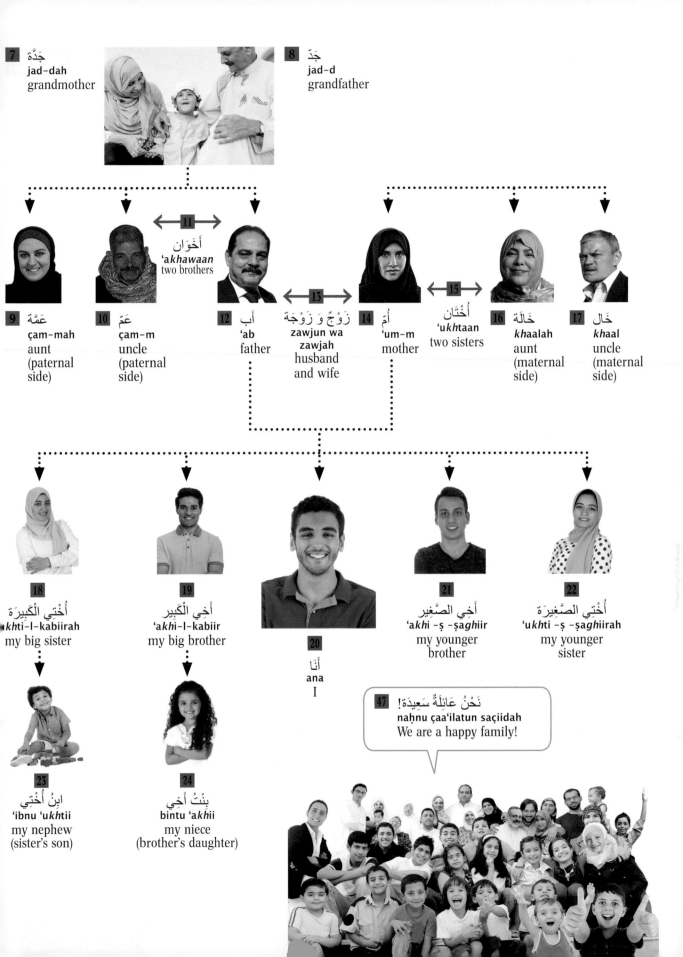

7 جَدَّة
jad-dah
grandmother

8 جَدّ
jad-d
grandfather

9 عَمَّة
çam-mah
aunt (paternal side)

10 عَمّ
çam-m
uncle (paternal side)

11 أَخَوَان
‘a*kh*awaan
two brothers

12 أَب
‘ab
father

13 زَوْجٌ وَ زَوْجَة
zawjun wa zawjah
husband and wife

14 أُمّ
‘um-m
mother

15 أُخْتَان
‘u*kh*taan
two sisters

16 خَالَة
***kh*aalah**
aunt (maternal side)

17 خَال
***kh*aal**
uncle (maternal side)

18
أُخْتِي الْكَبِيرَة
***kh*ti-l-kabiirah**
my big sister

19
أَخِي الْكَبِير
‘a*kh*i-l-kabiir
my big brother

20
أَنَا
ana
I

21
أَخِي الصَّغِير
‘a*kh*i -ṣ -ṣa*gh*iir
my younger brother

22
أُخْتِي الصَّغِيرَة
‘u*kh*ti -ṣ -ṣa*gh*iirah
my younger sister

23
ابنُ أُخْتِي
‘ibnu ‘u*kh*tii
my nephew (sister's son)

24
بِنْتُ أَخِي
bintu ‘a*kh*ii
my niece (brother's daughter)

47 نَحْنُ عَائِلَةٌ سَعِيدَة!
naḥnu çaa‘ilatun saçiidah
We are a happy family!

3 بَيْتِي
baytii
My House

1 غُرْفَةُ الْمَعِيشَة
ghurfatu -l-maçiishah
living room

2 شُرْفَة
shurfah
balcony

3 سُورُ الشُّرْفَة
suuru -sh-shurfah
balcony railing

4 سَقْف
saqf
ceiling

5 مَفَاتِيح
mafaatiiḥ
keys

6 لَوْحَة
lawḥah
painting

7 مِصْبَاح
miṣbaah
lamp

8 كُرْسِيّ
kursiy-y
chair

9 حَائِط
ḥa'iṭ
wall

10 تِلْفَاز
tilfaaz
TV

11 طَاوِلَةُ الْقَهْوَة
ṭaawilatu -l-qahwah
coffee table

12 سَجَّادَة
saj-jaadah
carpet

13 مُكَيِّفُ الْهَوَاء
mukay-yifu -l-hawaa'
air conditioner

14 طَاوِلَة
ṭaawilah
table

15 أَرِيكَة (كَنَبَة)
'ariikah (kanabah)
sofa

16 أَرْض
'arḍ
floor

17 سِتَارَة
sitaarah
curtain

18 نَافِذَة (شُبَّاك)
naafithzah (shub-baak)
window

19 وِسَادَة
wisaadah
pillow

20 سَرِير
sariir
bed

21 غُرْفَةُ النَّوْم
ghurfatu -n-nawm
bedroom

22 غُرْفَة
ghurfah
room

Additional Vocabulary

49 بَيْت
bayt
house

50 شَقَّة
shaq-qah
apartment

51 سَطْح
saṭḥ
roof

52 سَنْدَرَة
sandarah
attic

53 قَبو (بَدْرُوم)
qabu (badruum)
basement

54 مِرْآب (جَرَاج)
mir'aab (garaaj)
garage

55 قَابِسُ الضَّوْء (مِفْتَاحُ النُّور) (الْكُبْس)
qaabisu - ḍ-ḍaw' (miftaaḥu -n-nuur) ('alkubs)
light switch

56 مِقْبَسُ الْكَهْرَبَاء
miqbasu -l-kahrabaa'
electric socket

57 يَا لَهُ مِنْ بَيْتٍ جَمِيلٍ. أَوَدُّ أَنْ أَعِيشَ هُنَا!
yaa lahu min baytin jamiilin 'awad-du 'an 'açiisha hunaa
What a beautiful house. I would love to live here!

23 مَطْبَخ
maṭbakh
kitchen

24 مَايْكْرُوِيف
maykruwiiv
microwave

28 شَفَّاطُ الْمَطْبَخ
shaf-faaṭu -l-maṭbakh
cooker hood

25 خِزَانَةُ الْمَطْبَخ
khizaanatu -l-maṭbakh
kitchen cabinet

29 مِغْلَاة (كِيتِلْ)
mighlah (kiitil)
kettle

26 ثَلَّاجَة (بَرَّاد)
thal-laajah (bar-raad)
refrigerator

30 آلَةُ التَّحْمِيص (تُوسْتَرْ)
'aalatu -t-taḥmiiṣ (tustar)
toaster

27 فُرْن
furn
oven

31 مَوْقِد
mawqid
stove

32 غُرْفَةُ الدِّرَاسَة
ghurfatu -d-diraasah
study room

33 مِصْبَاحُ الطَّاوِلَة
miṣbaaḥu - ṭ-ṭaawilah
table lamp

34 دُرْج
durj
drawer

35 رَفُّ الْكُتُب
raf-fu -l-kutub
book shelf

36 مَكْتَب
maktab
desk/office

44 يُنَظِّف
yunaẓ-ẓif
to clean

45 مِصْعَد
miṣçad
elevator

46 بَاب
baab
door

37 دَوْرَةُ الْمِيَاه (حَمَّام)
dawratu -l-miyaah (ḥam-maam)
bathroom

38 غُرْفَةُ الْغَسِيل
ghurfatu -l- ghasiil
laundry room

47 نَبَاتٌ مَحْفُوظٌ بِوِعَاء (زَرْع)
nabaatun maḥfuuẓun biwiçaa' (zarç)
potted plant

41 دُش
dush
shower

39 صُنْبُور (حَنَفِيَّة)
ṣunbuur (ḥanafiy-yah)
tap

42 حَوْضُ الِاسْتِحْمَام (بَانْيُو)
ḥawḍu -l-istiḥmaam (banyuu)
bathtub

48 يَسْتَحِمّ
yastaḥim-m
to bathe

40 حَوْض
ḥawḍ
sink

43 مِقْعَدُ الْمِرْحَاض
miqçadu -l-mirḥaaḍ
toilet seat

58 كَمْ طَابَقًا فِي هَذَا الْبَيْتِ؟
kam ṭaabaqan fii hathza-l-bayt
How many floors does this house have?

59 أُرِيدُ أَنْ أَسْتَأْجِرَ شَقَّةً.
'uriidu 'an 'asta'jira shaq-qah
I want to rent an apartment.

60 يَا لَهُ مِنْ بَيْتٍ كَبِيرٍ!
yaa lahu min baytin kabiir
What a big house!

61 أَنَا أُرِيدُ أَنْ أَرَى الْمَطْبَخَ.
'ana 'uriidu 'an 'ara-l-maṭbakh
I want to see the kitchen.

4 جِسْمُ الإِنْسَان
jismu -l-‘insaan
The Human Body

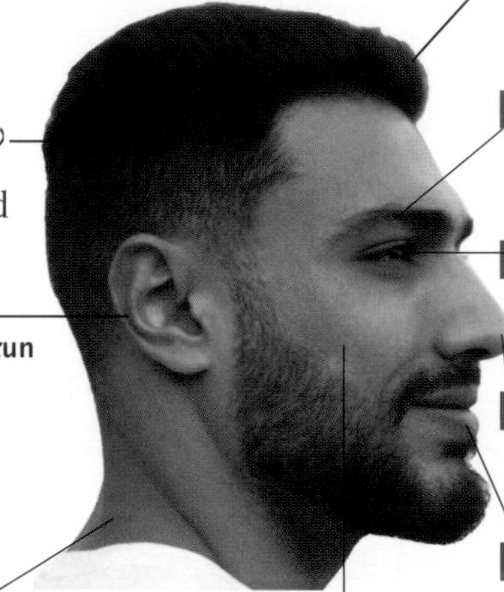

1 رَأْس
ra‘s
head

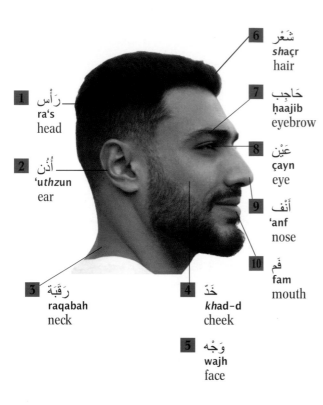

2 أُذُن
‘u*thz*un
ear

3 رَقَبَة
raqabah
neck

4 خَدّ
***kh*ad-d**
cheek

5 وَجْه
wajh
face

6 شَعْر
***sh*açr**
hair

7 حَاجِب
ḥaajib
eyebrow

8 عَيْن
çayn
eye

9 أَنْف
‘anf
nose

10 فَم
fam
mouth

12 أَسْنَان (م. سِنّ)
‘asnaan (s. sin-n)
teeth (s. a tooth)

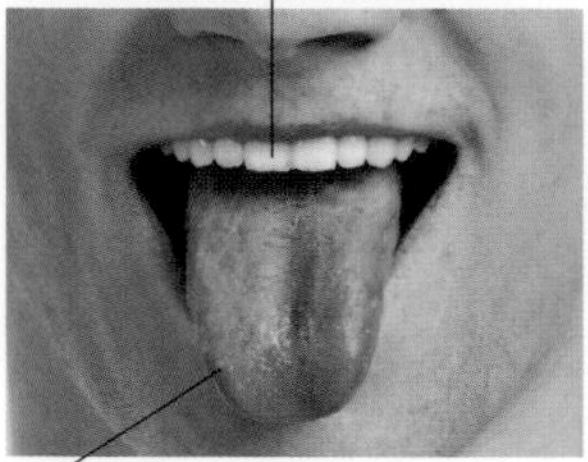

11 لِسَان
lisaan
tongue

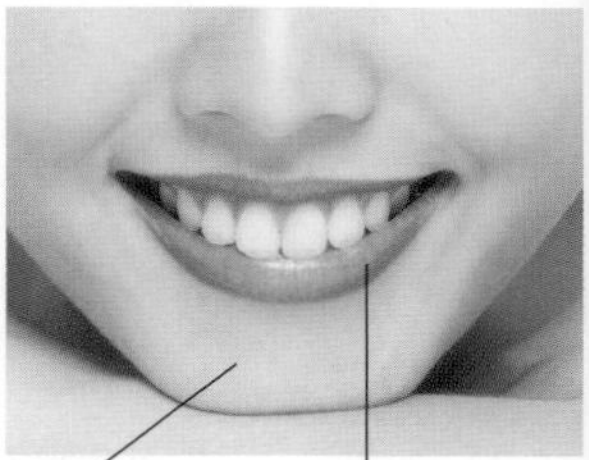

13 ذَقْن
***thz*aqn**
chin

14 شِفَاه
***sh*ifaah**
lips

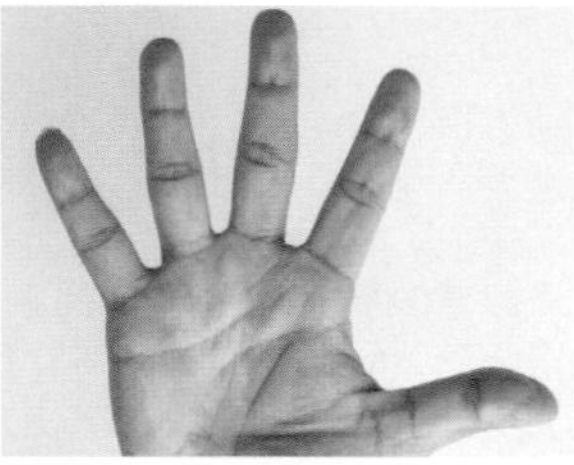

15 أَصَابِع (م.إِصْبَع)
‘aṣaabiç (s. ‘iṣbaç)
fingers (s. a finger)

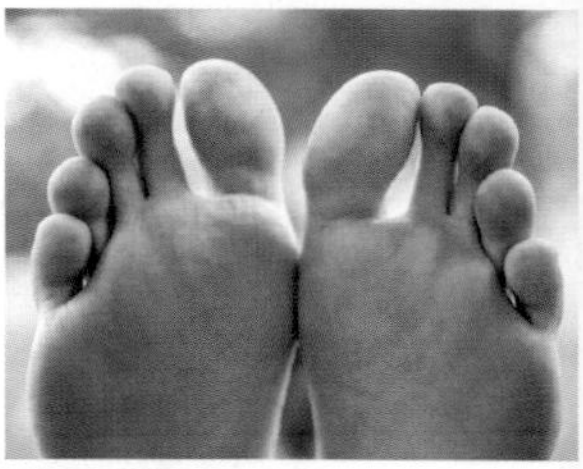

16 أَصَابِعُ الْقَدَم
‘aṣaabiçu -l-qadam
toes

50 كَمْ عُضْوًا فِي جَسَدِكَ يُمْكِنُكَ تَسْمِيَتُهُ؟
kam çuḍwan fii jasadika yumkinuka tasmiyatuh
How many parts of your (m) body can you (m) name?

51 كَيْفَ تَعْتَنِي بِجَسَدِكَ؟
kayfa taçtanii bijasadika
How do you (m) take care of your (m) body?

52 التَّدْخِينُ يَضُرُّ بِصِحَّتِكَ.
‘at-tad*kh*iinu yaḍur-ru biṣiḥ-ḥatika
Smoking is bad for your (m) health.

53 احْرِصْ عَلَى عَدَمِ الإِفْرَاطِ فِي الطَّعَامِ وَالشَّرَاب.
‘iḥriṣ çala çadami l-‘ifraaṭi fi ṭ -ṭaçaami wa *sh*-*sh*araab
Be careful not to eat and drink too much.

54 لَا تَأْكُلِ الْكَثِيرَ مِنَ الْحَلْوَى وَ الْوَجَبَاتِ الْخَفِيفَة.
laa ta‘kuli -l-ka*th*iira mina -l- ḥalwaa wa-l- wajabaati l*kh*a*fii*fah
Don’t eat too many sweets and snacks.

55 لِلْحِفَاظِ عَلَى صِحَّتِكَ؛ يَجِبُ عَلَيْكَ مُمَارَسَةُ اَلرِّيَاضَةِ كُلَّ يَوْم.
lilḥifaaẓi çalaa ṣiḥ-ḥatika, yajibu çalayka mumaarasatu -r-riyaaḍati kul-la yawm
To stay healthy, you should exercise every day.

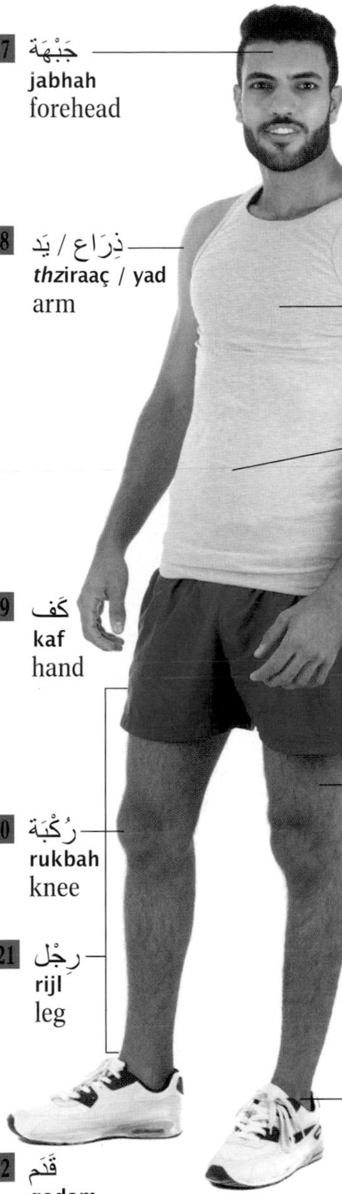

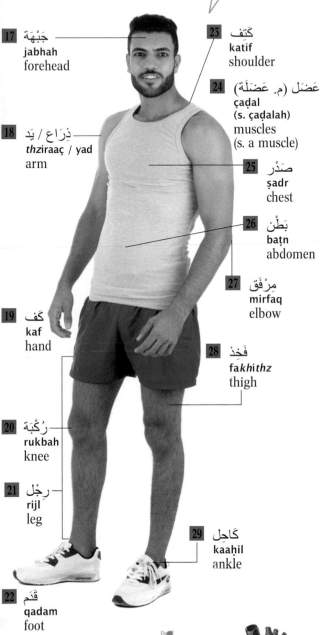

17 جَبْهَة
jabhah
forehead

18 ذِرَاع / يَد
***thz*iraaç / yad**
arm

19 كَف
kaf
hand

20 رُكْبَة
rukbah
knee

21 رِجْل
rijl
leg

22 قَدَم
qadam
foot

23 كَتِف
katif
shoulder

24 عَضَل (م. عَضَلَة)
çaḍal
(s. çaḍalah)
muscles
(s. a muscle)

25 صَدْر
ṣadr
chest

26 بَطْن
baṭn
abdomen

27 مِرْفَق
mirfaq
elbow

28 فَخِذ
fa*khithz*
thigh

29 كَاحِل
kaaḥil
ankle

Additional Vocabulary

36 أَعْضَاء
'açḍaa'
organs

37 الْجِهَازُ الْهَضْمِيّ
'al-jihaazu -l- haḍmiy-y
digestive system

38 الْجِهَازُ التَّنَفُّسِيّ
'al-jihaazu -t-tanaf-fusiy-y
respiratory system

39 الْجِهَازُ الْعَصَبِيّ
'al-jihaazu -l- çaṣabiy-y
nervous system

40 نِظَامُ الْهَيْكَلِ الْعَظْمِيّ
niẓaamu -l-haykali -l-çaẓmiy-y
skeletal system

41 جِلْد
jild
skin

42 دَم
dam
blood

43 الْأَوْعِيَةُ الدَّمَوِيَّة
'al-'awçiyatu -d-damawiy-yah
blood vessels

44 عَظْم
çaẓm
bones

45 شِرْيَان
***sh*iryaan**
artery

46 وَرِيد
wariid
vein

47 صِحَّة
ṣiḥ-ḥah
health

48 مَرَض
maraḍ
illness

49 مَعِدَة
maçidah
stomach

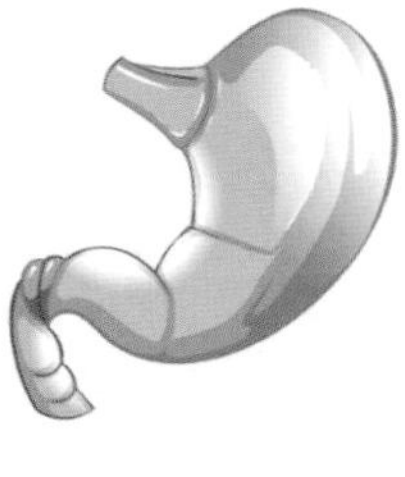

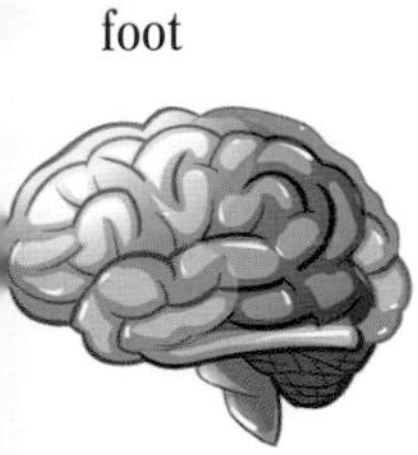

30 مُخّ
mu*kh*-*kh*
brain

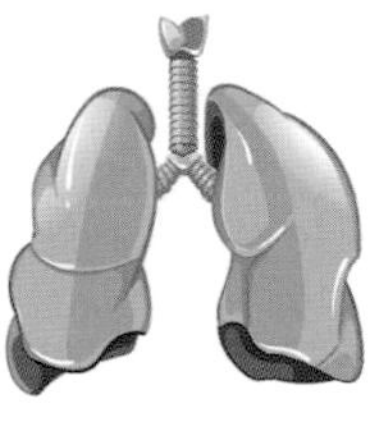

31 رِئَتَان
ri'ataan
lungs

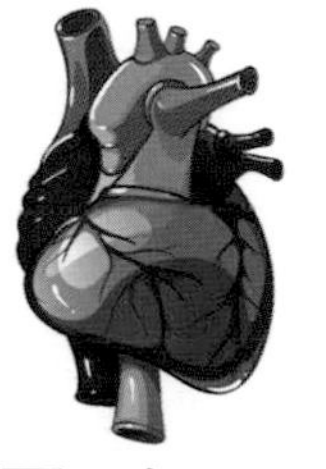

32 قَلْب
qalb
heart

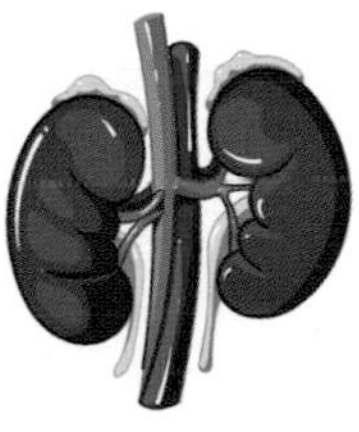

33 كُلَى
kulaa
kidneys

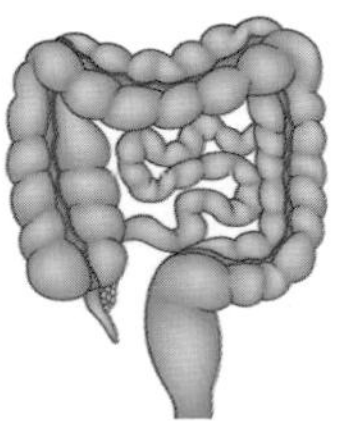

34 أَمْعَاء
'amçaa'
intestines

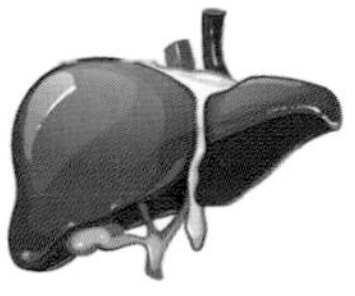

35 كَبِد
kabid
liver

5 الْعَدُّ وَالأَعْدَاد
'alçad-du wal'açdaad
Counting and Numbers

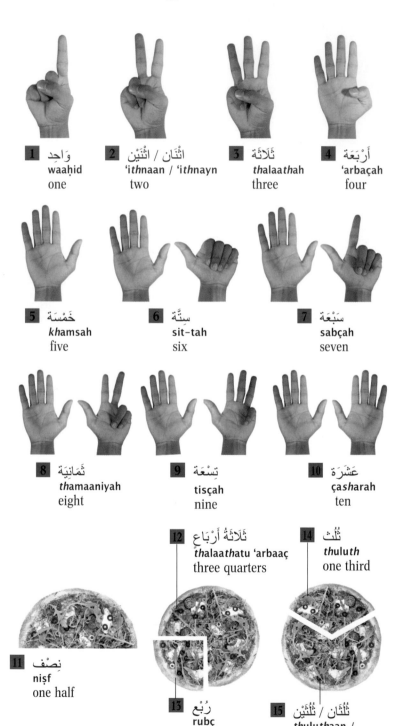

1 وَاحِد
waaḥid
one

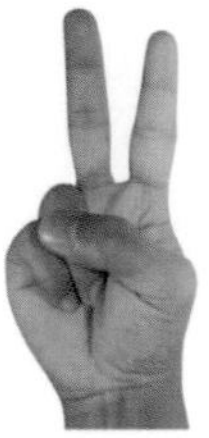

2 اثْنَان / اثْنَيْن
'ithnaan / 'ithnayn
two

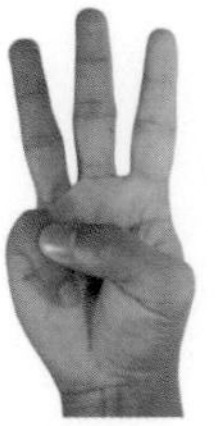

3 ثَلَاثَة
thalaathah
three

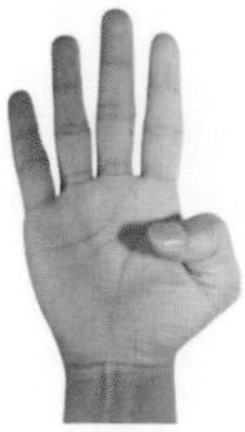

4 أَرْبَعَة
'arbaçah
four

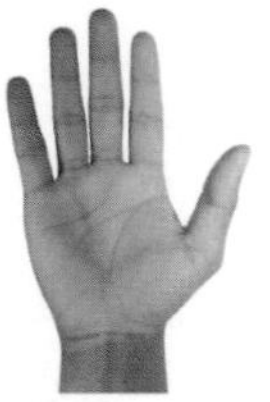

5 خَمْسَة
khamsah
five

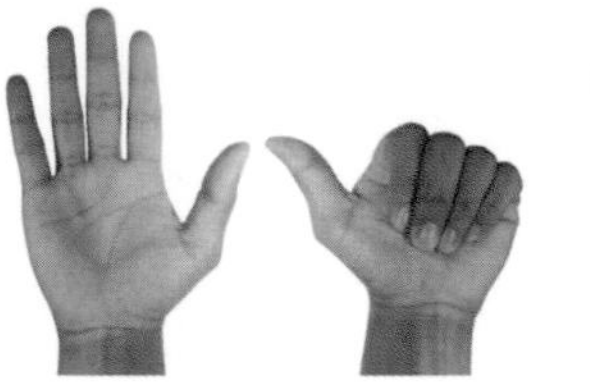

6 سِتَّة
sit-tah
six

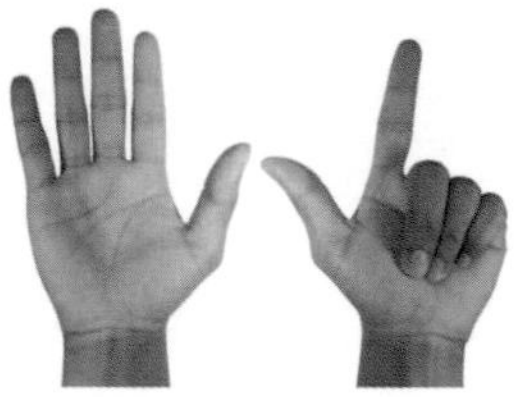

7 سَبْعَة
sabçah
seven

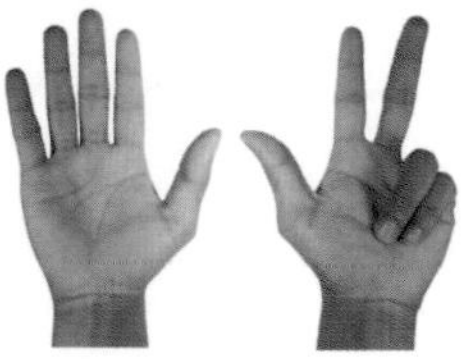

8 ثَمَانِيَة
thamaaniyah
eight

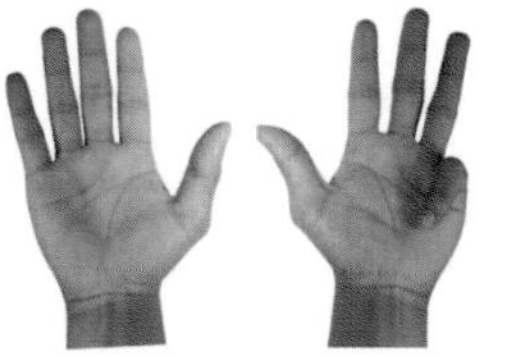

9 تِسْعَة
tisçah
nine

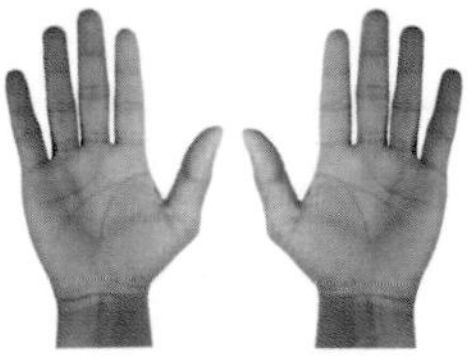

10 عَشَرَة
çasharah
ten

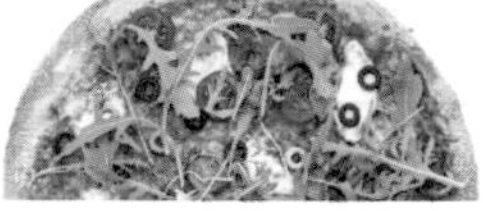

11 نِصْف
niṣf
one half

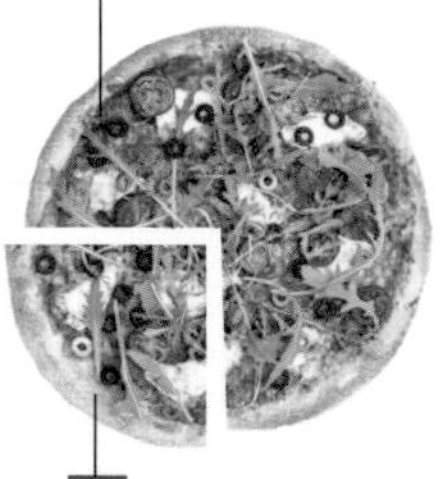

12 ثَلَاثَةُ أَرْبَاع
thalaathatu 'arbaaç
three quarters

13 رُبْع
rubç
one quarter

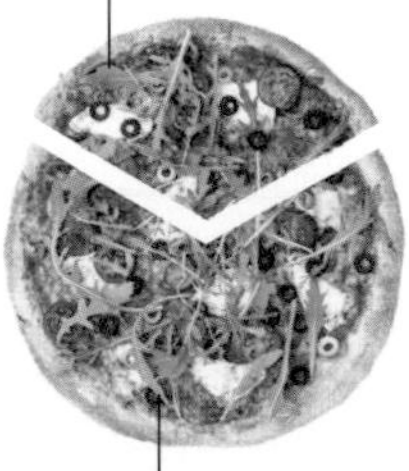

14 ثُلُث
thuluth
one third

15 ثُلُثَان / ثُلُثَيْن
thuluthaan / thuluthayn
two thirds

Cardinal Numbers
'al'açdaad الأَعْدَاد

0 صِفْر **ṣifr** zero
11 أَحَدَ عَشَر **'aḥada çashar** eleven
12 اثْنَا عَشَر **'ithnaa çashar** twelve
13 ثَلَاثَةَ عَشَر **thalaathata çashar** thirteen
14 أَرْبَعَةَ عَشَر **'arbaçata çashar** fourteen
15 خَمْسَةَ عَشَر **khamsata çashar** fifteen
16 سِتَّةَ عَشَر **sit-tata çashar** sixteen
17 سَبْعَةَ عَشَر **sabçata çashar** seventeen
18 ثَمَانِيَةَ عَشَر **thamaaniyata çashar** eighteen
19 تِسْعَةَ عَشَر **tisçata çashar** nineteen
20 عِشْرُون **çishruun** twenty
21 وَاحِدٌ وَعِشْرُون **waaḥidun wa çishruun** twenty-one
22 اِثْنَانِ وَعِشْرُون **'ithnaani wa çishruun** twenty-two
23 ثَلَاثَةٌ وَعِشْرُون **thalaathatun wa çishruun** twenty-three
24 أَرْبَعَةٌ وَعِشْرُون **'arbaçatun wa çishruun** twenty-four
25 خَمْسَةٌ وَعِشْرُون **khamsatun wa çishruun** twenty-five
26 سِتَّةٌ وَعِشْرُون **sit-tatun wa çishruun** twenty-six
27 سَبْعَةٌ وَعِشْرُون **sabçatun wa çishruun** twenty-seven
28 ثَمَانِيَةٌ وَعِشْرُون **thamaaniyatun wa çishruun** twenty-eight
29 تِسْعَةٌ وَعِشْرُون **tisçatun wa çishruun** twenty-nine
30 ثَلَاثُون **thalaathuun** thirty
40 أَرْبَعُون **'arbaçuun** forty
50 خَمْسُون **khamsuun** fifty
60 سِتُّون **sit-tuun** sixty
70 سَبْعُون **sabçuun** seventy
80 ثَمَانُون **thamaanuun** eighty
90 تِسْعُون **tisçuun** ninety
100 مِائَة **mi'ah** one hundred
1,000 أَلْف **'alf** one thousand

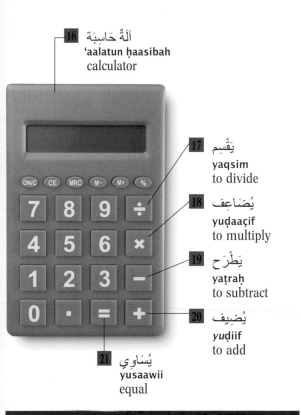

16 آلَةٌ حَاسِبَة
'aalatun ḥaasibah
calculator

17 يَقْسِم
yaqsim
to divide

18 يُضَاعِف
yuḍaaçif
to multiply

19 يَطْرَح
yaṭraḥ
to subtract

20 يُضِيف
yuḍiif
to add

21 يُسَاوِي
yusaawii
equal

Additional Vocabulary

22 كُلٌّ مِنْ
kul-lun min
both of

23 نِسْبَةٌ مِئَوِيَّة
nisbatun mi'awiy-yah
percent %

24 جُزْء
juz'
fraction (part)

25 أَرْقَامٌ زَوْجِيَّة
'arqaamun zawjiy-yah
even numbers

26 أَرْقَامٌ فَرْدِيَّة
'arqaamun fardiy-yah
odd numbers

27 يَعُدّ / يَحْسِب
yaçud-d / yaḥsib
to count

28 أَرْقَام
'arqaam
numbers

29 أَعْدَاد
'açdaad
digits

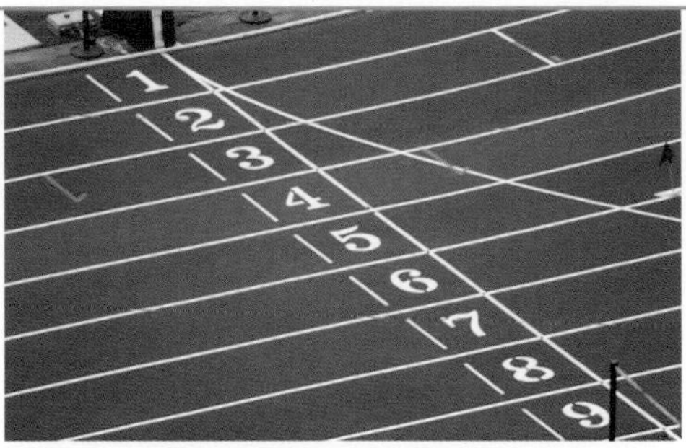

Ordinal Numbers
'al'açdaadu -t- tartiibiy-yah الأَعْدَادُ التَّرْتِيبِيَّة

1st الأَوَّل **'al'aw-wal** first
2nd الثَّانِي **'ath-thaanii** second
3rd الثَّالِث **'ath-thaalith** third
4th الرَّابِع **'ar-raabiç** fourth
5th الْخَامِس **'alkhaamis** fifth
6th السَّادِس **'as-saadis** sixth
7th السَّابِع **'as-saabiç** seventh
8th الثَّامِن **'ath-thaamin** eighth
9th التَّاسِع **'at-taasiç** ninth
10th الْعَاشِر **'alçaashir** tenth
11th الْحَادِيَ عَشَر **'alḥaadiya çashar** eleventh
12th الثَّانِيَ عَشَر **'ath-thaaniya çashar** twelfth
13th الثَّالِثَ عَشَر **'ath-thaalitha çashar** thirteenth
20th الْعِشْرُون **'alçishruun** twentieth
30th الثَّلاثُون **'ath-thalaathuun** thirtieth
40th الأَرْبَعُون **'al'arbaçuun** fourtieth
50th الْخَمْسُون **'al-khamsuun** fiftieth
60th السِّتُّون **'as-sit-tuun** sixtieth
70th السَّبْعُون **'as-sabçuun** seventieth
80th الثَّمَانُون **'ath-thamaanuun** eightieth
90th التِّسْعُون **'at-tisçuun** ninetieth
100th الْمِائَة **'almi'ah** one-hundredth
1,000th الأَلْف **'al'alf** one-thousandth

30 اثْنَان زَائِد أَرْبَعَة يُسَاوِي سِتَّة.
'ithnaan zaa'id 'arbaçah yusaawii sit-tah
Two plus four equals six.

31 أَحَدَ عَشَر نَاقِص خَمْسَة يُسَاوِي سِتَّة.
'aḥada çashar naaqiṣ khamsah yusaawii sit-tah
Eleven minus five equals six.

32 عَشَرَة فِي اثْنَىْ عَشَر يُسَاوِي مِائَة وَعِشْرِين.
çasharah fi-thnay çashar yusaawii mi'ah wa çishriin
Ten times twelve equals one hundred and twenty.

33 اِثْنَان وَأَرْبَعُون عَلَى ثَمَانِيَة يُسَاوِي خَمْسَة وَرُبْع.
'ithnaan wa 'arbaçuun çala thamaaniyah yusaawii khamsah wa rubç
Forty-two divided by eight equals five and a quarter.

6 الأَنْشِطَةُ الْيَوْمِيَّة
'al-'an*sh*iṭatu -l- yawmiy-yah
Daily Activities

5 يَقِف
yaqif
to stand

1 تَبْكِي
tabkii
she cries

2 يَضْحَك
yaḍḥak
to laugh

6 تَجْلِس
tajlis
she sits

3 يَسْتَمِعُ إِلَى
yastamiçu
'ilaa
to listen
to

4 تَنْظُرُ إِلَى
tanẓuru 'ilaa
she looks at

Additional Vocabulary

18 صَوْت
ṣawt
sound

19 يَسْأَل
yas'al
to ask

20 يَلْعَب
yalçab
to play

21 يَطْبُخ
yaṭbu*kh*
to cook

22 يَسْتَحِمّ
yastaḥim-m
to take a shower

23 أَغْسِلُ شَعْرِي
'a*gh*silu *sh*açrii
I wash my hair

24 يَتَنَفَّس
yatanaf-fas
to breathe

25 يَسْتَرْخِي
yastar*kh*ii
to relax

26 وَقْتُ فَرَاغ
waqtu faraa*gh*
leisure time

27 وَقْتُ الدِّرَاسَة
waqtu -d-diraasah
study time

28 يُجِيب
yujiib
to answer

29 يَغْضَب
ya*gh*ḍab
to get angry

30 يُصِرُّ عَلَى
yuṣir-ru çalaa
to insist on

31 يُوَافِق
yuwaafiq
to agree

32 يَطْلُب
yaṭlub
to request

33 يَوْمُ عَمَل
yawmu çamal
working day

34 عُطْلَةُ نِهَايَةِ الْأُسْبُوع
çuṭlatu nihaayati -l- 'usbuuç
weekend

35 يُغَادِرُ الْعَمَل
yu*gh*adiru -l- çamal
to leave work

36 يَذْهَبُ إِلَى الْمَدْرَسَة
ya*thz*habu 'ila -l- madrasah
to go to school

37 انْتِهَاءُ الْيَوْمِ الدِّرَاسِيِّ
'intihaa'u -l- yawmi -d-diraasiy-y
end of the school day

38 يَقُومُ بِالْأَعْمَالِ الْمَنْزِلِيَّة
yaquumu bi -l-'açmaali -l-manziliy-yah
to do household chores

39 يَتَنَاوَلُ الْفَطُور
yatanaawalu -l- faṭuur
to have breakfast

40 يَتَنَاوَلُ الْغَدَاء
yatanaawalu -l- *gh*adaa'
to have lunch

41 يَتَنَاوَلُ الْعَشَاء
yatanaawalu -l- ça*sh*aa'
to have dinner

42 أَحْتَاجُ إِلَى ثَمَانِي سَاعَاتٍ مِنَ النَّوْمِ كُلَّ يَوْم.
'aḥtaaju 'ilaa *th*amaanii saaçaatin mina -n-naw-mi kul-la yawm
I need eight hours of sleep every day.

7 يَنَام
yanaam
to sleep

8 يُشَاهِد
yu*sh*aahid
to watch

9 يَكْتُب
yaktub
to write

10 يَسْتَيْقِظ
yastayqiẓ
to wake up

11 يَغْسِلُ الْأَسْنَان
ya*gh*silu -l- 'asnaan
to brush teeth

12 يَتَكَلَّم
yatakal-lam
to talk

13 يَتَحَدَّثُ إِلَى
yataḥad-da*th*u 'ilaa
to speak to

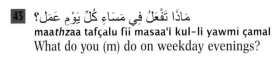

14 الْجَمِيعُ يَأْكُلُونَ مَعًا.
'aljamiiçu ya'kuluuna maçan
Everybody eats together

15 يَنْتَقِل
yantaqil
to move (from one place to another)

16 يُسَاعِد
yusaaçid
to help

17 يُمَشِّي الْكَلْب
yuma*sh*-*sh*i-l-kalb
to walk the dog

43 مَاذَا تَفْعَلُ فِي مَسَاءِ كُلِّ يَوْمِ عَمَل؟
maa*th*zaa tafçalu fii masaa'i kul-li yawmi çamal
What do you (m) do on weekday evenings?

44 مَاذَا تَفْعَلُ فِي عُطْلَةِ نِهَايَةِ الْأُسْبُوع؟
maa*th*zaa tafçalu fii çuṭlati nihaayati -l-'usbuuç
What do you (m) do on weekends?

45 مَا أَوَّلُ شَيْءٍ تَفْعَلُهُ فِي الصَّبَاح؟
maa 'aw-walu *sh*ay'in tafçaluhu fi - ṣ-ṣabaaḥ
What is the first thing you (m) do in the morning?

46 أَسْتَحِمُّ وَأَغْسِلُ أَسْنَانِي.
'astaḥim-mu wa 'a*gh*silu 'asnaanii
I take a shower and brush my teeth.

7 الْأَلْوَانُ وَالْأَشْكَالُ وَالْأَحْجَام
'al'alwaanu wa-l-'a*sh*kaalu wa-l-'aḥjaam
Colors, Shapes and Sizes

1 الأَلْوَان
'al'alwaan
colors

Note that the colors below are in the masculine form.

2 أَحْمَر
'aḥmar
red

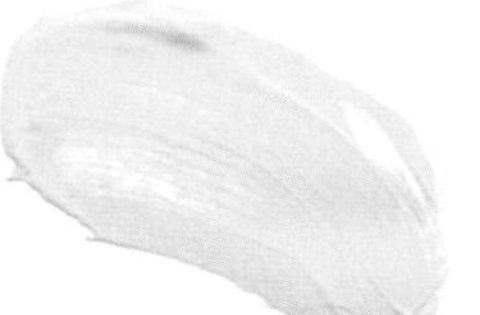

3 أَبْيَض
'abyaḍ
white

4 أَسْوَد
'aswad
black

5 أَصْفَر
'aṣfar
yellow

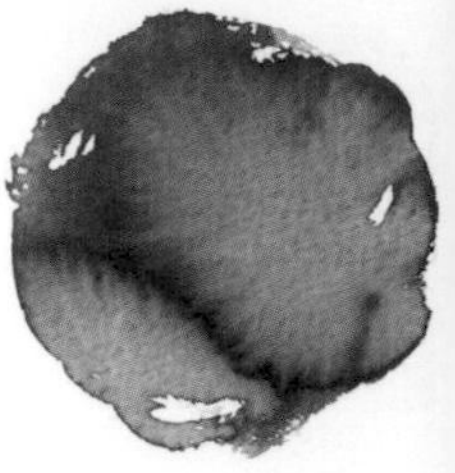

6 أَزْرَق
'azraq
blue

7 أَخْضَر
'a*kh*ḍar
green

8 بَنَفْسَجِيّ
banafsajiy-y
purple

9 بُنِّيّ
bun-niy-y
brown

10 رَمَادِيّ
ramaadiy-y
gray

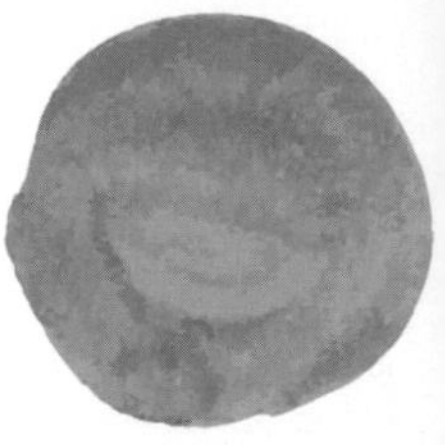

11 بُرْتُقَالِيّ
burtuqaaliy-y
orange

12 وَرْدِيّ
wardiy-y
pink

13 ذَهَبِيّ
***thz*ahabiy-y**
gold

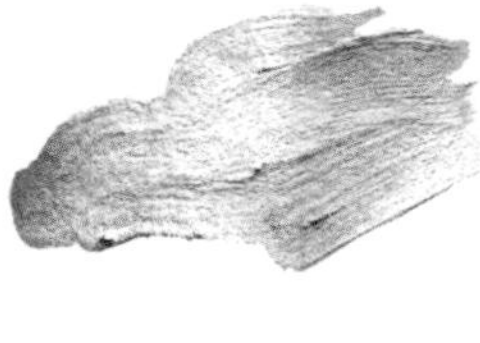

14 فِضِّيّ
fiḍ-ḍiy-y
silver

15 لَوْنٌ غَامِق
lawnun *gh*aamiq
dark color

16 لَوْنٌ فَاتِح
lawnun faatiḥ
light color

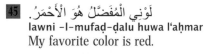

44 مَا لَوْنُكَ الْمُفَضَّلُ؟
maa lawnuka 'almufaḍ-ḍal
What is your (m) favorite color?

45 لَوْنِي الْمُفَضَّلُ هُوَ الْأَحْمَرُ.
lawni -l-mufaḍ-ḍalu huwa l'aḥmar
My favorite color is red.

17 قَوْسُ قُزَح
qawsu quzaḥ
a rainbow

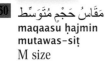

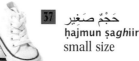

18 مُسْتَطِيل
mustaṭiil
a rectangle

19 دَائِرَة
daa'irah
a circle

20 ثُمَانِيُّ الْأَضْلَاعِ
*thu*maaniy-yu-l-
'aḍlaaç
an octagon

21 خُمَاسِيُّ الْأَضْلَاعِ
*khu*maasiy-yu-l-
'aḍlaaç
a pentagon

22 مُرَبَّع
mura*b*-*b*aç
a square

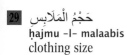

23 قَلْب
qalb
a heart

24 بَيْضَوِيّ
bayḍawiy-y
an oval

25 نَجْم
najm
a star

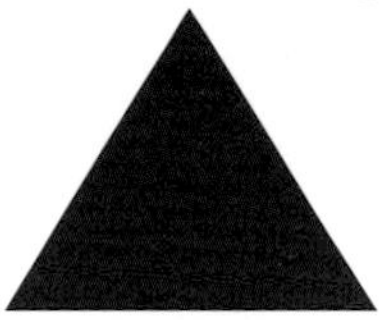

26 مُثَلَّث
mu*th*al-la*th*
a triangle

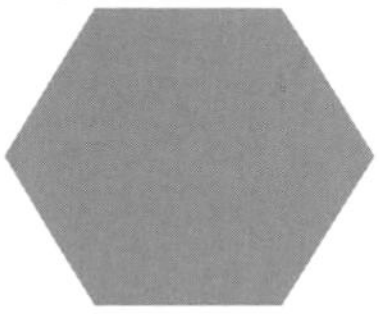

27 سُدَاسِيُّ الْأَضْلَاعِ
sudaasiy-yu-l-
'aḍlaaç
a hexagon

28 مُعَيَّن
muçay-yan
a rhombus

29 حَجْمُ الْمَلَابِس
ḥajmu -l- malaabis
clothing size

31 مَقَاسُ حَجْمٍ صَغِير
maqaasu ḥajmin
ṣaghiir
S size

32 مَقَاسُ حَجْمٍ صَغِيرٍ جِدًّا
maqaasu ḥajmin
ṣa*gh*iirin jid-dan
XS size

35 حَجْمٌ كَبِير
ḥajmun kabiir
large size

36 حَجْمٌ مُتَوَسِّط
ḥajmun mutawas-siṭ
medium size

37 حَجْمٌ صَغِير
ḥajmun ṣa*gh*iir
small size

30 مَقَاسُ حَجْمٍ مُتَوَسِّط
maqaasu ḥajmin
mutawas-siṭ
M size

33 مَقَاسُ حَجْمٍ كَبِير
maqaasu ḥajmin
kabiir
L size

34 مَقَاسُ حَجْمٍ كَبِيرٍ جِدًّا
maqaasu ḥajmin
kabiirin jid-dan
XL size

42 هَلْ لَدَيْكَ مَقَاسٌ أَكْبَر؟
hal ladayka maqaasun 'akbar
Do you (m) have a larger size?

43 هَلْ عِنْدَكِ نَفْسُ هَذَا بِأَلْوَانٍ مُخْتَلِفَة؟
hal çindaki nafsu ha*thz*aa bi'alwaanin mu*kh*talifah
Do you (f) have this in different colors?

Additional Vocabulary

38 شَكْل
*sh*akl
shape

39 حَجْم (مَقَاس)
ḥajm (maqaas)
size

40 أَكْبَر
'akbar
larger

41 أَصْغَر
'aṣ*gh*ar
smaller

8 الْمُتَنَاقِضَات
'almutanaaqiḍaat
Opposites

1 فَوْق ↔ تَحْت
fawq **taḥt**
up down

2 يَتَسَلَّم ↔ يُعْطِي
yatasal-lam **yuçṭii**
to receive to give

3 كَثِير ↔ قَلِيل
ka*th*iir **qaliil**
more (a lot) less (a few)

4 قَدِيم ↔ جَدِيد
qaadiim **jadiid**
old new

5 طَوِيل ↔ قَصِير
ṭawiil **qaṣiir**
tall short

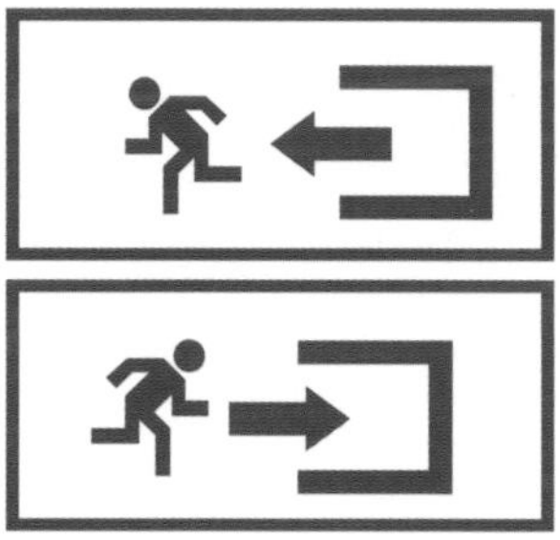

6 خُرُوج ↔ دُخُول
***kh*uruuj** **du*kh*uul**
exit enter

7 جَيِّد ↔ سَيِّئ
jay-yid **say-yi'**
good bad

8 نَشِيط ↔ كَسُول
na*sh*iiṭ **kasuul**
active idle

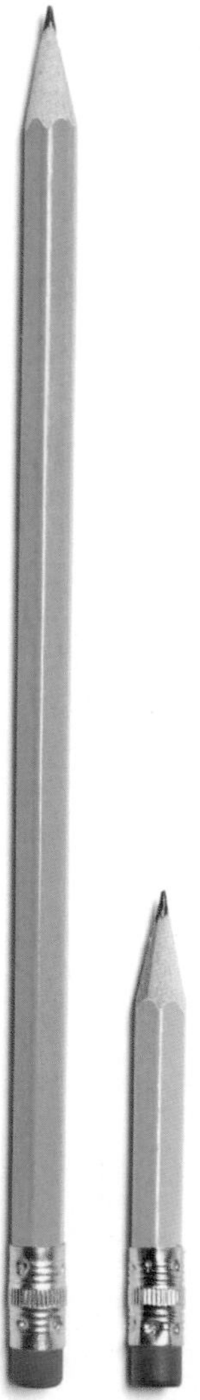

9 طَوِيل ↔ قَصِير
ṭawiil **qaṣiir**
long short

10 كَبِير ↔ صَغِير
kabiir — ṣa*gh*iir
old (age) — young (age)

11 كَبِير ↔ صَغِير
kabiir — ṣa*gh*iir
big — small (size)

12 مَفْتُوح ↔ مُغْلَق
maftuuḥ — mu*gh*laq
open — close

13 سَمِين ↔ نَحِيف
samiin — naḥiif
fat — skinny

Additional Vocabulary

14 يَأْخُذ ↔ يَضَع
ya'*khuthz* — yaḍaç
to take — to put

15 سَهْل ↔ صَعْب
sahl — ṣaçb
easy — difficult

16 يَمْلِك ↔ لَا يَمْلِك
yamlik — laa yamlik
to own — not to own

17 يَذْهَب ↔ يَأْتِي
ya*thz*hab — ya'tii
to go — to come

18 لَا ↔ نَعَمْ
laa — naçam
no — yes

19 جَوْعَان ↔ شَبْعَان
jawçaan — *sh*abçaan
hungry — (eat till) full

20 يَصِل ↔ يُغَادِر
yaṣil — yu*gh*aadir
to arrive — to depart/ leave

21 بِالْخَارِج ↔ بِالدَّاخِل
bil*kh*aarij — bid-daa*kh*il
outside — inside

22 مَاضِي ↔ مُسْتَقْبَل
maaḍii — mustaqbal
past — future

23 يَبْدَأ ↔ يَنْتَهِي
yabda' — yantahii
to begin — to end

24 بَعِيد ↔ قَرِيب
baçiid — qariib
far — near

25 صَحِيح ↔ خَطَأ
ṣaḥiiḥ — *kh*aṭa'
right — wrong

26 مُزَوَّر ↔ حَقِيقِيّ
muzaw-war — ḥaqiiqiy-y
fake — real

27 بَطِيء ↔ سَرِيع
baṭii' — sariiç
slow — fast

28 مُنْخَفِض ↔ عَالِي
mun*kh*afiḍ — çaalii
low — high

29 يُرْجِع ↔ يَقْتَرِض
yurjiç — yaqtariḍ
to return — to borrow

30 يَتَذَكَّر ↔ يَنْسَى
yata*thz*ak-kar — yansaa
to remember — to forget

31 سَعِيد ↔ حَزِين
saçiid — ḥaziin
happy — sad

32 مَفْتُوح ↔ مُغْلَق
maftuuḥ — mu*gh*laq
on (electricity) — off (electricity)

33 بَارِد وَسَاخِن هُمَا زَوْجَانِ مُتَنَاقِضَان.
baarid wa saa*kh*in humaa zawjaani mutanaaqiḍaan
Cold and hot is a pair of opposites.

34 الْمُتَنَاقِضُ هُوَ زَوْجٌ مِنَ الْكَلِمَاتِ الْمُتَنَاقِضَة.
'almutanaaqiḍu huwa zawjun mina-l-kalimaati -l-mutanaaqiḍah
An antonym is a pair of words with opposite meaning.

9 الْحَدِيثُ عَنِ الْفُلُوس / الْمَال

‘alḥadiithu çani-l-fuluus / ‘almaal

Talking About Money

Some Arabic countries share the name of paper and coin currency, but each has its own independent economy. For example, the paper currency pound is used in Egypt and Sudan, but Egyptian Pounds and Sudanese Pounds are not of the same monetary value in exchange for the US dollar.

1 عُمْلَةٌ وَرَقِيَّة
çumlatun waraqiy-yah
paper currency

2 عُمْلَةٌ مَعْدِنِيَّة
çumlatun maçdiniy-yah
coin currency

3 جُنَيْه
gunayh
Pound (Egypt, Sudan)

4 رِيَال
riyaal
Ryal (Saudi Arabia, Yemen, Oman, Qatar)

5 دِينَار
diinaar
Dinar (Jordan, Kuwait Libya, Bahrain, Algeria, Iraq)

6 دِرْهَم
dirham
Dirham (UAE)

7 لِيرَة
liirah
Lira (Syria, Lebanon)

8 قِرْش
qirsh
Cent (Egypt, Jordan, Syria)

9 فِلْس
fils
Fls (Bahrain, UAE)

10 هَلَلَة
halalah
Halala (Saudi)

11 سِنْتِيم
cintiim
Centime (Morocco, Algeria)

12 جُنَيْهٌ وَاحِد
gunayhun waaḥid
one pound

13 خَمْسَةُ رِيَالَاتٍ سُعُودِيَّة
***kh*amsatu riyaalaatin suçuudiy-yah**
5 Saudi Ryals

14 أَلْفُ لِيرَةٍ سُورِيَّة
‘alfu liiratin suuriy-yah
1000 Syrian Liras

15 عِشْرُونَ دِرْهَمًا إِمَارَاتِيًّا
çi*sh*ruuna dirhaman ‘imaaraatiy-yan
20 UAE Dirhams

16 خَمْسُونَ دِينَارًا أُرْدُنِيًّا
***kh*amsuuna diinaaran ‘urduniy-yan**
50 Jordanian Dinars

17 مِائَةُ جُنَيْهٍ مِصْرِيٍّ
mi‘atu gunayhin miṣriy-y
100 Egyptian pound

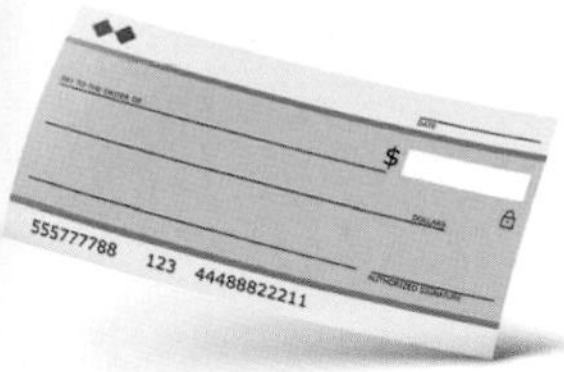

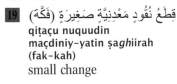

18 شِيك
shiik
check

19 قِطَعُ نُقُودٍ مَعْدِنِيَّةٍ صَغِيرَةٍ (فَكَّة)
qiṭaçu nuquudin maçdiniy-yatin ṣaghiirah (fak-kah)
small change

20 بِطَاقَةٌ ائْتِمَانِيَّة
biṭaaqatuni-'-timaaniy-yah
credit card

21 مُدَّخَرَات (ادِّخَار)
mud-dakharaat ('id-dikhaar)
savings

22 أَسْعَارُ الصَّرْف
'asçaaru-ṣ-ṣarf
currency exchange

23 يَسْحَبُ نُقُودًا
yasḥabu nuquudan
to withdraw money

Additional Vocabulary

24 نُقُود (مَال)
nuquud (maal)
money

25 سِعْر
siçr
price

26 خَصْم / تَنْزِيل
khaṣm / tanziil
discount

27 رَخِيص
rakhiiṣ
cheap

28 غَالِي
ghaalii
expensive

29 فَائِدَة
faa'idah
interest

30 اقْتِرَاض
'iqtiraaḍ
loan

31 دَيْن
dayn
debt

32 رَقْمُ الْحِسَاب
raqmu-l-ḥisaab
account number

33 إِيصَال
'iiṣaal
receipt

34 ضَرَائِب
ḍaraa'ib
taxes

35 نَقْدًا
naqdan
cash

36 قِسْط
qisṭ
installment

37 إِيدَاعٌ مَصْرِفِيّ (وَدِيعَةٌ بَنْكِيَّة)
'iidaaçun maṣrifiy-y (wadiiçatun bankiy-yah)
bank deposit

38 كَمْ سِعْرُه؟
kam siçruh
How much does this cost?

39 أَرْبَعَةٌ وَعِشْرُونَ جُنَيْهًا مِصْرِيًا وَخَمْسَةٌ وَتِسْعُونَ قِرْشًا.
'arbaçatun wa çishruuna gunayhan miṣriy-yan wa khamsatun wa tisçuuna qirshan
Twenty-Four Egyptian Pounds and ninety-five cents.

40 هَلْ يُوجَدُ خَصْمٌ؟
hal yuujadu khaṣm
Is there a discount?

41 طَيِّب، ١٠ فِي الْمِائَةِ خَصْم.
ṭay-yib çasharah fi-l-mi'ah khaṣm
OK, 10% discount.

10 الذَّهَابُ لِلتَّسَوُّق
‘athz-thzahaabu li-t-tasaw-wuq
Going Shopping

4 حَقِيبَةُ التَّسَوُّق
ḥaqiibatu-t-tasaw-wuq
shopping bag

1 تَشْتَرِي
tashtarii
she buys

43 كَمْ سِعْرُ هَذَا؟
kam siçru hathzaa
How much is it?

2 يَبِيع
yabiiç
to sell

3 يَتَسَوَّق
yatasaw-waq
to shop

5 سَاعَة
saaçah
watch

11 نَظَّارَة
naẓ-ẓaarah
glasses

14 قَمِيص
qamiiṣ
shirt

6 ثِيَاب
thiyaab
clothes

7 قَمِيصٌ نِسَائِيٌّ (بُلُوزَة)
qamiiṣun nisaa‘iy-y (buluuzah)
blouse

12 جَوَارِب (شَرَابَات)
jawaarib (sharaabaat)
socks

15 رَابِطَةُ عُنُق (كَرَافَتَّهْ)
raabiṭatu çunuq (karafat-tah)
necktie

9 سِرْوَالْ جِينْزْ (بَنْطَلُون جِينْزْ)
sirwaal jiinz (banṭaluun jiinz)
jeans

8 تَنُّورَة (جِيبَة)
tan-nuurah (jiibah)
skirt

10 سِرْوَال (بَنْطَلُون)
sirwaal (banṭaluun)
trousers

13 أَحْذِيَة
‘aḥthziyah
shoes

16 قُبَّعَة (طَاقِيَّة)
qub-baçah (ṭaaqiy-yah)
hat

Some useful shopping expressions:

46 أَيْنَ أَقْرَبُ مَرْكَزٍ لِلتَّسَوُّق؟
'ayna 'aqrabu markazin lit-tasaw-wuq
Where is the nearest shopping center?

47 هَلْ يُمْكِنُنِي تَجْرِبَتُهَا؟ (مُمْكِنْ أَقِيسْهَا؟)
hal yumkinunii tajribatuhaa? (mumkin 'qiishaa)
Can I try it on?

48 أَيْنَ غُرْفَةُ الْقِيَاس (حُجْرَةُ تَجْرِبَةِ الْمَلَابِس)؟
'ayna ghurfatu-l-qiyaas (ḥujraatu tajribati-l-malaabis)
Where is the fitting room?

49 هَذَا غَالٍ جِدًّا!
hathzaa ghaalin jid-dan
This is too expensive!

50 سَأَشْتَرِيه.
sa'ashtariih
I will buy it.

51 هَلْ تَقْبَلُ بِطَاقَاتِ الِائْتِمَانِ (الْكِرِيدِتْ كَارْدْ)؟
hal taqbalu biṭaaqaati-li'timaan ('alkridit kard)
Do you accept credit cards?

52 أَنَا سَأَدْفَعُ نَقْدًا.
'ana sa'adfaçu naqdaan
I will pay in cash.

53 هَلْ يُمْكِنُنِي الْحُصُولُ عَلَى إِيصَالِ الدَّفْع؟
hal yumkinuni-l-ḥuṣuulu çalaa 'iiṣaali-d-dafç
Could I have a receipt?

17 مُسْتَحْضَرَاتُ تَجْمِيل
mustaḥḍaraatu tajmiil
cosmetics

18 دُمَى (أَلْعَاب)
dumaa ('alçaab)
toys

19 حِزَام
ḥizaam
belt

20 وِشَاح (شَال)
wishaaḥ (shaal)
scarf

Additional Vocabulary

21 الْجُمُعَةُ الْبَيْضَاء
'aljumuçatu-l-bayḍaa'
White Friday

22 دُكَّان (مَتْجَر)
duk-kaan (matjar)
shop

23 مَتْجَرٌ مُتَعَدِّدُ الْأَقْسَام
matjarun mutaçad-didu-l-'aqsaam
department store

24 بُوتِيك (مَتْجَر)
buutiik (matjar)
boutique

25 مُوَظَّفُو الْمَتْجَر
muwaẓ-ẓafu-l-matjar
shop staff

26 مُحَاسِب (كَاشِير)
muḥaasib (kashiir)
cashier

27 تَوْصِيلٌ لِلْمَنَازِل
tawṣiilun lilmanaazil
home delivery

28 مُقَارَنَةُ الْأَسْعَار
muqaaranatu-l-'asçaar
comparing prices

29 التَّسَوُّقُ عَبْرَ الْإِنْتَرْنِت (التَّسَوُّق أُونْ لَايِنْ)
'at-tasaw-wuqu çabra-l-'intarnit ('at-tasaw-wuq 'un layin)
online shopping

30 بِطَاقَةُ ائْتِمَانْ (كِرِيدِتْ كَارْدْ)
biṭaaqatu 'timaan (kriidit kaard)
credit card

31 نَفْسُ الشَّيْء
nafsu-sh-shay'
the same thing

32 مَعًا
maçan
altogether

33 بِكُلِّ تَأْكِيد
bikul-li ta'kiid
certainly

34 بِصِفَةٍ عَامَّة
biṣifatin çaam-mah
generally

35 أَكْثَر وَ أَكْثَر
'akthar wa 'akthar
more; even more

36 قَرَار
qaraar
decision

37 آخَر
'aakhar
another

38 يَحْضُر
yaḥḍur
to bring

39 أَشْيَاء
'ashyaa'
things

40 فَاتُورَة
faatuurah
bill; invoice

41 مُعْفَاةٌ مِنَ الضَّرَائِب
muçfaatun mina-ḍ-ḍaraa'ib
tax free

42 اسْتِرْدَادُ الْمَالِ الْمَدْفُوع
'istirdaadu-l-maali-l-madfuuç
refund

44 هَلْ هُنَاكَ ضَرَائِبُ مُضَافَة؟
hal hunaaka ḍaraa'ibu muḍaafah
Are there any added taxes?

45 هَلْ مُمْكِنٌ اسْتِعَادَةُ الضَّرَائِبِ لَاحِقًا؟
hal mumkinun istiçaadatu- ḍ - ḍaraa'ibi laaḥiqan
Can I refund the taxes later?

11 الْحَيَاةُ فِي الْمَدِينَة
‘alḥayaatu fi-l-madiinah
Life in the City

1 فُنْدُق
funduk
hotel

2 مَطَار
maṭaar
airport

3 مَتْجَر (مَحَلّ)
matjar (maḥal-l)
shop

4 شَارِع
***sh*aariç**
street

5 سُوقٌ مَرْكَزِيٌّ (سُوبِرْمَارْكِتْ)
suuqun markazíy-y (super market)
supermarket

6 مَحَطَّةُ وَقُودٍ
maḥaṭ-ṭatu waquud
gas station

7 بَنْك
bank
bank

8 مَرْكَزُ الْمُؤْتَمَرَات
markazu-l-mu‘tamaraat
conference center

9 مَحَطَّةُ الْقِطَار
maḥaṭ-ṭatu -l- qiṭaar
train station

10 مُتْحَف (مَتْحَف)
mutḥaf (matḥaf)
museum

11 نَاطِحَةُ سَحَاب
naaṭiḥatu saḥaab
skyscraper

12 مَدِينَة
madiinah
city

13 مَبْنًى سَكَنِيّ
mabnan sakaniy-y
apartment building

14 مُتْحَفُ الْفَنّ
muthafu-l-fan-n
art museum

15 إسْتَاد
'istaad
stadium

16 مَكْتَبُ الْبَرِيد
maktabu-l-bariid
post office

17 قِسْمُ الشُّرْطَة
qismu-*sh*-*sh*urṭah
police station

18 طَرِيقٌ سَرِيع
ṭariiqun sariiç
expressway

19 صَالَةٌ رِيَاضِيَّةٌ (جِيمْ)
ṣaalatun riyaaḍiy-yah (jim)
gym

Additional Vocabulary

20 دَارُ عَرْضٍ سِينَمَائِيّ (سِينِمَا)
daaru çarḍin siinimaa'iy-y (siinimaa)
cinema

21 مِنْطَقَةُ الْأَعْمَالِ الْمَرْكَزِيَّة
minṭaqatu-l-'açmaali-l-markaziy-yah
central business district (CBD)

22 مَرْكَزُ تَسَوُّق (مُولْ)
markazu tasaw-wuq (muul)
shopping center; mall

23 مَمَرٌّ لِلْمُشَاة (رَصِيف)
mamar-run lilmu*sh*aah (raṣiif)
sidewalk

24 وَسَطُ الْبَلَد
wasaṭu-l-balad
downtown

25 ضَاحِيَة
ḍaaḥiyah
suburb

26 شَقَّة (بَيْت)
***sh*aq-qah (bayt)**
apartment (house)

27 جِسْر (كُوبْرِي)
jisr (kubrii)
bridge

28 زَاوِيَةُ الشَّارِع
zaawiyatu -*sh*-*sh*aariç
street corner

29 جَار
jaar
neighbor

30 آثَار
'aa*th*aar
monuments

31 كَنِيسَة
kaniisaah
church

32 مُشَاة
mu*sh*aah
pedestrian

33 عُبُورُ الْمُشَاة
çubuuru-l-mu*sh*aah
pedestrian crossing

34 مَسْجِد
masjid
mosque

38 هَلْ تَعِيشُ فِي مَدِينَةٍ أَمْ فِي ضَاحِيَة؟
hal taçii*sh*u fii madiinatin 'am fii ḍaaḥiyah
Do you (m) live in the city or in the suburb?

39 كَيْفَ تَذْهَبُ إِلَى الْعَمَل؟
kayfa ta*thz*habu 'ila-l-çamal
How do you (m) go to work?

40 كَمْ يَبْعُدُ الْمَطَارُ مِنْ وَسَطِ الْمَدِينَة؟
kam yabçudu-l-maṭaaru min wasaṭi-l-madiinah
How far is the airport from the downtown?

41 الْأُسْتَاذَةُ مُنَى تُرِيدُ أَنْ تَعِيشَ فِي الْمَدِينَة.
'al'ustaa*thz*atu munaa turiidu 'an taçii*sh*a fi-l-madiinah
Miss Mona wants to live in the city.

35 إِشَارَاتُ الْمُرُورِ الضَّوْئِيَّة
'i*sh*aaraatu-l-muruuri - ḍ-ḍaw'iy-yah
traffic lights

36 حَرَكَةُ السَّيْر (الْمُرُور)
ḥarakatu-s-sayr ('almuruur)
traffic

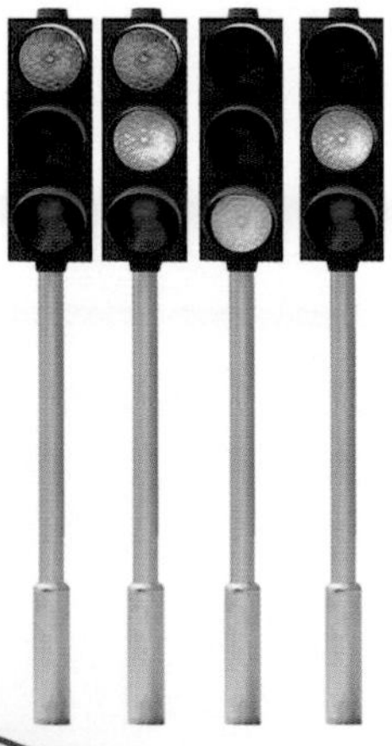

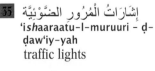

37 طَرِيق
ṭariiq
road

12 وَسَائِلُ النَّقْل
wasaa'ilu n-naql
Transportations

1 سَيَّارَة
say-yaarah
car

2 سَيَّارَةُ أُجْرَة (تَاكْسِي)
say-yaaratu 'ujrah (taxi)
taxi

3 سَائِق
saa'iq
driver

4 طَائِرَة
ṭaa'irah
airplane

5 شَاحِنَة
***sh*aaḥinah**
truck

6 شَاحِنَةُ النُّفَايَات
***sh*aaḥinatu-n-nufaayaat**
garbage truck

7 شَاحِنَةُ التَّوْصِيل
***sh*aaḥinatu-t-tawṣiil**
delivery van

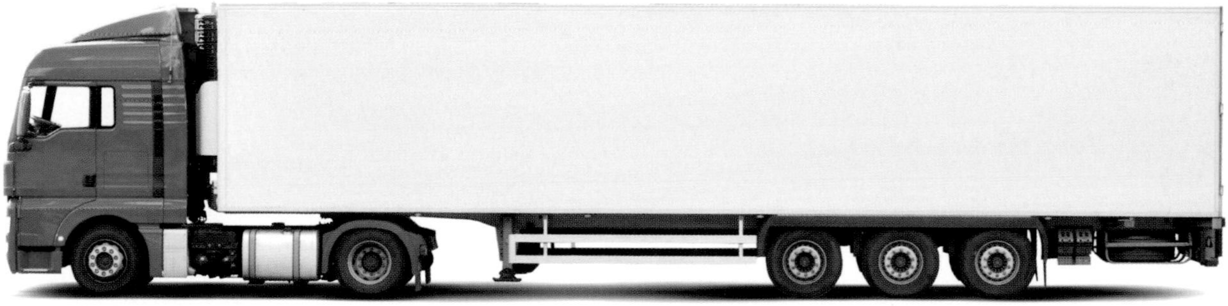

8 قِطَارٌ فَائِقُ السُّرْعَة
qiṭaarun faa'iqu -s-surçah
high speed train

9 دَرَّاجَةٌ بُخَارِيَّةٌ (مُوتُوسِيكِل)
dar-raajatun bu*kh*aariy-yah (mutusiikl)
motorcycle

10 سَيَّارَةٌ رِيَاضِيَّة
say-yaaratun riyaaḍiy-yah
sports car

11 مِتْرُو الأَنْفَاق
mitru-l-‘anfaaq
subway

12 حَافِلَةٌ عَامَّة (أُتُوبِيسْ عَام)
ḥaafilatun çaam-mah
(‘utubiis çaam)
public bus

13 مَوْقِفُ الأُتُوبِيس
mawqifu -l-‘utubiis
bus stop

14 سَفِينَة
safiinah
ship

15 قِطَار
qiṭaar
train

16 سَيَّارَةُ الإِطْفَاءِ
say-yaaratu
-l-‘iṭfaa‘
fire engine

17 تِرَام
tiraam
tram

18 دَرَّاجَة (عَجَلَة)
dar-raajah (çajalah)
bike

33 مَا أَفْضَلُ وَسِيلَةٍ لِلْوُصُولِ إِلَى وَسَطِ الْبَلَد؟
maa ‘afḍalu wasiilatin lilwuṣuuli ‘ilaa wasaṭi -l-balad
What is the best way to get downtown?

34 عَنْ طَرِيقِ اَلْحَافِلَة، أَوْ سَيَّارَةِ اَلأُجْرَة، أَوْ مِتْرُو اَلأَنْفَاق.
çan ṭariiqi -l-ḥaafilah ‘aw say-yaarati -l-‘ujrah ‘aw mitru -l-‘anfaaq
By bus, by taxi or take the subway.

35 كَيْفَ أَصِلُ إِلَى مَحَطَّةِ مِتْرُو الأَنْفَاق؟
kayfa ‘aṣilu ‘ilaa maḥaṭ-ṭati mitru -l-‘anfaaq
How do I get to the subway station?

Additional Vocabulary

19 يَسْتَقِلُّ الْحَافِلَة (يَرْكَبُ الْبَاص)
yastaqil-lu -l-ḥaafilah (yarkabu-l-baaṣ)
to take a bus

20 يَسْتَقِلُّ الْقِطَار (يَرْكَبُ الْقِطَار)
yastaqil-lu-l-qiṭaar (yarkabu-l-qiṭaar)
to ride a train

21 يَقُودُ سَيَّارَة
yaquudu say-yaarah
to drive a car

22 يَرْكَبُ دَرَّاجَة
yarkabu dar-raajah
to ride a bike

23 يَتَّجِهُ يَسَارًا (يَتَّجِهُ يَمِينًا)
yat-tajihu yasaaran (yat-tajihu yamiinan)
to turn left (to turn right)

24 طَرِيقُ اَلْحَافِلَةِ (طَرِيقُ اَلأُتُوبِيسْ \ اَلْبَاصْ)
ṭariiqu -l-ḥaafilah (ṭariiqu -l-‘utubiis \ ‘albaas)
bus route

25 يَسْتَدْعِي سَيَّارَةَ أُجْرَة (يَتَّصِل بِتَاكْسِي)
yastadçii say-yaarata ‘ujrah (yat-taṣil bitaaksii)
to call a taxi

26 انْطَلِقْ مُبَاشَرَةً
‘inṭaliq mubaa*sh*aratan
go straight

27 يُبْطِئ
yubṭi‘
to slow down

28 مُسَافِر (رَاكِب)
musaafir (raakib)
passenger

29 يُسْرِع
yusriç
to go faster

30 جَدْوَل
jadwal
schedule

31 شُبَّاكُ التَّذَاكِر
***sh*ub-baaku -t-ta*thz*aakir**
ticket counter

32 عَرَبَةُ الْحِصَان
çarabatu -l- ḥiṣaan
horse carriage

13 لسُّؤَالُ عَنْ الاِتِّجَاهَاتِ وَإِعْطَاءُ الاِتِّجَاهَات

'as-su'aalu çan li- t-tijaahaati wa 'içṭaa'u li- t-tijaahaat

Asking and Giving Directions

1 أَيْنَ؟
'ayna
where?

2 هُنَا
hunaa
here

3 هُنَاك
hunaak
there

4 فَوْق
fawq
above

5 تَحْت
taḥt
below

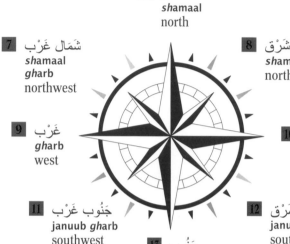

6 شَمَال
***sh*amaal**
north

7 شَمَال غَرْب
***sh*amaal *gh*arb**
northwest

8 شَمَال شَرْق
***sh*amaal *sh*arq**
northeast

9 غَرْب
***gh*arb**
west

10 شَرْق
***sh*arq**
east

11 جَنُوب غَرْب
januub *gh*arb
southwest

12 جَنُوب شَرْق
januub *sh*arq
southeast

13 جَنُوب
januub
south

14 أَمَام
'amaam
in front

15 خَلْف
***kh*alf**
behind

Some common phrases for asking and giving directions:

16 يَسْأَلُ عَنْ الاِتِّجَاهَات
yas'alu çan -li- t-tijaahaat
to ask for directions

21 إِعْطَاءُ الاِتِّجاهَات
'içṭaa'u - li t-tijaahaat
giving directions

17 أَنَا تَائِه! هَلْ يُمْكِنُ أَنْ تُسَاعِدَنِي؟
'ana taa'ih hal yumkinu 'an tusaaçidanii
I am lost. Can you (m) help me?

18 هَلْ هَذَا هُوَ الطَّرِيقُ إِلَى...؟
hal ha*thz*a huwa -ṭ-ṭariiqu 'ilaa ...
Is this the way to … ?

19 كَمْ يَبْعُد...؟
kam yabçud ...
How far?

20 هَلْ يُمْكِنُ أَنْ تُرِيَنِي عَلَى الْخَرِيطَةِ؟
hal yumkinu 'an turiyanii çala -l-*kh*ariiṭah
Can you (m) show me on the map?

22 أَعْتَذِرُ، لَا أَعْرِفُ.
'açta*thz*iru, laa 'açrif
I am sorry, I don't know.

23 فِي هَذَا الطَّرِيقِ.
fii ha*thz*a-ṭ-ṭariiq
It is this way.

24 فِي ذَاكَ الطَّرِيقِ.
fii *thz*aaka-ṭ-ṭariiq
It is that way.

25 إِنَّهُ عَلَى الْيَمِين (الْيَسَار).
'in-nahu çala -l-yamiin (lyasaar)
It's on the right (left).

26 إِنَّهُ بِجَانِب ...
'in-nahu bijaanib...
It's next to … .

28 وَسَط
wasaṭ
middle; center

27 الْجَانِبُ الأَيْسَر
'aljaanibu l'aysar
left side

29 الْجَانِبُ الأَيْمَن
'aljaanibu -l 'ayman
right side

30 اتَّجِه يَسَارًا
'it-tajih yasaaran
turn left (imperative)

31 انْطَلِقْ مُبَاشَرَةً
'inṭ-ṭaliq mubaa*sh*aratan
go straight (imperative)

32 اتَّجِه يَمِينًا
'it-tajih yamiinan
turn right (imperative)

33 خَارِج
***kh*aarij**
outside

34 دَاخِل
daa*kh*il
inside

Additional Vocabulary

35 تَائِه
taa'ih
being lost

36 اتِّجَاه
'it-tijaah
direction

37 مَسَافَة
masaafah
distance

38 كِيلُومِتْر
kiluu mitr
kilometer

39 مِيل
miil
mile

40 مِتْر
mitr
meter

41 قَدَم
qadam
foot

42 قَرِيب
qariib
near

43 بَعِيد
baçiid
far

44 مُقَابِل
muqaabil
against (opposing side)

45 الشَّرْق
'*sh*-*sh*arq
the east

46 الْجَنُوب
'aljanuub
the south

47 الْغَرْب
'al*gh*arb
the west

48 الشَّمَال
'*sh*-*sh*amaal
the north

49 جَانِب
jaanib
side

50 مُجَاوِر
mujaawir
nearby

51 مَكَان
makaan
place

52 جَانِبٌ وَاحِد
jaanibun waaḥid
one side

53 يُخْبِر
yu*kh*bir
to tell

54 يَمُرّ
yamur-r
to go through

55 يُغَادِر
yu*gh*aadir
to leave

56 كَمْ تَبَقَّى مِنَ الْوَقْت؟
kam tabaq-qaa mina -l- waqt
how much longer?

57 حَالًا
ḥaalan
immediately

58 يَسْمَح
yasmaḥ
to allow

59 فِي ذَلِكَ الْحِين
fii *thz*alika -l- ḥiin
at that time

60 يُفَكِّر
yufak-kir
to think

61 يَعْتَبِر
yaçtabir
to consider

62 يُسَاعِد
yusaaçid
to help

63 يَشْعُرُ بِالْقَلَق
ya*sh*çuru bilqalaq
to feel anxious

الْكَلامُ عَنِ الطَّقْس

14 'alkalaamu çani-ṭ-ṭaqs
Talking About the Weather

1 مِظَلَّة (شَمْسِيَّة)
miẓal-lah (*sh*amsiy-yah)
umbrella

2 مِعْطَفُ مَطَر
miçṭafu maṭar
raincoat

3 حِذَاءٌ طَوِيلٌ (بُوط)
ḥi*thz*aa'un ṭawiil (buuṭ)
boots

4 صَافِي
ṣaafii
clear (sky)

5 يَوْمٌ صَافِي
yawmun ṣaafii
clear day

6 غَائِم
***gh*aa'im**
overcast

7 ضَبَابِيّ (غَمَامِيّ)
ḍabaabiy-y (*gh*amaamiy-y)
cloudy

8 رِيَاح
riyaaḥ
wind

9 عَاصِف
çaaṣif
windy

10 مَطَر
maṭar
rain

11 تُمْطِر
tumṭir
is raining

12 بَرْق
barq
lightning

13 رَعْد
raçd
thunder

14 عَاصِفَةٌ رَعْدِيَّة
çaaṣifatun raçdiy-yah
thunderstorm

15 ثَلْج
***th*alj**
snow

16 تُثْلِج
tu*th*lij
to snow

17 إِعْصَار
'içṣaar
typhoon

39 الْيَوْمَ، الْجَوُّ جَمِيلٌ. غَدًا سَيَكُونُ الْجَوُّ مُمْطِرًا.
'alyawma 'aljaw-wu jamiil *gh*adan sayakuunu -l-ljaw-wu mumṭiran
It's a beautiful day today. Tomorrow will be rainy.

40 الْيَوْمَ، الطَّقْسُ حَارٌّ، وَلَكِنْ غَدًا سَيَكُونُ بَارِدًا.
'alyawma 'aṭ-ṭaqsu ḥaar-run wa laakin *gh*adan sayakuunu baaridan
The weather is hot today, but tomorrow will be cooler.

18 مِعْطَف
miçţaf
coat or jacket

19 سُتْرَة
sutrah
pullover / sweater

Additional Vocabulary

32 طَقْس
ţaqs
weather

33 نَشْرَةُ الْأَخْبَار
na*sh*ratu-l-'a*kh*baar
weather forecast

34 طَقْسٌ جَيِّد
ţaqsun jay-yid
good weather

35 طَقْسٌ سَيِّئ
ţaqsun say-yi'
bad weather

36 طَقْسٌ مُشْمِس
ţaqsun mu*sh*mis
sunny weather

37 تَلَوُّثُ الْهَوَاءِ
talaw-wu*th*u -l-hawaa'
air pollution

38 إِعْصَار
'içşaar
hurricane

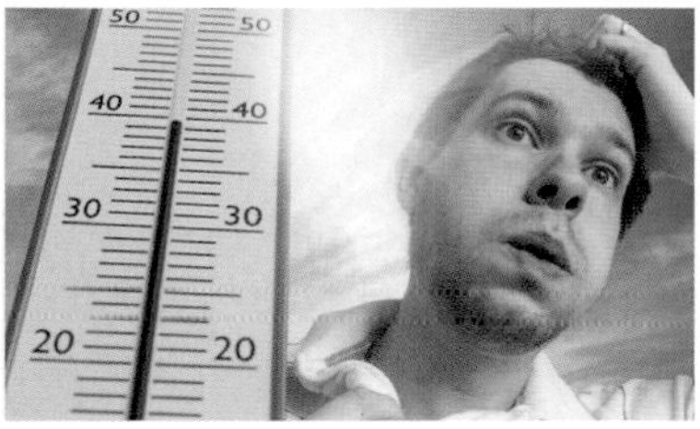

20 حَارّ
ḥaar-r
hot

21 طَقْسٌ حَارّ
ţaqsun ḥaar-r
hot weather

22 بَارِد
baarid
cold

23 طَقْسٌ بَارِد
ţaqsun baarid
cold weather

24 سَحَابَة
saḥaabah
cloud

25 ضَبَاب
ḍabaab
fog

26 شَمْس
***sh*ams**
sun

27 قَمَر
qamar
moon

28 عَاصِفَةٌ مُمْطِرَة
çaaşifatun mumţirah
rainstorm

29 وَابِل (مَطَرٌ كَثِير)
waabil (maţarun ka*th*iir)
hail

30 قُبَّعَة
qub-baçah
hat

31 قُفَّازَات (جَوَانْتِي)
quf-faazaat (gawaantii)
gloves

15 الإِخْبَارُ بِالْوَقْت

'al'ikhbaaru bi-l-waqt

Telling Time

1 سَاعَة
saaçah
hour

2 دَقِيقَة
daqiiqah
minute

3 ثَانِيَة
***th*aaniyah**
second

6 السَّاعَة
'as-saaçah
clock

4 السَّاعَةُ السَّادِسَة
'as-saaçatu - s-saadisah
6 o'clock

5 السَّاعَةُ السَّادِسَةُ وَخَمْسُ دَقَائِق
'as-saaçatu - s-saadisatu wa *kh*amsu daqaa'iq
five minutes past six

7 رُبْع
rubç
quarter (hour)

8 السَّاعَةُ السَّادِسَةُ وَخَمْسَ عَشْرَةَ دَقِيقَةً / السَّاعَةُ السَّادِسَةُ وَرُبْعٌ
'as-saaçatu - s-saadisatu wa *kh*amsa ça*sh*rata daqiiqah / as-saaçatu-s-saadisatu wa rubç
fifteen minutes past six

9 السَّاعَةُ السَّادِسَةُ وَنِصْفٌ
'as-saaçatu - s-saadisatu wa nisf
half past six

10 السَّاعَةُ السَّابِعَةُ إِلَّا خَمْسَ عَشْرَ ةَ دَقِيقَةً (رُبْع)
'as-saaçatu -s-saabiçatu 'il-la *kh*amsa ça*sh*rata daqiiqah (rubç)
fifteen minutes to seven

11 السَّاعَةُ السَّابِعَةُ إِلَّا خَمْسَ دَقَائِق
'as-saaçatu -s-saabiçatu 'il-la *kh*amsa daqaa'iq
five minutes to seven

37 كَمِ السَّاعَةُ؟
kami - s-saaçah
What is the time?

38 السَّاعَةُ الثَّامِنَةُ وَنِصْفٌ.
'as-saaçatu - *th*-*th*aaminatu wa niṣf
Half past eight.

39 آسِفَةٌ؛ لِأَنَّنِي مُتَأَخِّرَة.
'aasifatun li'an-nani muta'akh-khirah
Sorry, I'm late.

40 لَا بَأْس (أُوكِيه).
laa ba's ('ukayih)
It is OK.

12 مُنَبِّه
munab-bih
alarm clock

13 سَاعَةُ الْإِيقَاف (سْتُوب وَاتْش)
saaçatu -l- 'iiqaaf (stup waatsh)
stopwatch

14 سَاعَةٌ ذَكِيَّة
saaçatun *thz*akiy-yah
smartwatch

15 سَاعَةُ يَد
saaçatu yad
wrist watch

Additional Vocabulary

17 وَقْت
waqt
time

18 الصَّبَاحُ الْبَاكِر
'aṣ-ṣabaaḥu-l-baakir
early morning

19 فِي الصَّبَاح
fi - ṣ-ṣabaaḥ
in the morning; a.m.

20 الظُّهْر
'ẓ-ẓuhr
noon

21 بَعْدَ الظُّهْر
baçda -ẓ-ẓuhr
in the afternoon; p.m.

22 مُنْتَصَفُ اللَّيْل
muntaṣafu - l-layl
midnight

23 دَقِيق
daqiiq
punctual

24 مُبَكِّرًا
mubak-kiran
early

25 مُتَأَخِّرًا
muta'akh-khiran
late

26 سَاعَة
saaçah
o'clock

27 فِيمَا بَعْدُ (لَاحِقًا)
fiimaa baçd (laaḥiqan)
later

28 قَبْل
qabl
before

29 بَيْن
bayn
between; among

30 لَحْظَةٌ قَصِيرَة
laḥẓatun qaṣiirah
a brief moment

31 مُنْذُ لَحْظَة
mun*thz*u laḥẓah
a moment ago

32 فِي الْمَاضِي
fi -l-maaḍii
in the past

33 مِرَارًا وَتَكْرَارًا
miraaran wa takraaran
frequently

34 بَعْدَ لَحْظَة
baçda laḥẓah
in a moment

35 مُفَاجِئ (عَاجِل)
mufaaji' (çaajil)
sudden

36 أَخِيرًا
'a*kh*iiran
finally

41 أَرَاكَ فِي السَّاعَةِ الثَّالِثَةِ بَعْدَ الظُّهْر!
'araaka fi - s-saaçati - *th*-*th*aali*th*ati baçda - ẓ -ẓuhr
See you (m) at 3 p.m.!

16 لَيْل
layl
night

16 السَّنَوَاتُ وَالتَّوَارِيخ

‘as-sanawaatu wa-t-tawaarii*kh*

Years and Dates

4 تَقْوِيم (نَتِيجَة)
taqwiim (natiijah)
calendar

1 سَنَة (عَام)
sanah (çaam)
year

2 شَهْر
***sh*ahr**
month

3 يَوْم
yawm
day

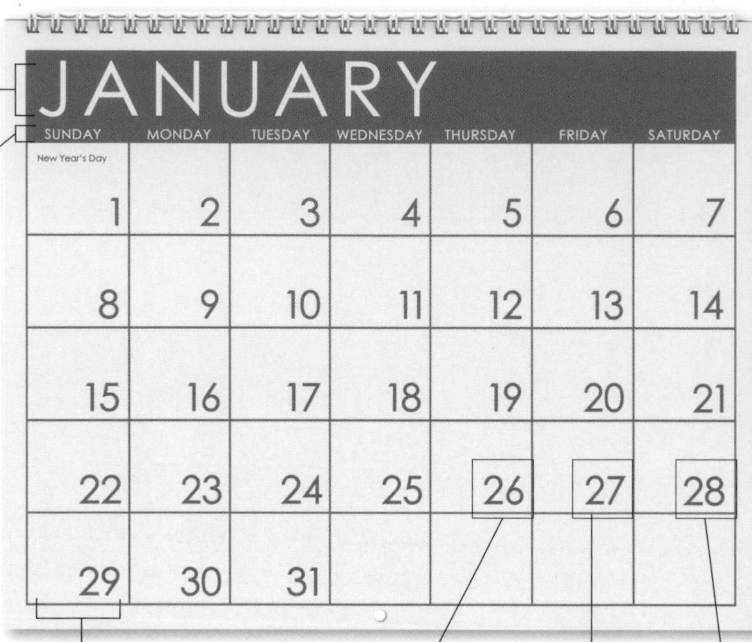

JANUARY
SUNDAY MONDAY TUESDAY WEDNESDAY THURSDAY FRIDAY SATURDAY
New Year's Day
1 2 3 4 5 6 7
8 9 10 11 12 13 14
15 16 17 18 19 20 21
22 23 24 25 26 27 28
29 30 31

5 يَوْمُ الْأَحَد
yawmu -l-‘aḥad
Sunday

6 أَمْس
‘ams
yesterday

7 الْيَوْم
‘alyawm
today

8 غَدًا
***gh*adan**
tomorrow

9 يَوْمُ الْأَحَد **yawmu -l-‘aḥad** Sunday
10 يَوْمُ الِاثْنَيْن **yawmu -l-i*th*nayn** Monday
11 يَوْمُ الثُّلَاثَاء **yawmu *th*-*th*ulaa*th*aa‘** Tuesday
12 يَوْمُ الْأَرْبِعَاء **yawmu -l -‘arbiçaa‘** Wednesday
13 يَوْمُ الْخَمِيس **yawmu -l -*kh*amiis** Thursday
14 يَوْمُ الْجُمُعَة **yawmu -l -jumuçah** Friday
15 يَوْمُ السَّبْت **yawmu -s - sabt** Saturday

45 أُحِبُّ أَنْ أَحْتَفِظَ بِمُذَكِّرَاتٍ.
‘uḥib-bu ‘an ‘aḥtafiẓa bimu*thz*ak-kiraat
I like to keep a diary.

46 الْيَوْمُ هُوَ الْجُمُعَة، السَّابِعُ وَالْعِشْرُونَ مِنْ يَنَايِر.
‘alyawmu huwa -l-jumuçah ‘as-saabiçu wa-l-çi*sh*ruuna min yanaayir
Today is Friday, January 27.

47 أَمْسِ كَانَ الْخَمِيس، السَّادِسُ وَالْعِشْرُونَ مِنْ يَنَايِر.
‘amsi kaana -l-*kh*amiis ‘as-saadisu wa -l-çi*sh*ruuna min yanaayir
Yesterday was Thursday, January 26.

48 غَدًا سَيَكُونُ السَّبْت، الثَّامِنُ وَالْعِشْرُونَ مِنْ يَنَايِر.
***gh*adan sayakuunu -s-sabt ‘a*th*-*th*aaminu wa-l-çi*sh*ruuna min yanaayir**
Tomorrow will be Saturday, January 28.

How to express years, months and dates in Arabic:

Read from left to right, saying the thousands moving forward.

2022 is أَلْفَانِ وَاثْنَانِ وَعِشْرُون **'alfaani wa thnaani wa çishruun**

2021 is أَلْفَانِ وَوَاحِدٌ وَعِشْرُون **'alfaani wa waaḥidun wa çishruun**

1988 is أَلْفٌ وَتِسْعُمِائَةٌ وَثَمَانِيَةٌ وَثَمَانُون **'alfun wa tisçumi'atun wa thamaaniyatun wa thamaanuun**

The 12 months of the year in Arabic are:

16 January يَنَايِر **yanaayir**
17 February فِبْرَايِر **fibraayir**
18 March مَارِس **maaris**
19 April إِبْرِيل **'ibriil**
20 May مَايُو **maayuu**
21 June يُونْيُو **yunyuu**
22 July يُولْيُو **yulyuu**
23 August أُغُسْطُس **'ughusṭus**
24 September سِبْتَمْبِر **sibtambir**
25 October أُكْتُوبَر **'uktuubar**
26 November نُوفَمْبِر **nuvambir**
27 December دِيسَمْبِر **diisambir**

Use the ordinal number when saying dates:

February 5 الْخَامِسُ مِنْ فِبْرَايِر **'alkhamisu min fibraayir**

March 31 الْوَاحِدُ وَالثَّلَاثُونَ مِنْ مَارِس **'alwaaḥidu wa th-thalaathuuna min maaris**

April 1 الأَوَّلُ مِنْ إِبْرِيل **al'aw-walu min 'ibriil**

July 4 الرَّابِعُ مِنْ يُولْيُو **'ar-raabiçu min yulyuu**

December 25 الْخَامِسُ وَالْعِشْرُونَ مِنْ دِيسَمْبِر **'al'khaamisu wa 'alçishruuna min diisambir**

49 مَتَى عِيدُ مَوْلِدِكِ؟
mataa çiidu mawlidik
When is your (f) birthday?

50 عِيدُ مَوْلِدِي هُوَ الْوَاحِدُ وَالثَّلَاثُونَ مِنْ يَنَايِر.
çiidu mawlidii huwa -l-waaḥidu wa-th-thalaathuuna min yanaayir
My birthday is on January 31.

Additional Vocabulary

28 يَوْمٌ مِنَ الشَّهْر
yawmun mina - sh-shahr
day of a month

29 أُسْبُوع
'usbuuç
week

30 سَنَوَاتُ الْعُمْر
sanawaatu -l-çumr
years of life

31 الأُسْبُوعُ الْمَاضِي
'al'usbuuçu -l-maaḍii
last week

32 الأُسْبُوعُ الْقَادِم
'al'usbuuçu- l-qaadim
next week

33 الشَّهْرُ الْمَاضِي
'ash-shahru -l-maaḍii
last month

34 الشَّهْرُ الْقَادِم
'ash-shahru -l-qaadim
next month

35 السَّنَةُ الْمَاضِيَة
'as-sanatu -l-maaḍiyah
last year

36 الْعَامُ السَّابِق
'alçaamu -s-saabiq
the year before

37 هَذَا الْعَام
hathza -l-çaam
this year

38 الْعَامُ الْقَادِم
'alçaamu -l-qaadim
next year

39 الْعَامُ بَعْدَ الْقَادِم
'alçaamu baçda -l-qaadim
the year after next

40 يَوْمِيَّات (مُذَكِّرَاتٌ)
yawmiy-yaat (muthzakiraat)
diary

41 سَنَةٌ كَبِيسَة
sanatun kabiisah
leap year

42 عَقْد
çaqd
decade (10 years)

43 قَرْن
qarn
century (100 years)

44 أَلْفِيَّة
'alfiy-yah
millennium (1000 years)

17 فُصُولُ السَّنَة

fuṣuulu -s-saanah

The Seasons of the Year

1 الرَّبِيع
‘ar-rabiiç
spring

2 الصَّيْف
‘aṣ-ṣayf
summer

3 الْخَرِيف
‘al*kh*ariif
autumn/fall

4 الشِّتَاء
‘a*sh*-*sh*itaa‘
winter

5 دَافِئ
daafi‘
warm

6 نَسِيمٌ لَطِيف
nasiimun laṭiif
a gentle breeze

7 أَزْهَارُ الْخَوْخ
‘azhaaru -l-*kh*aw*kh*
peach blossoms

8 يُزْهِر
yuzhir
to blossom

9 تُمْطِرُ رَذَاذًا
tumṭiru ra*thz*aa*thz*an
to drizzle

10 ظِلُّ الشَّمْس
ẓil-lu -*sh*-*sh*ams
sun shade

11 اللَّعِبُ بِالْمَاء
‘al-laçibu bi-l-maa‘
playing with water

12 يَصْنَعُ رَجُلَ الْجَلِيد
yaṣnaçu rajula -l-jaaliid
to make a snowman

The changing colors of the seasons.
تَغْيُّرُ أَلْوَانِ الْفُصُول taghy-yuru 'alwaani-l-fuṣuul

أَزْهَارُ الرَّبِيع	خُضْرَةُ الصَّيْف	أَوْرَاقُ الْخَرِيف	ثَلْجُ الشِّتَاءِ
'azhaaru -r-rabiiç	khuḍratu -ṣ-ṣayf	'awraaqu-l-khariif	thalju-sh-shitaa'
spring blossoms	summer greenery	autumn foliage	winter snow

13 يَحْصُد
yaḥṣud
to harvest

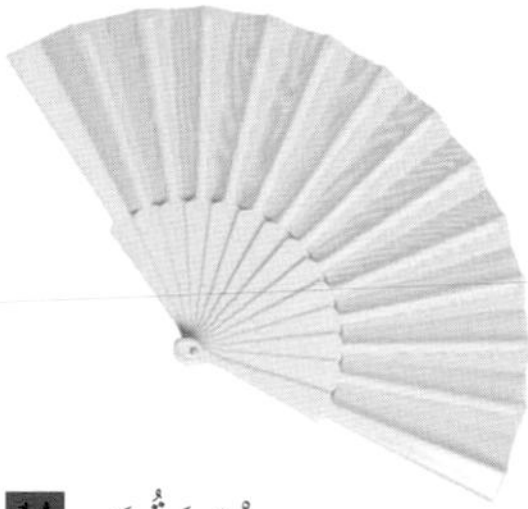

14 مِرْوَحَةُ يَد
mirwaḥatu yad
hand fan

15 تَرَاشُقُ كُرَةِ الثَّلْج
taraashuqu kurati -th-thalj
snowball fights

16 كِرِيم (دِهَان) حِمَايَةِ مِنْ حُرُوقِ الشَّمْس
kiriim (dihaan) ḥimaayatin min ḥuruuqi-sh-shams
sunblock lotion

17 مَحَاصِيل
maḥaaṣiil
crops

Additional Vocabulary

18 الْمَوَاسِمُ الْأَرْبَعَةُ (الْفُصُول)
'almawaasimu-l-'arbaçah ('alfuṣuul)
four seasons

19 سَابِق
saabiq
former

20 فِعْلِيًّا
fiçliy-yan
actually

21 أَوَدُّ أَنْ أَذْهَبَ إِلَى الشَّاطِئِ، وَأَلْعَبَ بِالْخَارِجِ.
'awad-du 'an 'athzhaba 'ila sh-shaaṭi' wa 'alçaba bil-khaarij
I'd like to go to the beach and play outdoors.

22 كَمْ مَوْسِمًا (فَصْلًا) فِي السَّنَةِ؟
kam mawsiman (faṣlan) fi -s-sanah
How many seasons are there in a year?

23 هُنَاكَ أَرْبَعَةُ مَوَاسِمَ فِي السَّنَةِ.
hunaaka 'arbaçatu mawaasima fi-s-sanah
There are four seasons in a year.

24 مَا مَوْسِمُكَ الْمُفَضَّل؟
maa mawsimuka -l-mufaḍ-ḍal
What is your (m) favorite season?

25 مَوْسِمِي (فَصْلِي) الْمُفَضَّلُ هُوَ الصَّيْف.
mawsimii (faṣlii) 'almufaḍ-ḍalu huwa-ṣ-ṣayf
My favorite season is summer.

18 الاِحْتِفَالُ بِالأَعْيَاد
‘aliḥtifaalu bil‘açyaad
Celebrating the Holidays

1 مِهْرَجَان
mihrajaan
festival

2 عَامٌ جَدِيد
çaamun jadiid
New Year

3 أَلْعَابٌ نَارِيَّة
‘alçaabun naariy-yah
fireworks

4 رَأْسُ السَّنَةِ الْمِيلَادِيَّة
ra‘su -s-sanati -l-miilaadiy-yah
New Year's Day

5 لَيْلَةُ رَأْسِ السَّنَةِ الْمِيلَادِيَّةِ
laylatu ra‘si- s-sanati -l-miilaadiy-yah
New Year's Eve

6 عِيدُ الْفِطْر
çiidu -l-fiṭr
Eid Al fitr

7 عِيدُ الأَضْحَى
çiidu -l -‘aḍḥaa
Eid Al ‘adHa

8 السَّنَةُ الْهِجْرِيَّة
‘as-sanatu -l-hijriy-yah
Islamic Year

9 رَمَضَان
ramaḍaan
Ramadan

10 أَحَدُ الشَّعَانِين (السَّعَف)
‘aḥadu -*sh*-*sh*açaaniin (‘as-saçaf)
Palm Sunday

11 كَحْكُ الْعِيد
kaḥku -l-çiid
Eid Cookies

12 فَسِيخ
fasii*kh*
salted fish

13 كُنَافَة
kunaafah
kunafa

14 عِيدُ الأَب
çiidu -l- ‘ab
Father's Day

15 عِيدُ الأُمّ
çiidu -l-‘um-m
Mother's Day

16 عِيدُ الْحُبِّ
çiidu -l-ḥub-b
Valentine's Day

17 شُكُولَاتَة
*sh*ukulaatah
chocolates

18 وَرْد
ward
roses

19 عِيدُ الشُّكْرِ
çiidu -*sh*-*sh*ukr
Thanksgiving

20 هَالُووِين
haaluuwiin
Halloween

21 شَمُّ النَّسِيم
*sh*am-mu -n-nasiim
Easter Day

22 عِيدُ الإِسْتِقْلَال
çiidu -l- istiqlaal
Independence Day

Additional Vocabulary

26 الْمَوْلِدُ النَّبَوِيُّ الشَّرِيف
'almawlidu -n-nabawiy-yu -*sh*-*sh*ariif
Prophet Muhamed Birthday celebration

27 إِجَازَةُ الصَّيْفِ
'ijaazatu -ṣ-ṣayf
summer vacation (break)

28 إِجَازَةُ الشِّتَاءِ
'ijaazatu -*sh*-*sh*itaa'
winter vacation (break)

29 إِجَازَةُ انْتِهَاءِ السَّنَةِ الدِّرَاسِيَّةِ
'ijaazatu -ntihaa'i
-s-sanati -d-diraasiy-yah
end of the school year holiday

30 عِيدٌ (ذِكْرَى سَنَوِيَّةٌ)
çiid (*thz*ikraa sanawiy-yah)
anniversary

31 شَهْرُ الْعَسَل
*sh*ahru -l- çasal
honeymoon

32 عِيدُ مِيلَاد
çiidu miilaad
birthday

33 يَحْضُرُ عِيدَ مِيلَاد
yaḥḍuru çiida miilaad
to attend a birthday party

34 الْحَجّ
'alhaj-j
alhajj
(pilgrimage)

35 عِيدُ مِيلَادٍ سَعِيد!
çiidu miilaadin saçiid
Happy birthday!

23 هَدِيَّة
hadiy-yah
gift

36 عِيدٌ مِيلَادٍ مَجِيد!
çiidun miilaadin
majiid
Merry Christmas!

24 الْكِرِيسْمَاس
'alkriismaas
Christmas

25 سَانْتَا كُلُوز
saanta kuluuz
Santa Claus

37 يُرْجَى الِانْضِمَامُ إِلَيْنَا فِي إِفْطَارِ رَمَضَان.
yurja- l- inḍimaamu 'ilaynaa fii 'ifṭaari ramaḍaan
Please join us for the Ramadan Iftar.

38 كُلُّ عَامٍ وَأَنْتَ بِخَيْر!
kul-lu çaamin wa 'anta bi*kh*ayr
Happy Year!

19 أُحِبُّ أَنْ أَتَعَلَّمَ

‘uḥib-bu ‘an ‘ataçal-lam

I Love to Learn

1 امْتِحَان (امْتِحَانَات)
‘imtiḥaan (‘imtiḥaanaat)
exam (exams)

2 قِرَاءَة
qiraa‘ah
reading

3 يَتَعَلَّم
yataçal-lam
to learn

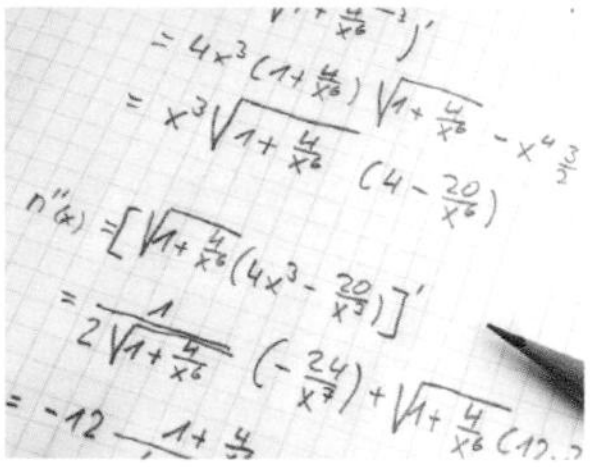

4 رِيَاضِيَّات
riyaaḍiy-yaat
mathematics

5 تَرْبِيَةٌ بَدَنِيَّة
tarbiyatun badaniy-yah
physical education

6 يُجِيب
yujiib
to answer

7 كِتَاب
kitaab
book

8 الْأَخْبَار
‘al‘a*kh*baar
the news

9 جَرِيدَة
jariidah
newspaper

10 مَجَلَّة
majal-lah
magazine

11 قَامُوس
qaamuus
dictionary

12 خِطَاب
***kh*iṭaab**
letter

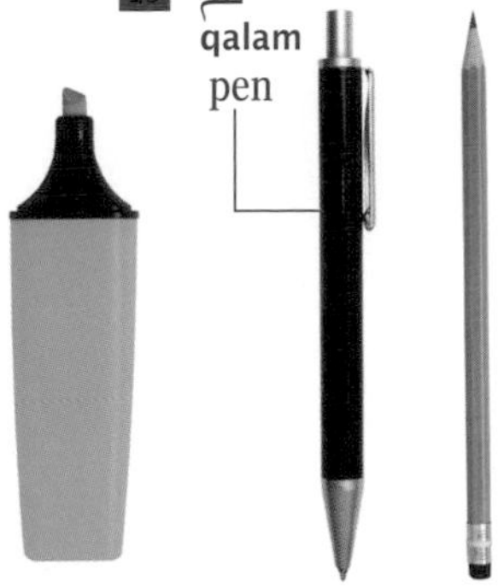

13 قَلَم
qalam
pen

14 مِمْحَاة
mimḥaah
eraser

15 قَلَمُ تَحْدِيد (مَارْكَر)
qalamu taḥdiid (maarkar)
marker pen

16 مِبْرَاة (بَرَّايَة)
mibraah
(bar-raayah)
pencil sharpener

17 مِسْطَرَة
misṭarah
ruler

18 دَفْتَر
daftar
notebook

19 قَلَمُ تَمْيِيز (هَايْلَيْتَر)
qalamu tamyiiz
(haaylaytar)
highlighter

20 قَلَمُ رَصَاص
qalamun raṣaaṣ
pencil

21 مِقَص
miqaṣ-ṣ
scissors

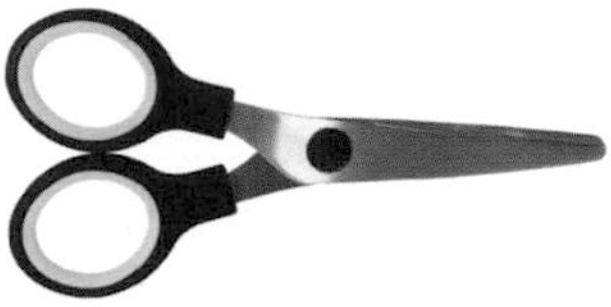

Additional Vocabulary

22 يَفْهَم
yafham
to understand

23 يُمَارِس
yumaaris
to practice

24 يُرَاجِع
yuraajiç
to review

25 أَدَب
'adab
literature

26 تَارِيخ
taarii*kh*
history

27 كَلِمَة
kalimah
word

28 قِصَّة
qiṣ - ṣah
story

29 حُبّ
ḥub-b
love

30 هَنْدَسَة
handasah
geometry

31 عُلُوم
çuluum
science

32 اقْتِصَاد
'iqtiṣaad
economics

33 جَبْر
jabr
algebra

34 فِيزِيَاء
fiiziyaa'
physics

35 كِيمِيَاء
kiimiyaa'
chemistry

36 جُغْرَافِيَا
ju*gh*raafiyaa
geography

37 اخْتِبَار
'i*kh*tibaar
test

38 مَوْهِبَة
mawhibah
talent

39 قُدْرَة
qudrah
ability

40 يَتَحَسَّن
yataḥas-san
to improve

41 أَعْلَى
'açlaa
top (higher)

42 يَدْرُس
yadrus
to study

43 هَدَف
hadaf
purpose / objective

44 عِلْمُ الْأَحْيَاء
çilmu -l-'aḥyaa'
biology

45 صَفٌّ دِرَاسِيٌّ
ṣaf-fun diraasiy-y
grade (level at school)

46 سُؤَال (مُشْكِلَة)
su'aal (mu*sh*kilaah)
question (problem)

47 عَمَلٌ مَنْزِلِيّ (وَاجِب)
çamalun manziliy-y (waajib)
homework

48 دِرَاسَاتٌ اجْتِمَاعِيَّة
diraasaatun - ijtimaaçiy-yah
social studies

49 حِسَابُ التَّفَاضُلِ وَالتَّكَامُل
ḥisaabu -t-tafaaḍuli wa-t-takaamul
calculus

50 مُهِمَّةٌ مَنْزِلِيَّة (وَاجِب)
muhim-matun manziliy-yah (waajib)
assignment

51 مُسْتَوى
mustawaa
level (of achievement)

53 مَا مَادَّتُكَ الدِّرَاسِيَّةُ الْمُفَضَّلَة؟
maa maad-datuka -d-diraasiy-yatu -l-mufaḍ-ḍalah
What is your (m) favorite subject?

54 أُحِبُّ الْأَدَبَ وَالتَّارِيخ.
'uḥib-bu -l-'adaba wa -t-taarii*kh*
I like literature and history.

52 أُحِبُّ الْكُتُب!
'uḥib-bu -l-kutub
I love books!

20 فِي الْمَدْرَسَة
fi -l- madrasah
At School

1 سَبُّورَةٌ بَيْضَاء
sab-buuratun bayḍaa‘
whiteboard

2 سَبُّورَة
sab-buurah
board

3 مَكْتَبَة
maktabah
library

4 فَصْلٌ دِرَاسِيّ
faṣlun diraasiy-y
classroom

5 يُعَلِّمُ (يُدَرِّسُ)
yuçal-lim (yudar-ris)
to teach

6 مُعَلِّمَة (مُدَرِّسَة)
muçal-limah (mudar-risah)
teacher (f)

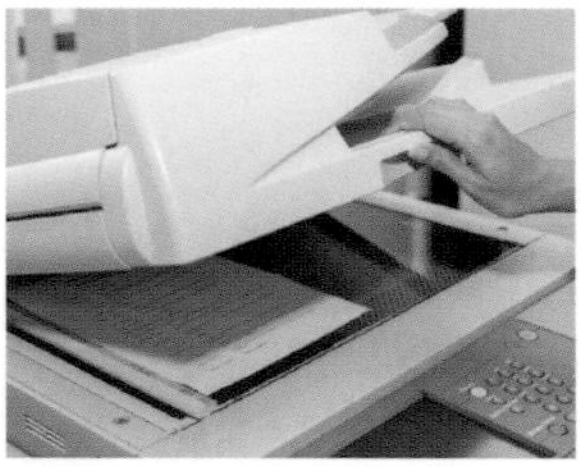

7 آلَةُ تَصْوِيرِ مُسْتَنَدَاتٍ
‘aalatu taṣwiiri mustanadaat
photocopier

9 ارْفَعْ يَدَك
‘rfaç yadak
raise your hand

12 عُلُوم
çuluum
science

11 آلَةٌ حَاسِبَةٌ
‘aalatun ḥaasibah
calculator

8 يُصَوِّرُ مُسْتَنَدَاتٍ
yuṣaw-wiru mustanadaat
to photocopy

10 دُكْتُورٌ جَامِعِيٌّ (أُسْتَاذ)
duktuurun jaamiçiy-y (‘ustaa*thz*)
professor

13 زُمَلَاءُ الصَّفّ
zumalaa‘u - ṣ-ṣaf-f
classmates

14 قَاعَةُ الْمُحَاضَرَات
qaaçatu -l- muḥaaḍaraat
lecture hall

15 طَالِب
ṭaalib
student

49 هَلْ تُرِيدِينَ الْمُسَاعَدَةَ فِي وَاجِبَاتِك؟
hal turiidiina lmusaaçadata fii waajibaatik
Do you (f) need help with your (f) assignment?

Additional Vocabulary

16 مَوْضُوع
mawduuç
topic

17 مَاهِر
maahir
clever

18 مُدِير
mudiir
principal

19 دَرَجَات
darajaat
grades

20 ذَكِيّ
*thz*akiy-y
intelligent

21 قَاعَة (مَسْرَح)
qaaçah (masraḥ)
auditorium

22 مَعْمَل
maçmal
laboratory

23 دَفْتَرُ التَّدْرِيبَات
daftaru-t-tadriibaat
workbook

24 كِتَابٌ مَدْرَسِيّ
kitaabun madrasiy-y
textbook

25 صَفٌّ لَيْلِيّ
ṣaf-fun layliy-y
night class

26 مَدْرَسَة
madrasah
school

27 مَدْرَسَةٌ خَاصَّةٌ
madrasatun *kh*aaṣ-ṣah
private school

28 مَدْرَسَةٌ عَامَّة
madrasatun çaam-mah
public school

29 حَضَانَة
ḥaḍaanah
nursery school

30 مَدْرَسَةٌ ابْتِدَائِيَّة
madrasatun-ibtidaa'iy-yah
elementary school

31 مَدْرَسَةٌ مُتَوَسِّطَة
madrasatun mutawas-siṭah
middle school

32 مَدْرَسَةٌ ثَانَوِيَّة
madrasatun *th*aanawiy-yah
high school

33 جَامِعَة
jaamiçah
university

34 كُلِّيَّة
kul-liy-yah
college

35 يَتَخَصَّصُ فِي
yata*kh*aṣ-ṣaṣu fii
to major in

36 يَتَخَرَّج
yata*kh*ar-raj
to graduate

37 الْحُرُوفُ الأَبْجَدِيَّة
'alḥuruufu -l-'abjadiy-yah
alphabet

38 مَعْمَلُ حَاسِبٍ آلِيّ (مَعْمَل كُمْبِيُوتَر)
maçmalu ḥaasibin 'aaliy-y (maçmal ḳumbiyuutar)
computer lab

39 يَدْرُسُ فِي مَدْرَسَةٍ ابْتِدَائِيَّة
yadrusu fi madrasatin -i-btidaa'iy-yah
to go to elementary school

40 السَّنَةُ الأُولَى فِي الْكُلِّيَّة
'as-sanatu-l-'uulaa fi -l-kul-liy-yah
freshman year in college

41 السَّنَةُ الثَّانِيَةُ فِي الْكُلِّيَّة
'as-sanatu -*th*-*th*aaniyatu fi -l-kul-liy-yah
sophomore year in college

42 السَّنَةُ الثَّالِثَةُ فِي الْكُلِّيَّة
'as-sanatu *th*-*th*aali*th*atu fi -l-kul-liy-yah
junior year in college

43 سَنَةُ التَّخَرُّجِ مِنَ الْكُلِّيَّة
sanatu -t-ta*kh*ar-ruji mina -l-kul-liy-yah
senior year in college

44 فِي أَيِّ عَامٍ أَنْتَ؟
fii 'ay-yi çaamin 'ant
What year are you (m) in?

45 أَنَا فِي السَّنَةِ الثَّانِيَةِ فِي الْكُلِّيَّةِ.
'ana fi -s-sanati -*th*-*th*aaniyati fi -l-kul-liy-yah
I'm a sophomore in college.

46 مَا تَخَصُّصُكَ؟
maa ta*kh*aṣ-ṣuṣuk
What is your (m) major?

47 أَنَا مُتَخَصِّصٌ فِي الرِّيَاضِيَّاتِ.
'ana muta*kh*aṣ-ṣiṣun fi-r-riyaaḍiy-yaat
I am majoring in math.

48 أَنْتَ بِالتَّأْكِيدِ ذَكِيٌّ جِدًّا!
'anta bi-t-ta'kiidi *thz*akiy-yun jid-dan
You must be very smart!

21 تَعَلُّمُ اللُّغَةِ الْعَرَبِيَّة
taçal-lumu -l-lu*gh*ati -l-çarabiy-yah
Learning the Arabic Language

1 اللُّغَةُ الْعَرَبِيَّةُ لَيْسَتْ صَعْبَةً لِتَتَحَدَّثَهَا.
'al-lu*gh*atu -l-çarabiy-yatu laysat ṣaçbatan litataḥad-da*th*ahaa
Arabic is not a difficult language to speak.

2 وَلَكِنَّهَا تَحْتَاجُ إِلَى وَقْتٍ لِتَعَلُّمِهَا.
wa laakin-nahaa taḥtaaju 'ilaa waqtin litaçal-lumihaa
But it takes time to learn it.

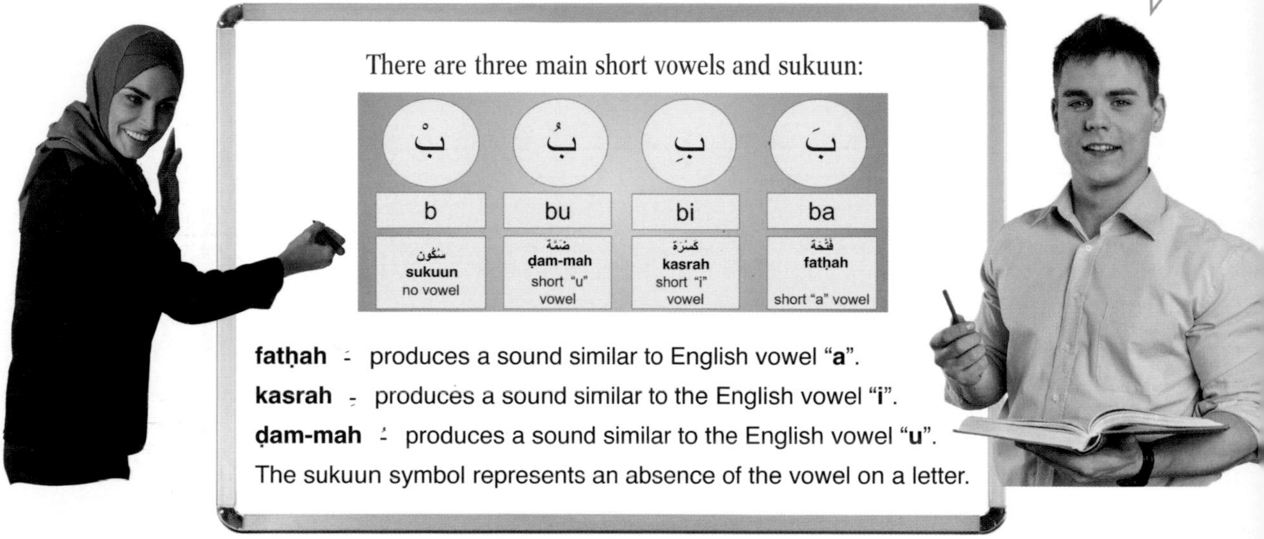

There are three main short vowels and sukuun:
بْ بُ بِ بَ
b bu bi ba
سُكُون sukuun no vowel
ضَمَّة ḍam-mah short "u" vowel
كَسْرَة kasrah short "i" vowel
فَتْحَة fatḥah short "a" vowel
fatḥah َ produces a sound similar to English vowel "a".
kasrah ِ produces a sound similar to the English vowel "i".
ḍam-mah ُ produces a sound similar to the English vowel "u".
The sukuun symbol represents an absence of the vowel on a letter.

3 بِطَاقَاتٌ تَعْلِيمِيَّة
biṭaaqaatun taçliimiy-yah
flashcards

4 اللُّغَةُ الْعَرَبِيَّةُ تُكْتَبُ بِخَطٍّ مُتَّصِلٍ.
'al-lu*gh*atu -l-çarabiy-yatu tuktabu bi*kh*aṭ-ṭin mut-taṣil
Arabic is written in cursive.

5 فَنُّ الْخَطّ
fan-nu -l-*kh*aṭ-ṭ
calligraphy

Additional Vocabulary

6 اسْم
'ism
noun

7 فِعْل
fiçl
verb

8 صِفَة
ṣifah
adjective

9 حَال
ḥaal
adverb

10 حَرْفُ جرّ
ḥarfu jar-r
preposition

11 إِضَافَة
'iḍaafah
annexation

12 كَلِمَة
kalimah
word

13 جُمْلَة
jumlah
sentence

14 عِبَارَة
çibaarah
phrase

15 مَقَالَةٌ قَصِيرَة
maqaalatun qaṣiirah
short essay

16 قَصِيدَة
qaṣiidah
poem

17 مَقَالَة
maqaalah
essay

18 ثَقَافَة
*th*aqaafah
culture

19 نَحْو
naḥw
grammar

20 تَرْجَمَة
tarjamah
translation

21 لُغَوِيَّات
lu*gh*awiy-yaat
linguistics

22 دَرْس
dars
lesson

23 مُهِمَّة
muhim-mah
assignment / task

24 كِتَابُ تَدْرِيبَات
kitaabu tadriibaat
exercise book

25 بَسِيط
basiiṭ
simple

26 يَفْهَم
yafham
to understand

27 سَهْل
sahl
easy

28 صَعْب
ṣaçb
difficult

29 تَدْرِيب
tadriib
drill (academic)

30 يَجْتَهِد
yajtahid
to strive

31 يُعِدّ
yuçid-d
to prepare

32 خَبَر
*kh*abar
predicate

33 مُبْتَدَأ
mubtada'
subject (in a nominal sentence)

34 تَعْبِيرٌ اصْطِلَاحِيّ
taçbiirun i-ṣṭilaaḥiy-y
idiom

35 مُقَرَّرٌ تَعْلِيمِيّ
muqar-rarun taçliimiy-y
course; curriculum

36 اللُّغَةُ الْعَرَبِيَّةُ الْفُصْحَى الْمُعَاصِرَة
'al-lu*gh*atu -l- çarabiy-yatu -l- fuṣḥa -l- muçaaṣirah
Modern Standard Arabic (MSA)

37 لَهَجَات
lahajaat
dialects (of different Arabic countries)

38 عَلَامَاتُ التَّشْكِيل
çalaamaatu -t-ta*sh*kiil
diacritics; tone marks

39 مُفْرَدَات (كَلِمَات)
mufradaat (kalimaat)
vocabulary

40 حَرَكَاتٌ قَصِيرَة
ḥarakaatun qaṣiirah
short vowels

41 حَرَكَاتٌ طَوِيلَة
ḥarakaatun ṭawiilah
long vowels

42 جُمْلَةٌ اسْمِيَّة
jumlatun ismiy-yah
a nominal sentence

43 جُمْلَةٌ فِعْلِيَّة
jumlatun fiçliy-yah
a verbal sentence

44 فَاعِل
faaçil
a subject (doer of an action)

45 مَفْعُولٌ بِهِ
mafçuulun bih
an object

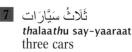

22 تَرَاكِيبُ حِسَابِيَّة
taraakiibu ḥisaabiy-yah
Counting Words

Also known as "measure words"

1 كِيسَانِ مِنَ السُّكَّر
kiisaani mina -s-suk-kar
two bags (packets) of sugar

2 ثَلَاثَةُ كُتُب
***th*alaa*th*atu kutub**
three books

3 زَوْجٌ وَاحِدٌ مِنَ الْأَحْذِيَة
zawjun waaḥidun mina -l-'aḥ*thz*iyah
one pair of shoes

4 خَمْسُ تَذَاكِر
***kh*amsu ta*thz*aakir**
five tickets

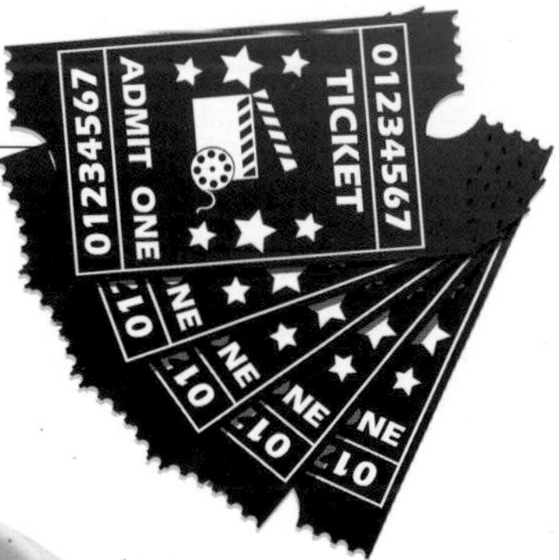

5 ثَمَانِي قِطَعٍ مِنَ الْمَلَابِس
***th*amaanii qiṭaçin mina -l-malaabis**
eight pieces of clothing

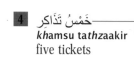

6 وِعَاءُ حِسَاءٍ وَاحِد
wiçaa'u ḥisaa'in waaḥid
one bowl of soup

8 كُرْسِيٌّ وَاحِد
kursiy-yun waaḥid
one chair

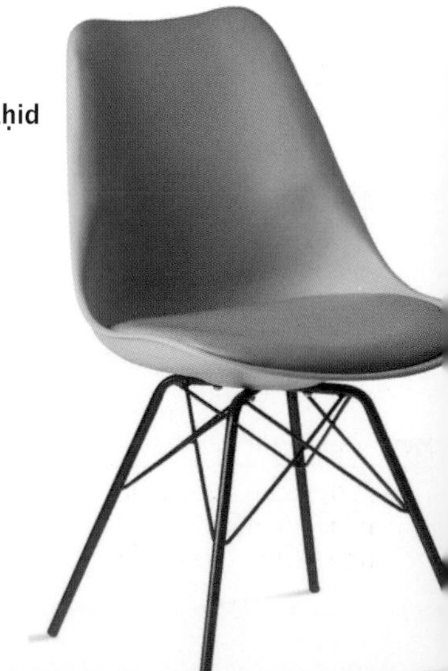

7 ثَلَاثُ سَيَّارَات
***th*alaa*th*u say-yaaraat**
three cars

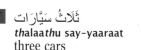

Counting words or measure words are used to quantify things, just as in English when we say "three sheets of paper" or "two cups of coffee."

Some common measure words in Arabic are listed below.

MEASURE WORDS		MAIN USES	EXAMPLES
عُبُوَّة	çubuw-wah	packet	13 اشْتَرَيْتُ عُبُوَّةً مِنَ الشَّاي. 'ishtaraytu çubuw-watan mina sh-shaay I bought a packet of tea.
طَرْد	ṭard	package	14 جَاءَنِي طَرْدٌ مِنْ صَدِيق. jaa'anii ṭardun min ṣadiiq I received a package from a friend.
حُزْمَة	ḥuzmah	a bundle	15 حُزْمَةٌ مِنَ الْوَرَقِ ḥuzmatun mina lwaraq a bundle of papers
زَوْجٌ مِنْ	zawjun min	objects that comes in pairs	16 زَوْجٌ مِنَ الْأَحْذِيَة zawjun mina l'aḥthziyah a pair of shoes
لِتْر	litr	liter	17 لِتْرُ مَاءٍ litru maa' a liter of water
كِيلُوغرَام	kiiluu ghiraam	kilogram	18 كِيلُوغِرَامٍ مِنَ الذَّهَبِ kiilu ghiraamin mina thz-thzahab a kilogram of gold
مِيْل	miil	mile	19 مِيلٌ وَاحِدٌ مِنَ الْمَنْزِلِ miilun waaḥidun mina lmanzil a mile from home
كِيلُومِتْر	kiluu mitr	kilometer	20 كِيلُو مِتْرٍ وَاحِدٌ مِنَ الْجَامِعَةِ kiilu mitrin waaḥidun mina ljaamiçah a kilometer from the university
قِطْعَة	qiṭçah	piecc	21 قِطْعَةُ شُكُولَاتَة qiṭçatu shukulaatah a piece of chocolate

9 مَجْمُوعَةٌ وَاحِدَةٌ مِنَ النَّاس
majmuuçatun waaḥidatun mina -n-naas
one group of people

10 سِتَّةُ أَشْخَاص
sit-tatu 'ashkhaaṣ
six people

11 مَبْنًى مِنْ أَرْبَعَةِ طَوَابِق
mabnan min 'arbaçati ṭawaabiq
four-story building

12 كُوبَان مِنَ الشَّاي
kuubaani mina -sh-shaay
two cups of tea

23 الْحَاسِبُ الْآلِيّ وَالإِنْتَرْنِت
'lhaasibu l'aaliy-y wa -l-'intarnit
Computer and the Internet

Most of the technological words have both standardized translation and colloquial, Arabized pronunciation of the English words.

1 حَاسِبٌ آلِيّ (كُمْبِيُوتَر)
ḥaasibun 'aaliy-y (kumbiyuutar)
computer

2 شَاشَة
shaashah
screen

3 كُمْبِيُوتَر لَوْحِيّ (تَابْلِتْ)
kumbiyuutar lawḥiy-y (taablit)
tablet

7 مِنَ السَّهْلِ الِاتِّصَالُ بِالإِنْتَرْنِتْ فِي الشَّرْقِ الأَوْسَطِ.
mina -s-sahl -i- t-tiṣaalu bil'intarnit fi -*sh*-*sh*arqi -l- 'awsaṭ
It is easy to get online in the Middle East.

4 حَاسُوبٌ مَكْتَبِيّ (كُمْبِيُوتَرْ)
ḥaasuubun maktabiy-y (kumbiyuutar)
desktop computer

5 لَوْحَةُ مَفَاتِيح (كِي بُورْدْ)
lawuḥatu mafaatiiḥ (kii burd)
keyboard

6 حَاسُوبٌ مَحْمُول (لَابْ تُوبْ)
ḥaasuubun maḥmuul (laab tuub)
laptop

10 فَأْرَة (مَاوِسْ)
fa'rah (maawis)
mouse

8 لُعْبَةُ فِيدِيُو (فِيدْيُو جِيمْ)
luçbatu vidiyuu (vidiyuu gim)
video game

9 وِسَادَةُ الْفَأْرَة (مَاوِسْ بَادْ)
wisaadatu -l- fa'rah (maawis baad)
mousepad

11 مَاسِحٌ ضَوْئِيّ (سْكَانَر)
maasiḥun ḍaw'iy-y (scaanar)
scanner

12 قُرْصٌ مَضْغُوط (سِي دِي) دِي فِي دِي
qursun maḍ*gh*uuṭ (sii dii) dii vii dii
CD/DVD

13 فِلَاشَة يُو إِسْ بِي
filaa*sh*ah yu 'is bii
USB flash drive

14 مَنَافِذ (بُورْتِسْ)
manaafi*thz* (puurtis)
ports

15 بَرِيدٌ إِلِكْتِرُونِيّ (إِيمِيلْ)
bariidun 'iliktiruuniy-y ('iimiil)
email

Additional Vocabulary

16 دُخُولٌ إِلَى الْإِنْتَرْنِتّ (أَكْسِيسْ لِلنِّتْ)
du*kh*uulun ‘ila -l-‘intarnit (‘aksis lin-nit)
Internet access

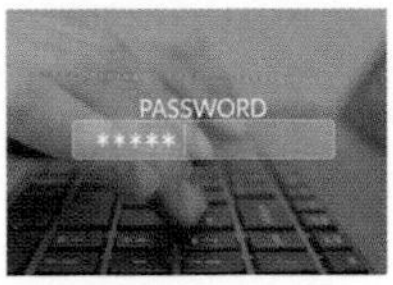

17 كَلِمَةُ الْمُرُورِ (بَاسْوُرْدْ)
kalimatu -l-muruur (baaswurd)
password

18 يُرْسِلُ بَرِيدًا إِلِكْتِرُونِيًّا (إِيمِيلْ)
yursilu bariidan ‘iliktiruuniy-yan (‘iimiil)
to send email

19 غُرْفَةُ الدَّرْدَشَةِ (شَاتْ رُووُمْ)
***gh*urfatu -d-darda*sh*ah (*sh*aat ruum)**
chat room

20 دَرْدَشَةٌ عَبْرَ الْإِنْتَرْنِتّ (شَاتْ)
darda*sh*atun çabra -l-‘intarnit (*sh*aat)
online chat

21 مَوْقِعٌ إِلِكْتِرُونِيّ (وِيبْ سَايِتْ)
mawqiçun ‘iliktiruuniy-y (wib saayit)
website

22 شَبَكَة (نِيتْ وُرْكِينْجْ)
***sh*abakah (nit wurking)**
networking

23 يُسَجِّلُ الدُّخُول
yusaj-jilu -d-du*kh*uul
to sign in

24 بَرْنَامَج (سُوفْتْ وِيرْ)
barnaamaj (suft wiir)
software

25 نِظَامُ تَشْغِيل
ni*th*zaamu ta*sh*g*h*iil
operating system

26 فَيْرُوس (فَايْرَسْ)
vayruus (vaayras)
virus

27 مِلَفّ (فَايِلْ)
milaf-f (faayil)
file

28 صَفْحَةُ الْوِيب
ṣafḥatu -l-wib
web page

29 تَصْمِيمُ الْمَوَاقِع
taṣmiimu -l-mawaaqiç
web design

30 (URL) عُنْوَانُ الْوِيب
çunwaanu -l-wib (yu ar il)
web address/URL

31 تَطْبِيق
taṭbiiq
application (computer program)

32 يَنْقُر (كلِيكْ)
yanqur (kilik)
to click

33 تَحْمِيل (دَاوِنْلُوُودْ)
taḥmiil (daawinluud)
to download

34 يَتَّصِلُ بِالْإِنْتَرْنِتْ
yat-taṣilu bil‘intarnit
to connect to the internet

35 مُتَّصِلٌ بِالإِنْتَرنِت (أُونْ لايِنْ)
mut-taṣilun bil‘itarnit (‘un layin)
connected to the internet (online)

36 بِطَاقَةُ الشَّبَكَة
biṭaaqatu -*sh*-*sh*abakah
network card

37 وَسَائِطُ مُتَعَدِّدَة
wasaa‘iṭu mutaçad-didah
multimedia

38 مُدَوَّنَة
mudaw-wanah
blog

39 مُتَصَفِّح
mutaṣaf-fih
browser

40 أَمْنُ الشَّبَكَات
‘amnu -*sh*-*sh*abakaat
network security

41 بَحْثٌ عَلَى الْإِنْتَرْنِتّ
baḥ*th*un çala -l-‘intarnit
online search

42 وَايْ فَايْ
waay faay
wifi

43 شَبَكَةُ الْكَابِل
***sh*abakatu -l- kaabil**
cable network

44 هِوَايَتِي هِيَ اللَّعِبُ عَلَى الْإِنْتَرْنِتْ (أُونْ لايِنْ).
hiwaayatii hiya -l-laçibu çala -l-‘intarnit (‘un layin)
My hobby is online gaming.

45 دَعُونَا نُدَرْدِشْ عَلَى الْإِنْتَرْنِتْ (نَتَكَلَّمُ أُونْ لَايِنْ).
daçuunaa nudardi*sh* çala -l-‘intarnit (natakal-lam ‘un layin)
Let’s chat online.

46 مَا التَّطْبِيقُ (آبْ) الَّذِي تَسْتَخْدِمُهُ؟ أَنَا أَسْتَخْدِمُ الْفِيسْبُوك.
maa -t-taṭbiiq (‘aab) ‘al-la*th*zii tasta*kh*dimuh? ‘ana ‘asta*kh*dimu -l-fisbuuk
What app do you (m) use? I use Facebook.

47 حَسَنًا، أُرْسِلُ لَكَ الْمُسْتَنَدَاتِ الآنَ.
ḥasanan, ‘ursilu laka -l- mustanadaati -l-‘aan
Okay, I’m sending you (m) the documents now.

24 أُحِبُّ هَاتِفِي الذَّكِيّ
'uḥib-bu haatifi *thz*-*thz*akiy-y
I Love My Smartphone!

1 هَاتِفٌ ذَكِيّ (تِلِيفُونٌ ذَكِيٌّ) (سِمَارْتْ فُونْ)
haatifun *thz*akiy-y (tiliifuun *thz*akiy-y) (smaart fuun)
smartphone

2 أَصْدِقَاءُ عَبْرَ الإِنْتَرْنِت (أُون لَايْن)
'aṣdiqaa'u çabra l'intarnit
online friends

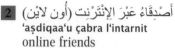

3 التَّسَوُّقُ عَبْرَ الْإِنْتَرْنِتْ
'at-tasaw-wuqu çabra l-'intarnit
online shopping

4 مَقَاهِي الْإِنْتَرْنِتْ (كَافِيهْ النِّتْ)
maqaahi -l-'intarnit (kaafiih 'in-nit)
Internet cafes

5 إِكْس
'iks
X

6 وَاتْسْ آبْ
waats 'aab
WhatsApp

7 هَاتِف (تِلِيفُونْ) أَنْدرُويدْ
haatif (tiliifuun) 'andruuyid
Android phone

8 هَاتِف آبِل (آيْفُونْ)
haatif 'aabil ('aayfuun)
Apple phone (iPhone)

9 جَوَّال (مُوبَايِلْ)
jaw-waal (mubaayil)
mobile phone

10 يُجْرِي مُكَالَمَةً هَاتِفِيَّةً
yujrii mukaalamatan haatifiy-yah
to make a phone call

11 يَتَلَقَّى مُكَالَمَةً هَاتِفِيَّةً
yatalaq-qaa mukaalamatan haatifiy-yah
to receive a phone call

Additional Vocabulary

21 شَبَكَةُ الْإِنْتَرْنِتْ
***sh*abakatu -l-'intarnit**
Internet

22 رَسَائِلُ نَصِّيَّةٌ
rasaa'ilu naṣ-ṣiy-yah
texting

23 عَامِّيَّةُ الْإِنْتَرْنِتْ
çaam-miy-yatu -l-'intarnit
Internet slang

24 فِيدِيُو
vidiyuu
video

25 لُغَةُ الْإِنْتَرْنِتْ
lu*gh*atu -l-'intarnit
Internet language

26 رَمْزُ (رَقْمُ) الْبَلَد
ramzu (raqmu) lbalad
country code

27 رَمْزُ (رَقْمُ) الْمِنْطَقَةِ
ramzu (raqmu) lminṭaqah
area code

28 رَقْمُ الْهَاتِفِ (التِّلِيفُونْ)
raqmu -l- haatif ('at-tilifuun)
telephone number

29 مُكَالَمَةٌ دَوْلِيَّةٌ
mukaalamatun dawliy-yah
long distance call (international call)

30 شَرِيحَةُ الْجَوَّال
***sh*ariiḥatu -l- jaw-waal**
SIM card

31 شَاحِنُ الْجَوَّالِ (اَلْهَاتِف)
***sh*aaḥinu -l- jaw-waal ('alhaatif)**
phone charger

32 بِطَاقَاتُ الْجَوَّال (اَلْهَاتِف)
biṭaaqaatu -l- jaw-waal ('alhaatif)
phone cards

12 إِشَارَةٌ قَوِيَّة
'ishaaratun qawiy-yah
strong signal

13 إِشَارَةٌ ضَعِيفَة
'ishaaratun ḍaçiifah
weak signal

14 سِلْفِي
silfii
selfie

15 أَمَازُون
'amaazuun
Amazon

16 يَاهُوو
yaahuu
Yahoo

17 فِيسْ بُوك
fiis buk
Facebook

18 جُوجَل
googal
Google

19 آبِل
'aabil
Apple

20 مَايِكْرُوسُوفْت
mayikruusuft
Microsoft

Some common telephone phrases:

33 أَهْلًا، هَذَا (اسْمٌ).
'ahlan hathzaa (name)
Hello, This is (name).

34 هَلْ يُمْكِنُنِي التَّحَدُّثُ إِلَى (اسْمٍ)؟
hal yumkinuni -t-taḥaduthu 'ilaa (name)
May I speak to (name)?

35 رَجَاءً، اطْلُبْ مِنْهُ \ مِنْهَا الرَّدَّ عَلَى مُكَالَمَاتِي.
rajaa'an 'uṭlub minhu / minha 'ar-rad-da çalaa mukaalamaatii
Please ask him/her to answer my calls.

36 هَلِ الْوَقْتُ مُنَاسِبٌ لِلتَّحَدُّثِ الْآنَ؟
hali -l-waqtu munaasibun lit-taḥad-duthi -l-'aan
Is it a good time to talk now?

37 هَلْ يُمْكِنُكَ التَّحَدُّثُ بِصَوْتٍ عَالٍ؟
hal yumkinuka -t-taḥad-duthu biṣawtin çaalin
Could you (m) speak up?

38 عُذْرًا، لَقَدِ اتَّصَلْتُ بِالرَّقْمِ الْخَطَأ.
çuthzran, laqadi -t-taṣaltu bir-raqmi -l-khaṭa'
Sorry, I dialed the wrong number.

39 انْتَظِرْ لَحْظَةً، مِنْ فَضْلِكَ.
'intathzir laḥthzatan min faḍlik
Please wait a moment.

40 يُرْجَى تَرْكُ رِسَالَةٍ.
yurjaa tarku risaalah
Please leave a message.

41 مَنِ الْمُتَّصِلُ، مِنْ فَضْلِكَ؟
mani -l- mut-taṣil min faḍlik
Who's calling, please?

42 هَلْ يُمْكِنُكَ التَّحَدُّثُ بِشَكْلٍ أَبْطَأَ قَلِيلًا؟
hal yumkinuka -t-taḥad-duthu bishaklin 'abṭa'a qaliilan
Could you (m) speak a little slower?

25 فِي الْعَمَل
fi-l-çamal
At Work

9 مُهَنْدِسٌ مِعْمَارِيّ
muhandisun miçmaariy-y
architect

10 عَامِلَةُ التِّلِيفُون
çaamilatu -t-tiliifuun (f)
telephone operator

1 مُحَامِي
muḥaamii
lawyer

2 قَاضِيَة
qaaḍiyah
judge (f)

3 مُمَوِّل
mumaw-wil
financier

4 مُهَنْدِس
muhandis
engineer

15 مَكْتَب
maktab
office

5 مُحَاسِب
muḥaasib
accountant

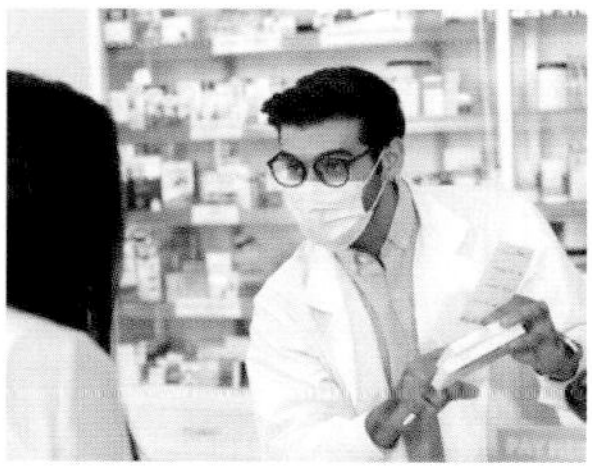
6 صَيْدَلَانِيّ (صَيْدَلِيّ)
ṣaydalaaniy-y (ṣaydaliy-y)
pharmacist

7 فَنَّانَة
fan-naanah
artist (f)

8 مُوسِيقِيّ
musiiqiy-y
musician

16 سِكِرْتِيرَة
sikirtiirah
secretary (f)

17 مُدِير
mudiir
manager

11 طَاهِي (شِيف)
ṭaahii (*sh*iif)
chef

12 مُصَوِّرٌ فُوتُوغْرَافِيّ
muṣawir-run futuu*gh*raafiy-y
photographer

13 طَيَّار
ṭay-yaar
pilot

14 طَبِيبَةُ الْأَسْنَان (دُكْتُورَةُ الْأَسْنَان)
ṭabiibatu -l- ʻasnaan
(duktuuratu -l-ʻasnaan)
dentist (f)

18 رَجُلُ الْإِطْفَاء
rajulu -l- ʻiṭfaaʻ
firefighter

19 مُزَارِع
muzaariç
farmer

Additional Vocabulary

20 شَرِكَة
*sh*arikah
company

21 رَائِدُ أَعْمَال
raaʻidu ʻaçmaal
entrepreneur

22 يُفَتِّش
yufaat-ti*sh*
to inspect

23 كُلِّيَّة
kul-liy-yah
college

24 عَمَل
çamal
work

25 مُوَظَّف
muwaẓ-ẓaf
employee

26 مُتَدَرِّب
mutadar-rib
trainee

27 يَتَدَرَّب
yatadar-rab
to intern

28 عَمَلٌ إِضَافِيّ
çamalun
ʻiḍaafiy-y
overtime work

29 طَرِيقَة
ṭariiqah
method / way

30 فُرْصَة
furṣah
opportunity

31 دَائِمًا
daaʻiman
always

32 يَذْهَبُ إِلَى الْعَمَل
ya*thzh*abu ʻilaa lçamal
to go to work

33 عَمَلٌ بِنِظَامِ الْوَرْدِيَّات
çamalun biniẓaami -l- wardiy-yaat
shift work

34 مُزَوِّدُ الْخِدْمَة
muzaw-widu -l-*kh*idmah
service provider

35 مَرْكَزٌ وَظِيفِيّ
markazun waẓifiy-y
position

36 مَا طَبِيعَةُ الْعَمَلِ الَّذِي تَقُومُ بِهِ؟
ma ṭabiiçatu -l- çamali -l-la*thz*i taquumu bih?
What sort of work do you (m) do?

37 أَنَا أَتَدَرَّبُ لِأَكُونَ طَبِيبًا (دُكْتُور).
ʻana ʻatadar-rabu liʻakuuna ṭabiiban (duktuur)
I am training to be a doctor.

38 أَنَا أَذْهَبُ إِلَى الْعَمَلِ السَّاعَة ٨:٤٥ صَبَاحًا كُلَّ يَوْمٍ.
ʻana ʻa*thzh*abu ʻila lçamali s-saaçata *th-th*aaminata wa *kh*amsatan wa ʻarbaçiina daqiiqatin ṣabaaḥan kul-la yawm
I go to work at 8:45 a.m. every morning.

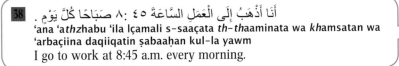

26 الْمُوسِيقَى وَالرَّقْص
'almuusiiqaa wa -r-raqṣ
Music and Dance

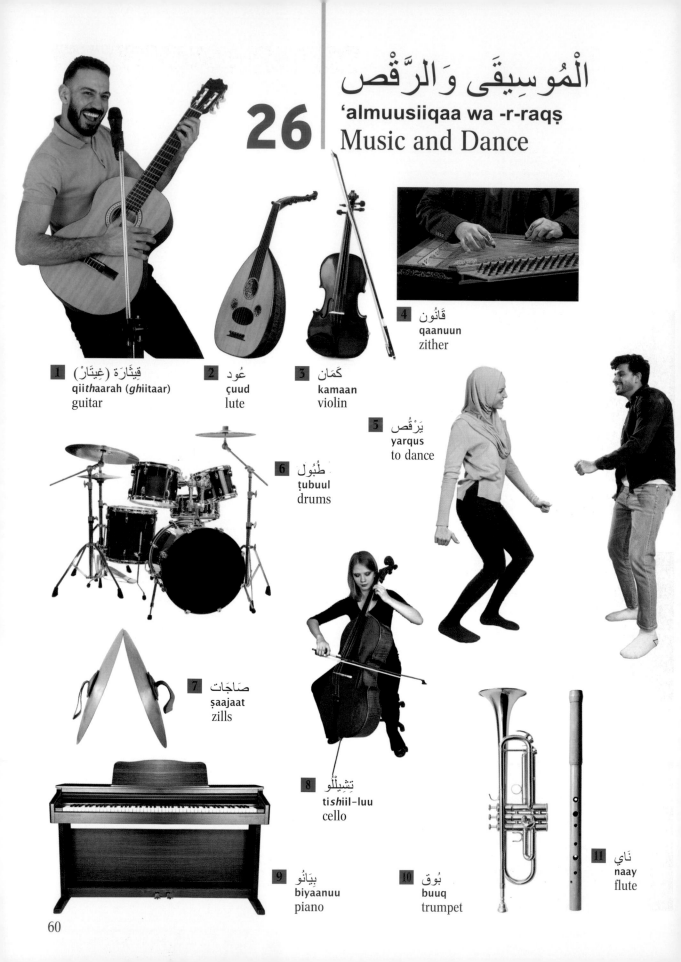

4 قَانُون
qaanuun
zither

1 قِيثَارَة (غِيتَار)
qii*th*aarah (*gh*iitaar)
guitar

2 عُود
çuud
lute

3 كَمَان
kamaan
violin

5 يَرْقُص
yarqus
to dance

6 طُبُول
ṭubuul
drums

7 صَاجَات
ṣaajaat
zills

8 تِشِيلْلُو
ti*sh*iil-luu
cello

9 بِيَانُو
biyaanuu
piano

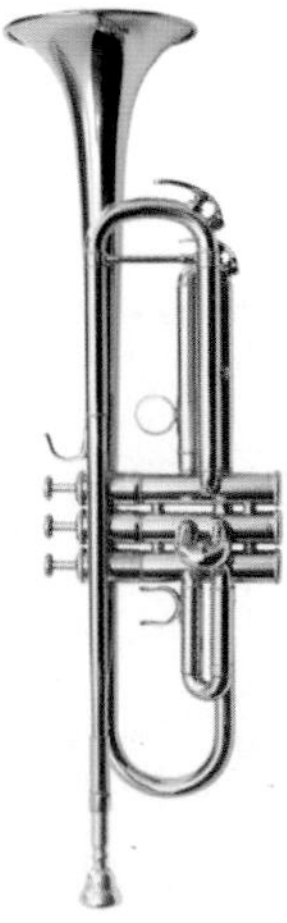

10 بُوق
buuq
trumpet

11 نَاي
naay
flute

12 كَارْيُوكِي
karyuukii
karaoke

13 يُغَنِّي
yu*gh*an-nii
to sing

14 مُغَنِّي
mu*gh*an-nii
singer

15 حَفْلَةٌ مُوسِيقِيَّة
ḥaflatun musiiqiy-yah
concert

16 جُمْهُور
jumhuur
audience

17 أُوبِرَا
'ubiraa
opera

18 مُمَثِّل
muma*th*-*th*il
actor

19 مُمَثِّلَة
muma*th*-*th*ilah
actress

20 فِرْقَةٌ مُوسِيقِيَّة
firqatun musiiqiy-yah
musical band

Additional Vocabulary

21 يُقَيِّم (يُقَدِّر)
yuqay-yim (yuqad-dir)
to appreciate

22 سَمَّاعَاتُ الْأُذُن
sam-maaçaatu -l- 'u*thz*un
earbuds

23 يَعْزِف
yaçzif
to play (a musical instrument)

24 يَعْزِفُ آلَةً مُوسِيقِيَّة
yaçzifu 'aalatan musiiqiy-yah
to play an instrument

25 يَسْتَمِعُ إِلَى
yastamiçu 'ilaa
to listen to

26 الرَّقْص
'ar-raqṣ
dance (performance art)

27 مُوسِيقَى الْبُوبْ
musiiqa -l- bub
pop music

28 أُورْكِسْتِرَا
'urkistiraa
orchestra

29 هِوَايَة
hiwaayah
hobby

30 مَشْهُور
ma*sh* huur
famous

31 يُعَبِّر
yuçab-bir
to express

32 بَرْنَامَج
barnaamaj
program

33 يَسْتَمْتِعُ بِـ
yastamtiçu bi
to enjoy

34 مُوسِيقَى
musiiqaa
music

35 يُؤَدِّي
yu'ad-dii
to perform

36 هَلْ تَسْتَطِيعِينَ أَنْ تَعْزِفِي عَلَى الْغِيتَار؟
hal tastaṭiiçiina 'an taçzifi çala -l-*gh*itaar
Can you (f) play the guitar?

37 مَا نَوْعُ الْمُوسِيقَى الَّتِي تُفَضِّلِينَهَا؟
maa nawçu -l- musiiqa -l-latii tufaḍiliinahaa
What kind of music do you (f) prefer (like)?

27 زِيَارَةُ عِيَادَةِ الطَّبِيب
ziyaaratu çiyaadati -ṭ-ṭabiib
Visiting a Doctor's Clinic

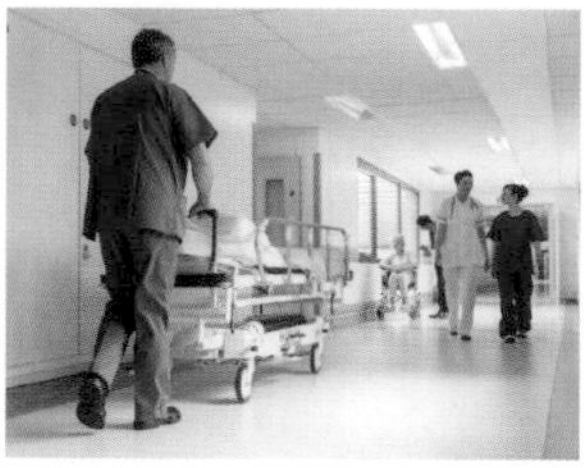

1 مُسْتَشْفَى
mustashfaa
hospital

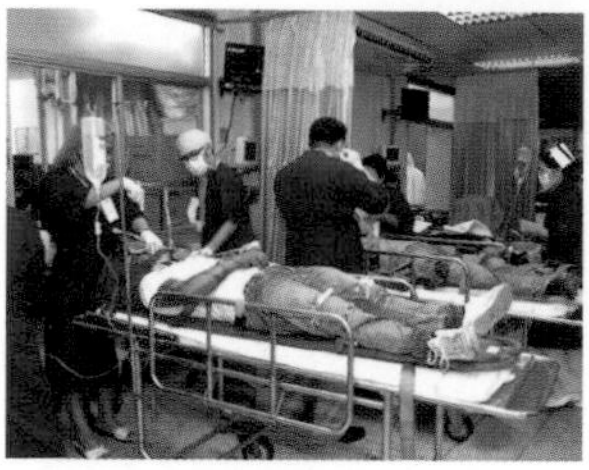

2 غُرْفَةُ الطَّوَارِئ
***gh*urfatu - ṭ-ṭawaari'**
emergency room

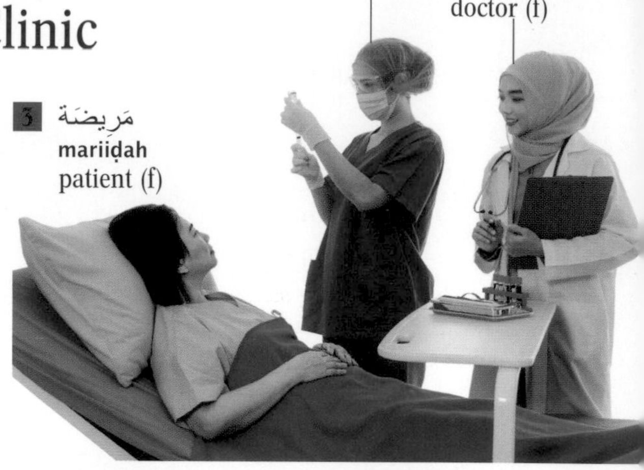

3 مَرِيضَة
mariiḍah
patient (f)

4 مُمَرِّضَة
mumar-riḍah
nurse (f)

5 طَبِيبَةٌ (دُكْتُورَة)
ṭabiibah (duktuura
doctor (f)

6 يَسْحَبُ الدَّم
yasḥabu -d-dam
to draw blood

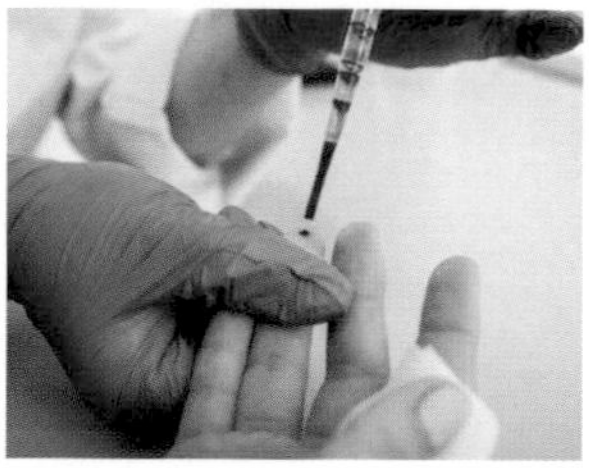

7 اخْتِبَارُ دَم
'ik*h*tibaaru dam
blood test

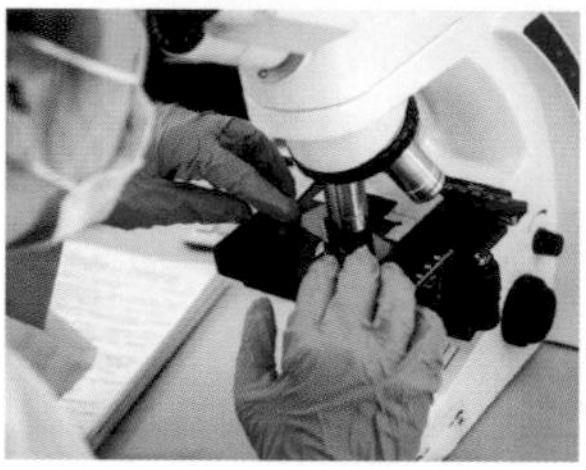

8 فَحْصٌ مَخْبَرِيّ
faḥṣun ma*kh*bariy-y
laboratory test

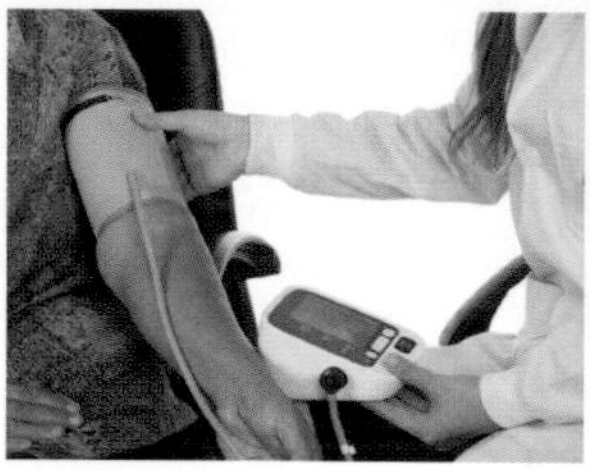

9 ضَغْطُ الدَّم
ḍa*gh*ṭu-d-dam
blood pressure

10 يُصَابُ بِنَزْلَةِ بَرْد
yuṣaabu binazlati bard
to catch a cold

11 يَسْعُل
yasçul
to cough

12 حُمَّى
ḥum-maa
fever

13 يَمْرَض
yamraḍ
to fall sick

14 يَتَنَاوَلُ الدَّوَاء
yatanaawalu -d-dawaa'
to take medicine

15 دَوَاء
dawaa'
medicine

16 أَقْرَاصُ الدَّوَاءِ
'aqraaṣu -d-dawaa'
pills

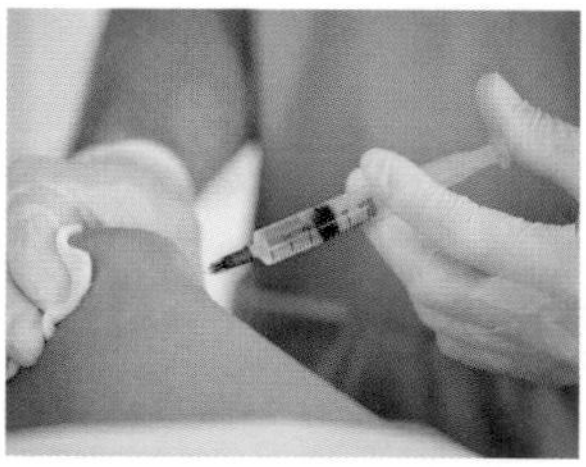

17 حَقْن
ḥaqn
injection

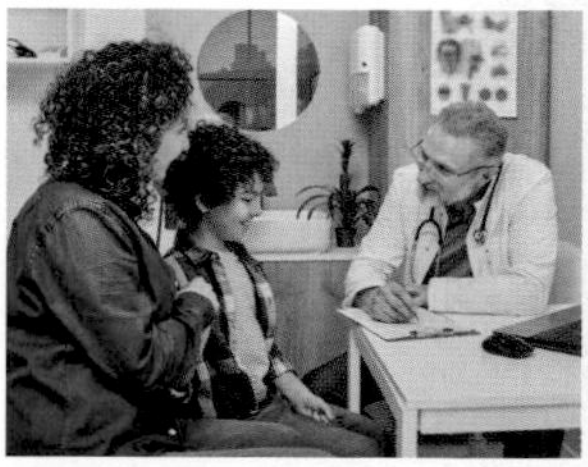

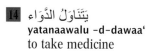

18 غُرْفَةُ اسْتِشَارَةِ الطَّبِيب
***gh*urfatu -sti*sh*aarati ṭ-ṭabiib**
doctor's consultation room

Additional Vocabulary

19 مَوْعِد
mawçid
appointment

20 حَادِثَة
ḥaadithah
accident

21 يُؤْلِم
yu'lim
it hurts

22 مُتْعَب
mutçab
tired

23 مُنْهَك
munhak
worn out (exhausted)

24 يَشْعُر
yashçur
to feel

25 جُرْح
jurḥ
wound

26 قَطْع
qaṭç
cut

27 طَوَارِئ
ṭawaari'
emergency

28 أَمَل
'amal
hope

29 مُطَهِّر
muṭah-hir
antiseptic

30 مَرْهَم (دِهَان)
marham (dihaan)
ointment

31 سَيَّارَةُ الإِسْعَاف
say-yaaratu -l-'isçaaf
ambulance

32 وَصْفَةٌ طِبِّيَّة
waṣfatun ṭib-biy-yah
prescription

33 مُتَعَلِّقٌ بِـ
mutaçal-liqun bi
pertaining to

34 هَامّ (مُهِمّ)
haam-m (muhim-m)
important

35 عِدَّةَ مَرَّات
çid-datu mar-raat
several times

36 قَلِق
qaliq
anxious; worried

37 يَكْتَشِفُ
yaktashif
to discover

38 رَئِيسِيّ
ra'iisiy-y
main

39 غُرْفَةُ الانْتِظَار
ghurfatu -lintiẓaar
waiting room

40 طِبُّ الأَسْنَان
ṭib-bu -l-'asnaan
dentistry

41 الطِّبُّ الْعَامّ
'aṭ-ṭib-bu -l- çaam-m
general medicine

42 الْجِرَاحَةُ الْعَامَّة
'aljiraaḥatu -l-çaam-mah
general surgery

43 طِبُّ الأَطْفَال
ṭib-bu -l- 'aṭfaal
pediatrics

44 طِبُّ النِّسَاء
ṭib-bu -n-nisaa'
gynecology

45 طِبُّ الأَوْرَام
ṭib-bu -l-'awraam
oncology

46 عِلَاجٌ طَبِيعِيّ
çilaajun ṭabiiçiy-y
physiotherapy

47 طِبُّ الأَعْصَاب
ṭib-bu -l-'açṣaab
neurology

48 طِبُّ الإِشْعَاع
ṭib-bu -l-'ishçaaç
radiology

49 أَنْفٌ وَأُذُنٌ وَ حَنْجَرَة
'anf wa 'uthzun wa ḥanjarah
ear, nose and throat

50 طِبُّ الرَّمَد (الْعُيُون)
ṭib-bu -r-ramad ('alçuyuun)
ophthalmology

51 طِبُّ الأَمْرَاضِ الْجِلْدِيَّة
ṭib-bu -l- 'amraaḍi ljildiy-yah
dermatology

52 يَقْلَقُ بِشَأْن
yaqlaqu bi-sha'n
to be concerned about

53 يَشْعُرُ بِالطُّمَأْنِينَة
yashçuru biṭ-ṭuma'niinah
to feel reassured

54 حَقِيبَةُ الإِسْعَافَاتِ الأَوَّلِيَّة
ḥaqiibatu l 'isçaafaati -l- 'aw-waliy-yah
first aid kit

55 ضِمَادَة
ḍimaadah
bandage

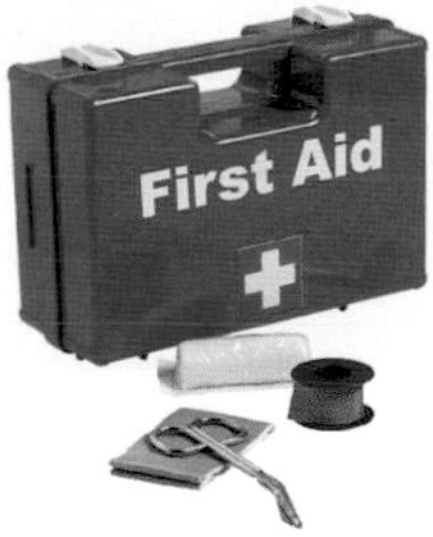

56 مَاذَا تَشْتَكِي؟
maathzaa tashtakii
What brings you (m) today? (What are your concerns)?

57 أُعَانِي مِنْ حُمَّى وَالْتِهَابٍ فِي الْحَلْق.
'uçaanii min ḥum-maa wa ltihaabin fi -l-ḥalq
I have a fever and a sore throat.

58 أَنَا لَسْتُ عَلَى مَا يُرَام.
'ana lastu çalaa maa yuraam
I am not feeling well.

59 أَرْغَبُ فِي رُؤْيَةِ طَبِيب (دُكْتُور).
'arghabu fii ru'yati ṭabiib (duktuur)
I would like to see a doctor.

60 هَلْ لَدَيْكَ مَوْعِد؟
hal ladayka mawçid
Do you (m) have an appointment?

28 حِمَايَةُ بِيئَتِنَا
ḥimaayatu bii‘atinaa
Protecting Our Environment

1 حَدِيقَة
ḥadiiqah
garden

2 زَهْرَة
zahrah
flower

6 سَيَّارَةٌ كَهْرُبَائِيَّة
say-yaaratun kahrubaa‘iy-yah
electric car

3 مُنْتَزَه
muntazah
park

4 تَلَوُّث
talaw-wu*th*
pollution

5 عُشْب
çu*sh*b
grass

7 مُحِيط
muḥiiṭ
ocean

8 نَهْر
nahr
river

9 طَاقَةٌ شَمْسِيَّة
ṭaaqatun *sh*amsiy-yah
solar energy

10 هَادِئ
hadi‘
quiet

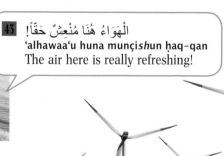

43 الْهَوَاءُ هُنَا مُنْعِشٌ حَقًّا!
‘alhawaa‘u huna munçi*sh*un ḥaq-qan
The air here is really refreshing!

11 هَوَاء
hawaa‘
air

12 طَاقَةُ الرِّيَاح
ṭaaqatu -r-riiaaḥ
wind power

13 حَوَاجِزُ رَمْلِيَّة
ḥawaajizu ramliy-yah
sand break

14 غَابَة
***gh*aabah**
forest

16 غَازٌ طَبِيعِيّ
***gh*aazun ṭabiiçiy-y**
natural gas

17 طَاقَةٌ نَوَوِيَّة
ṭaaqatun nawawiy-yah
nuclear energy

15 شَجَرَة
***sh*ajarah**
tree

44 هَلْ تَقُومِينَ بِإِعَادَةِ التَّدْوِيرِ؟
hal taquumiina bi 'içaadati-t-tadwiir
Do you (f) recycle?

45 أَنَا أُعِيدُ تَدْوِيرَ اَلزُّجَاجِ وَالْوَرَقِ وَالْبِلَاسْتِيك.
'ana 'uçiidu tadwiira -z-zujaaji wa-l-waraqi wa-l-bilaastik
I recycle glass, paper and plastic.

Additional Vocabulary

18 نَظِيف
naẓiif
clean

19 نَبَات
nabaat
plant

20 إِعَادَةُ التَّصْنِيع
'içaadatu - t-taṣniiç
recycling

21 طَاقَةٌ نَظِيفَة
ṭaaqatun naẓiifah
clean energy

22 نَفْط
nafṭ
oil

23 فَحْم
faḥm
coal

24 جَوْدَةُ الْهَوَاء
jawdatu -l-hawaa'
air quality

25 مُؤَشِّر
mu'a*sh*-*sh*ir
index

26 مَاء
maa'
water

27 بِيئَة
bii'ah
environment

28 قِنَاع
qinaaç
mask

29 تَغْيِيرَات
ta*gh*yiiraat
changes

30 أَرْض
'arḍ
earth; ground

31 بِوَاسِطَة
biwaasiṭah
by

32 بِسَبَب
bisabab
because of

33 لِغَرَضِ (لِـ)
li*gh*araḍi (li)
for the purpose of

34 مُكْتَمِل
muktamil
complete

35 يُحَقِّق (يُنْجِز)
yuḥaq-qiq (yunjiz)
to accomplish

36 يُؤَثِّرُ عَلَى (فِي)
yu'a*th*-*th*iru çalaa (fii)
to affect

37 وَلَكِنْ
wa laakin
but

38 وَمَعَ ذَلِكَ
wa maça *thz*aalik
however

39 بِالطَّبْعِ (بِكُلِّ تَأْكِيد)
biṭ-ṭabçi (bikul-li ta'kiid)
of course

40 إِذَا (لَوْ)
'i*thz*aa (law)
if

41 عَلَى الرَّغْمِ مِن
çala -r-ra*gh*mi min
although

42 نَتِيجَةً لِـ
natiijatan li
as a result of

29 مَمْلَكَةُ الْحَيَوَانَات
mamlakatu lḥayawaanaat
The Animal Kingdom

3 زَرَافَة
zaraafah
giraffe

1 حَدِيقَةُ الْحَيَوَانِ
ḥadiiqatu -l- ḥayawaan
zoo

2 حِمَارٌ وَحْشِيّ
ḥimaarun waḥshiy-y
zebra

4 نَمِر
namir
tiger

5 أَسَد
'asad
lion

40 هَذَا الْحَيَوَانُ أَصْغَرُ مِنْ ذَلِك.
haathza -l-ḥayawaanu 'aṣgharu min thzaalik
This animal is smaller than that one.

41 هَلْ تُحِبُّ أَنْ تَذْهَبَ إِلَى حَدِيقَةِ الْحَيَوَان؟
hal tuḥib-bu 'an tathzhaba 'ilaa ḥadiiqati -l-ḥayaawaan
Do you (m) like going to the zoo?

42 يُوجَدُ الْعَدِيدُ مِنَ الْحَيَوَانَاتِ فِي حَدِيقَةِ الْحَيَوَان.
yuujaadu -l-çadiidu mina -l- ḥayawaanaatl fll ḥadiiqati -l-ḥayawaan
There are many animals in the zoo.

6 دُبّ
dub-b
bear

10 دَيْنَاصُور
daynaaṣuur
dinosaur

7 قِرْد
qird
monkey

8 غُورِيلّا
ghuril-la
gorilla

9 بَانْدَا
baandaa
panda

11 مَاعِز
maaçiz
goat

12 خَرُوف
***kh*aruuf**
sheep

13 بَقَرَة
baqarah
cow

14 فِيل
fiil
elephant

15 حِصَان
ḥiṣaan
horse

16 ذِئْب
***thz*i'b**
wolf

17 ثُعْبَان
***th*uçbaan**
snake

18 طَاوُوس
ṭaawuus
peacock

19 دَجَاج
dajaaj
chicken

20 طَائِر
ṭaa'ir
bird

21 كَلْب
kalb
dog

22 قِطَّة
qiṭ-ṭah
cat

23 تِنِّين
tin-niin
dragon

24 بَعُوض
baçuuḍ
mosquitoes

25 ذُبَابَة
***thz*ubaabah**
housefly

26 نَحْلَة
naḥlah
bee

27 فَرَاشَة
faraa*sh*ah
butterfly

28 سَمَك
samak
fish (pl)

Additional Vocabulary

29 لِتَكُونَ خَائِفًا
litakuuna *kh*aa'ifan
to be afraid

30 لَطِيف
laṭiif
cute; adorable

31 هُوَ - هِيَ
huwa (m) – hiya (f)
it

32 جِدًّا
jid-dan
very

33 لِلْغَايَة
lil*gh*aayah
extremely

34 نَفْس
nafs
same

35 تَطَابُق
taṭaabuk
identical

36 يُشْبِه
yu*sh*bih
to resemble

37 يَظْهَر
yaẓhar
to appear

38 يَجْرُؤ
yajru'
to dare

39 غَرِيب
***gh*ariib**
strange

30 هَيَّا نُحَافِظْ عَلَى لِيَاقَتِنَا

hay-yaa nuḥaafiẓ çala liyaaqatinaa

Let's Keep Fit!

1 تِنِسْ طَاوِلَة
tinis ṭaawilah
table tennis

2 يَلْعَبُ كُرَةَ الْقَدَم
yalçabu kurata -l-qadam
to play soccer

3 الرُّجْبِي
'ar-rujbii
rugby

4 تَسَلُّقُ الْجِبَال
tasal-luqu -l-jibaal
mountain climbing

5 تِنِسُ الرِّيشَة
tinisu -r-riishah
badminton

6 تَتَمَرَّن
tatamar-ran
she exercises

7 بِيسْبُول
bisbuul
baseball

8 جَرْيٌ لِمَسَافَاتٍ طَوِيلَة
jaryun limasaafaatin ṭawiil-lah
long-distance running

9 عَدْو
çadw
sprint

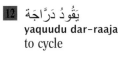

10 جَرْي
jary
running

11 دَرَّاجَة
dar-raajah
bicycle

12 يَقُودُ دَرَّاجَة
yaquudu dar-raajah
to cycle

13 مُنَافَسَة
munaafasah
competition

14 خَطُّ النِّهَايَة
khaṭu -n-nihaayah
finish line

15 جُولْف
julf
golf

16 التَّزَحْلُقُ عَلَى الْجَلِيد
'at-tazaḥluqu çala -l- jaliid
ice-skating

17 التَّزَلُّج
'at-tazal-luj
skiing

18 تَجْدِيف
tajdiif
rowing

19 سِبَاحَة
sibaaḥah
swimming

20 الكُرَةُ الطَّائِرَة
'alkuraatu -ṭ-ṭaa'irah
volleyball

21 الْمَشْي
'almashy
walking

Additional Vocabulary

25 رِيَاضَات
riyaaḍaat
sports

26 قَمِيصٌ رِيَاضِيّ
qamiiṣun riyaaḍiy-y
sports shirt

27 حِذَاءٌ رِيَاضِيّ
ḥithzaa'un r-riyaaḍiy-y
sports shoes; sneakers

28 كُرَة
kurah
ball

29 صِحِّيّ
siḥ-ḥiy-y
healthy

22 تَلْعَبُ كُرَةَ السَّلَّة
talçabu kurata -s-sal-lah
she plays basketball

23 تِنِس
tinis
tennis

24 مِضْرَبُ تِنِس
miḍrabu tinis
tennis racket

30 هَلْ تَرْغَبُ فِي مُمَارَسَةِ الرِّيَاضَة؟
hal targhabu fii mumaarasati -r-riyaaḍah
Would you (m) like to exercise?

31 مَا الرِّيَاضَاتُ الَّتِي تُمَارِسُهَا؟
maa -r-riyaaḍaatu -l-latii tumaarisuhaa
What sports do you (m) play?

32 أُحِبُّ الْهَرْوَلَةَ وَلَعِبَ كُرَةِ السَّلَّةِ.
'uḥib-bu -l-harwalata wa laçiba kurati -s-sal-lah
I like to jog and play basketball.

31 هَلْ تُحِبُّ السَّفَر؟
hal tuḥib-bu -s-safar
Do You Like Traveling?

3 مُسَافِرَة
musaafirah
traveler (f)

4 أَمْتِعَة
'amtiçah
luggages

5 حَقِيبَةُ سَفَر
ḥaqiibatu safar
suitcase

1 فُنْدُق
funduk
hotel

2 خَرِيطَة
***kh*ariiṭah**
map

6 مُرْشِدٌ سِيَاحِيّ
mur*sh*idun siyaaḥiy-y
tour guide

7 مَنَاطِقُ جَذْبٍ سِيَاحِيّ
manaaṭiqu ja*th*zbin siyaaḥiy-y
areas of tourist attractions

8 جَوَازُ سَفَرٍ
jawaazu safar
passport

9 بِطَاقَةُ صُعُودِ الطَّائِرَة
biṭaaqatu ṣuçuudi - ṭ-ṭaa'irah
boarding pass

10 السَّفَرُ بِالطَّائِرَة
'as-safaru bi-ṭ-ṭaa'irah
travel by airplane

11 السَّفَرُ بِالْقِطَار
'as-safaru bilqiṭaar
travel by rail

12 فِي رِحْلَةٍ بَحْرِيَّة
fii riḥlatin baḥriy-yah
on a cruise

13 فِي حَافِلَةِ الرِّحْلَات
fii ḥaafilati -r-riḥlaat
on a traveling bus

14 مَتْجَرُ بَيْعِ تَذْكَارَات
matjaru bayçi ta*th*zkaaraat
souvenir shop

15 آلَةُ تَصْوِير (كَامِيرَا)
'aalatu taṣwiir (kamiraa)
camera

16 صُورَةٌ فُوتُوغْرَافِيَّة
ṣuratun futu*gh*raafiy-yah
photograph

Additional Vocabulary

17 رِحْلَة
rihlah
a trip

18 يُسَافِر
yusaafir
to travel

19 عُطْلَة (إِجَازَة)
çutlah (‘ijaazah)
vacation

20 تَذْكِرَةُ طَيَرَان
tathzkiratu tayaraan
plane ticket

21 حَجْزٌ فُنْدُقِيّ
hajzun funduqiy-y
hotel reservation

22 عُمْلَة
çumlah
currency

23 تَأْشِيرَة
ta‘shiirah
visa

24 كِتَابُ دَلِيلِ السَّفَر
kitaabu daliili -s-safar
travel guidebook

25 وَكَالَةُ السَّفَر
wakaalatu -s-safar
travel agency

26 لِقَاح
liqaah
vaccination

27 جُمْرُك
jumruk
customs

28 مَعَالِمُ سِيَاحِيَّة
maçaalimu siyaahiy-yah
sightseeing

29 بِطَاقَةٌ بَرِيدِيَّة
bitaaqatun bariidiy-yah
postcard

30 وَايْ فَايْ مَجَّانِيّ
waay faay maj-jaaniy-y
free wifi

31 مُتْحَف
muthaf
museum

32 شَاطِئُ بَحْر
shaati‘u bahr
beach

33 نَصْبٌ تَذْكَارِيّ
nasbun tathzkariy-y
memorial monument

34 مَحَطَّةُ الْقِطَار
mahat-tatu -l-qitaar
train station

35 مَطْعَم
matçam
restaurant

36 يجِد
yajid
to find

37 يَأْخُذ
ya‘khuthz
to take

38 مَطَار
mataar
airport

39 نُزُلُ الشَّبَاب (بُيُوتُ الشَّبَاب)
nuzulu -sh-shabaab (buyuutu-sh-shabaab)
youth hostel

40 دَارُ الضِّيَافَة / نُزُل
daaru - d-diyaafah/nuzul
guesthouse / lodge

41 مَرْكَزُ الْمَعْلُومَاتِ السِّيَاحِيَّة
markazu -l-maçluumaati -s-siyaahiy-yah
tourist information center

42 مَرْكَزُ الرِّحْلَاتِ الْبَحْرِيَّة
markazu -r-rihlaati -l-bahriy-yah
cruise center

43 أَيْنَ تُرِيدِينَ أَنْ تَذْهَبِي فِي الإِجَازَة؟
‘ayna turiidiina ‘an tathzhabii fi -l-‘ijaazah
Where do you (f) like to go on vacation?

44 أُحِبُّ أَنْ أَذْهَبَ إِلَى مِصْر.
‘uhib-bu ‘an ‘athzhaba ‘ilaa misr
I like to go to Egypt.

45 أُرِيدُ تَذْكِرَةً إِلَى الإِسْكَنْدَرِيَّة، وَتَكُونُ ذَهَابًا وَعَوْدَة، مِنَ الدَّرَجَةِ الثَّانِيَة.
‘uriidu tathzkiratan ‘ila-l-‘iskandariy-yah, wa takuunu thzahaaban wa çawdah, mina -d-darajati -th-thaaniyah
I’d like a second class two-way ticket to Alexandria.

46 هُوَ قَامَ بِرِحْلَةٍ حَوْلَ الْعَالَم.
huwa qaama birihlatin hawla -l-çaalam
He made a round-the-world trip.

47 أُحِبُّ أَنْ أُسَافِرَ عَلَى نَفْسِ شِرْكَةِ الطَّيَرَان؛ لِلْحُصُولِ عَلَى نِقَاطِ الأَمْيَال.
‘uhib-bu ‘an ‘usaafira çalaa nafsi shirkati -t-tayaraan; lilhusuuli çalaa niqaati -l- ‘amyaal
I like to fly on the same airline to get mileage points.

32 دُوَلُ الْعَالَم
duwalu -l-çaalam
Countries of the World

1 بَعْضُ الدُّوَلِ فِي الشَّرْقِ الأَوْسَط
baçḍu -d-duwali fi -*sh*-*sh*arqi -l-'awsaaṭ
Some countries in the Middle East

2 مِصْر
miṣr
Egypt

3 الْمَغْرِب
'alma*gh*rib
Morocco

4 سُورِيَّا
suuriy-yaa
Syria

5 تُونِس
Tuunis
Tunisia

6 لُبْنَان
lubnaan
Lebanon

7 فِلَسْطِين
filasṭiin
Palestine

8 الْعِرَاق
'alçiraaq
Iraq

9 قَطَر
qaṭar
Qatar

10 الإِمَارَاتُ الْعَرَبِيَّةُ الْمُتَّحِدَة
'al'imaaratu -l- çarabiy yatu -l-mut-taḥidah
UAE

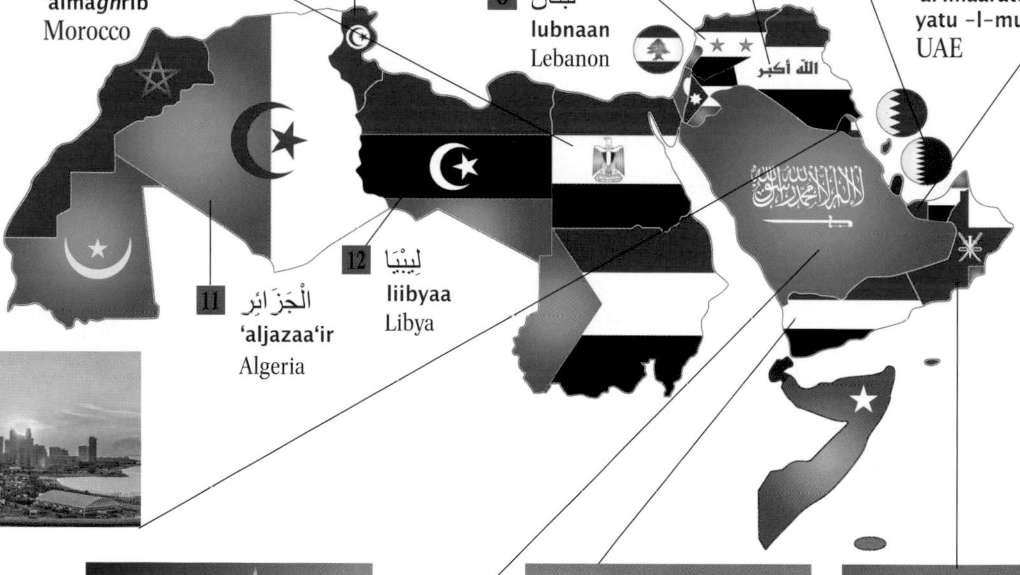

11 الْجَزَائِر
'aljazaa'ir
Algeria

12 لِيبْيَا
liibyaa
Libya

13 كُوَيْت
kuwayt
Kuwait

14 الْمَمْلَكَةُ الْعَرَبِيَّةُ السُّعُودِيَّةُ (السُّعُودِيَّة)
'almamlakatu -l-çarabiy-yatu -s-suçuudiy-yah ('as-suçuudiy-yah)
Saudi Arabia

15 الْيَمَن
'alyaman
Yemen

16 عُمَان
çumaan
Oman

17 الْقَارَّاتُ السَّبْعُ فِي الْعَالَم
'alqaar-raatu -s-sabçu fi-l-çaalam
Seven continents of the world

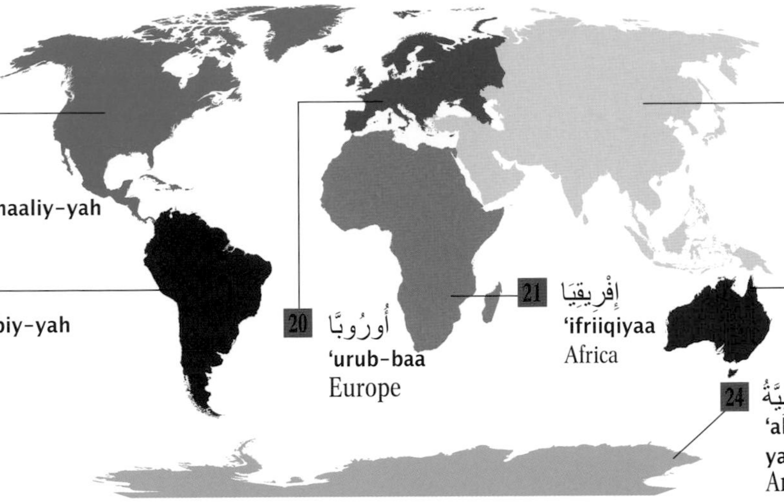

18 أَمْرِيكَا الشَّمَالِيَّة
'amriika -*sh*-*sh*amaaliy-yah
North America

19 أَمْرِيكَا الْجَنُوبِيَّة
'amriika -l-januubiy-yah
South America

20 أُورُوبَّا
'urub-baa
Europe

21 إِفْرِيقِيَا
'ifriiqiyaa
Africa

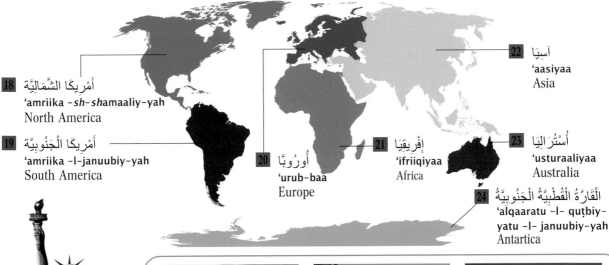

22 آسِيَا
'aasiyaa
Asia

23 أُسْتُرَالِيَا
'usturaaliyaa
Australia

24 الْقَارَّةُ الْقُطْبِيَّةُ الْجَنُوبِيَّةُ
'alqaaratu -l- quṭbiy-yatu -l- januubiy-yah
Antartica

25 الْجَزَائِرُ
'aljazaa'ir
Algeria

26 تُونِس
Tuunis
Tunisia

27 الْمَغْرِب
'alma*gh*rib
Morocco

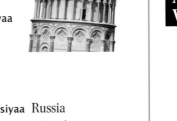

28 الْوِلايَاتُ الْمُتَّحِدَةُ الأَمْرِيكِيَّةُ (أَمْرِيكَا)
'alwilaayaatu -l-mut-taḥidatu-l- 'amriikiy-yah ('amriika)
America

29 الْهِنْد
'alhind
India

30 أُسْتُرَالِيَا
'austuraaliyaa
Australia

كَنَدَا **kanadaa** Canada
الدِّنِمَارْك **ad-dinimaark** Denmark
فِنْلَنْدَا **finlandaa** Finland
أَلْمَانْيَا **'almaanyaa** Germany
إِنْجِلْتِرَا **'ingiltira** Great Britain
أَيِرْلَنْدَا **'ayirlandaa** Ireland
لُوكْسُمْبُورْغ **luksumbuur*gh*** Luxembourg
هُولَنْدَا **huulandaa** Netherlands
نِيُوزِيلانْدَا **niyuuzilandaa** New Zealand
النُّرْوِيج **an-nurwiij** Norway
بُولَنْدَا **buulandaa** Poland

31 إِيطَالِيَا
'iiṭaaliyaa
Italy

رُوسِيَا **ruusiyaa** Russia
السُّوِيد **as-suwiid** Sweden
سُوِيسْرَا **suwisraa** Switzerland
الْفَاتِيكَان **'alfaatiikaan** Vatican

Additional Vocabulary

32 الْكُرَةُ الأَرْضِيَّة
'alkuratu-l-'arḍiy-yah
globe

33 الْعَالَم
'alçaalam
world

33 لُغَات
lu*gh*aat
Languages

In Arabic, start with the word "language" before saying the language name itself.
Example: The Arabic language: اللُّغَةُ الْعَرَبِيَّة
(Language is لغة)

1 اللُّغَةُ الإِنْجِلِيزِيَّة
'al-lu*gh*atu -l- 'injiliiziy-yah
English

2 اللُّغَةُ الْفَرَنْسِيَّة
'al-lu*gh*atu -l- faransiy-yah
French

3 اللُّغَةُ الرُّوسِيَّة
'al-lu*gh*atu -r-ruusiy-yah
Russian

4 اللُّغَةُ الأَلْمَانِيَّة
'al-lu*gh*atu -l- 'almaaniy-yah
German

5 اللُّغَةُ الإِيطَالِيَّة
'al-lu*gh*atu -l- 'iiṭaaliy-yah
Italian

6 اللُّغَةُ الإِسْبَانِيَّة
'al-lu*gh*atu -l-'isbaaniy-yah
Spanish

7 اللُّغَةُ التُّرْكِيَّة
'al-lu*gh*atu t-turkiy-yah
Turkish

8 اللُّغَةُ الْيَابَانِيَّة
'al-lu*gh*atu -l- yaabaaniy-yah
Japanese

9 اللُّغَةُ الْعَرَبِيَّة
'al-lu*gh*atu -l-çarabiy-yah
Arabic

10 اللُّغَةُ الْيُونَانِيَّة
'al-lughatu
-l-yuunaaniy-yah
Greek

11 اللُّغَةُ الْعِبْرِيَّة
'al-lu*gh*atu -l-
çibriy-yah
Hebrew

12 اللُّغَةُ الْفِيتْنَامِيَّة
'al-lu*gh*atu -l-
fiitnaamiy-yah
Vietnamese

13 اللُّغَةُ الْهِنْدِيَّة
'al-lu*gh*atu -l-hindiy-yah
Hindi

14 اللُّغَةُ الإِنْدُونِيسِيَّة
'al-lu*gh*atu -l-'induuniisiy-yah
Indonesian

15 اللُّغَةُ التَّايْلانْدِيَّة
'al-lu*gh*atu -t-taaylaandiy-yah
Thai

16 اللُّغَةُ الْكُورِيَّة
'al-lu*gh*atu -l-kuuriy-yah
Korean

17 اللُّغَةُ التَّاغْلُوغِيَّة
'al-lu*gh*atu -t-
taa*gh*luu*gh*iy-yah
Tagalog

18 اللُّغَةُ الْبُرْتُغَالِيَّة
'al-lu*gh*atu -l-
burtu*gh*aaliy-yah
Portuguese

19 لُغَةُ الْمَانْدِرِينْ الصِّينِيَّة
lu*gh*atu-l-maandiriin
'aṣ - ṣiiniy-yah
Mandarin Chinese

20 مَا لُغَتُكَ الْأُمُّ؟
maa lu*gh*atuka -l-'um-m
What is your (m) mother language?

21 كَمْ لُغَةً تَتَحَدَّثُ؟
kam lu*gh*atan tataḥad-dath
How many languages do you (m) speak?

34 هَلْ تُحِبُّ الطَّعَامَ الْعَرَبِيَّ؟

hal tuḥib-bu ṭ-ṭaçaama lçarabiy-y

Do You Like Arabic Food?

1 مَطْعَمٌ عَرَبِيٌّ
maṭçamun çarabiy-y
Arabic restaurant

2 طَاهِي (طَبَّاخ)
ṭaahii (ṭab-baakh)
chef (cook)

3 نَادِلَة (جَرْسُونَهْ)
naadilah (garsuunah)
waitress

4 قَائِمَةُ الطَّعَام
qaa'imatu ṭ-ṭaçaam
menu

5 كَبْسَة
kabsah
kabsa

6 كُشَرِي
kusharii
kushary

7 خُبْز
khubz
bread

8 أَصَابِع (إِصْبَع)
'aṣaabiç ('iṣbaç)
fingers (a finger)

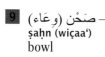

9 صَحْن (وِعَاء)
ṣaḥn (wiçaa')
bowl

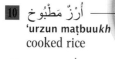

10 أُرْزٌ مَطْبُوخ
'urzun maṭbuukh
cooked rice

11 أُرْزٌ أَبْيَض
'urzun 'abyaḍ
white rice

12 طَبَق
ṭabaq
plate

13 شَوْكَة
shawkah
fork

14 سِكِّين
sik-kiin
knife

15 مِلْعَقَة
milçaqah
spoon

16 طَعْمِيَّة
ṭaçmiy-yah
falafel

17 رِنْجَة
ringah
herring

18 فُول
fuul
fava beans

19 مَحْشِي وَرَقِ عِنَب
maḥ*sh*ii waraqi çinab
stuffed grape leaves

20 مَلْفُوف (مَحْشِي كُرُنْب)
malfuuf (maḥ*sh*i kurunb)
stuffed cabbage

21 الْبَقْلَاوَة
'albaqlaawah
baklava

22 كُفْتَة
kuftah
kofta

23 شَاوِرْمَا
***sh*aawirmaa**
shawarma

24 خُضَار مَطْبُوخ (طَبِيخ)
***kh*uḍaar maṭbuukh (ṭabiikh)**
cooked vegetable

25 دَجَاج
dajaaj
chicken

Additional Vocabulary

26 حِسَاء (شُورْبَة)
ḥisaa' (*sh*urbah)
soup

27 نَبَاتِيّ
nabaatiy-y
vegetarian

28 يَطْلُب
yaṭlub
to order

29 اخْتِيَار
'i*kh*tiyaar
choice

30 خَاصّ
***kh*aaṣ-ṣ**
special

31 أَيْضًا
'ayḍan
also; too

32 نَادِل (جَرْسُون)
naadil (garsuun)
waiter

33 تَقْرِيبًا
taqriiban
almost

34 يُحِبُّ الْجَمِيعُ أَكْلَ الطَّعَامِ الْعَرَبِيِّ.
yuḥib-bu -l-jamiiçu 'akla ṭ-ṭaçaami -l- çarabiy-y
Everyone likes to eat Arabic food.

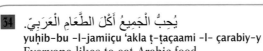

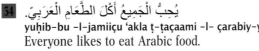

35 أَدْعُوكَ لِتَنَاوُلِ الْعَشَاءِ اللَّيْلَة.
'adçuuka litanaawuli -l-ça*sh*aa'i -l-laylah
I am inviting you (m) for dinner tonight.

36 هَذَا رَائِع! أُرِيدُ أَنْ آكُلَ طَعَامًا عَرَبِيًّا.
haa*thz*a raa'iç 'uriidu 'an 'aakula ṭaçaaman çarabiy-yan
That is great! I want to eat Arabic food.

37 آنِسَةُ...
'aanisah ...
Miss...
(name)

35 أَشْهَرُ الطَّعَامِ الْغَرْبِيّ
'ashharu ṭ-ṭaçaami lgharbiy-y
Popular Western Foods

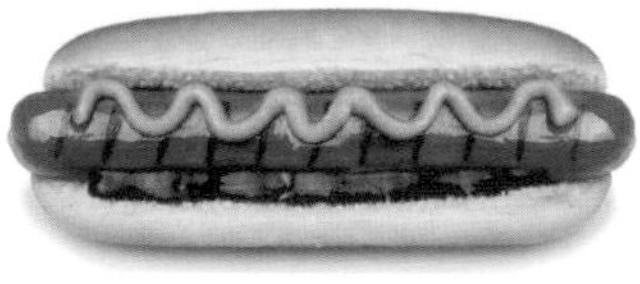

1 نَقَانِق
naqaaniq
hot dog

2 سَانْدُوِيتْش
sandwiitsh
sandwich

3 بِيتْزَا
biitzaa
pizza

4 مَعْكَرُونَة (مَكَرُونَة) (اسْبَاكِتِّي)
maçkaruunah (makaruunah) ('isbaakit-tii)
pasta; spaghetti

5 دُونَات
duunaat
donuts

6 خُبْزُ بَاجِيت
khubzu baajit
baguette

7 بُوظَة (آيِسْ كِرِيمْ)
buuẓah ('aayis kiriim)
ice cream

8 مُهَلَّبِيَّة
muhal-labiy-yah
pudding

9 لَازَانْيَا
laazaanyaa
lasagne

10 دِيكٌ رُومِيّ
diikun ruumiy-y
turkey

11 فَطِيرَةُ تُفَّاح
faṭiiratu tuf-faaḥ
apple pie

12 لَحْمُ خِنْزِير
laḥmu khinziir
ham

15 شَرِيحَةُ لَحْم (سِتِيكْ)
shariiḥatu laḥm (stiik)
steak

13 سَلَطَة
salaṭah
salad

14 بَطَاطِس مَهْرُوسَة
baṭaaṭis mahruusah
mashed potatoes

16 سُجُق
sujuq
sausage

17 فَطُورٌ غَرْبِيّ
faṭuurun gharbiy-y
Western breakfast

18 عَصِيرُ فَوَاكِه
çaṣiiru fawaakih
fruit juice

19 قَهْوَة
qahwah
coffee

20 لَحْمٌ مُقَدَّد
laḥmun muqad-dad
bacon

21 خُبْزٌ مُحَمَّص (تُوسْت)
ghubzun muḥam-maṣ (tuust)
toast

26 هَمْبُرْغَر
hamburghar
hamburger

27 بَطَاطِس مَقْلِيَّة
baṭaaṭis maqliy-yah
french fries

22 كَعْكَة (كِيكَة)
kaçkah (kiikah)
cake

23 جُبْن
jubn
cheese

24 حُبُوب (الْكُورْن فِلِيكْس\ سِيرْيَال)
ḥubuub ('alkuurn fliks/ siiryaal)
cereal

25 دَقِيقُ الشُّوفَان
daqiiqu -sh-shuufaan
oatmeal

Additional Vocabulary

28 طَعَامٌ عَلَى النَّمَطِ الْغَرْبِيّ
ṭaçaamun çala -n-namaṭi -l-gharbiy-y
Western-style food

29 طَيِّبُ الْمَذَاق (لَذِيْذ)
ṭay-yibu -l- mathzaaq (lathziithz)
tasty (delicious)

30 فَطِيرَة (بَانْ كِيك)
faṭiirah (baan kiik)
pancakes

31 الشِّوَاءُ (الْبَارْبِكْيُو)
'ash-shiwaa' ('albaarbikyuu)
barbecue

32 يَشْوِي
yashwii
to barbecue

33 يَخْبِز
yakhbiz
to bake

34 زِبْدَة
zibdah
butter

35 زَبَادِي
zabaadii
yogurt

36 كَاتْشَب
kaatshab
ketchup

37 مَاكْدُونَالْدِز هُوَ مَطْعَمٌ شَهِيرٌ لِلْوَجَبَاتِ السَّرِيعَةِ فِي الشَّرْقِ الأَوْسَطِ.
maakduunaaldz huwa maṭçamun shahiirun lilwajabaati -s-sariiçati fi -sh-sharqi -l- 'awsaṭ
McDonalds is a popular fast food restaurant in the Middle East.

38 الأَطْفَالُ يُحِبُّونَ الْهَامْبُرْغَر وَالْبَطَاطِسَ الْمَقْلِيَّة.
'al'aṭfaalu yuḥib-buuna -l- haamburghar wa lbaṭaaṭisa -l-maqliy-yah
Children like hamburgers and french fries.

39 هَلْ تُفَضِّلُ الأَكْلَ الْعَرَبِيَّ أَمِ الْغَرْبِيّ؟
hal tufaaḍ-ḍilu -l-'akla -l-çarabiy-ya 'ami -l-gharbiy-y
Do you (m) prefer Arabic food or Western food?

36 الْمَشْرُوبَات
‘almashruubaat
Drinks

1 مَشْرُوب
mashruub
beverage

2 مِيَاهٌ مَعْدِنِيَّة
miyaahun maçdiniy-yah
mineral water

3 عَصِيرُ فَوَاكِه
çaşiiru fawaakih
fruit juice

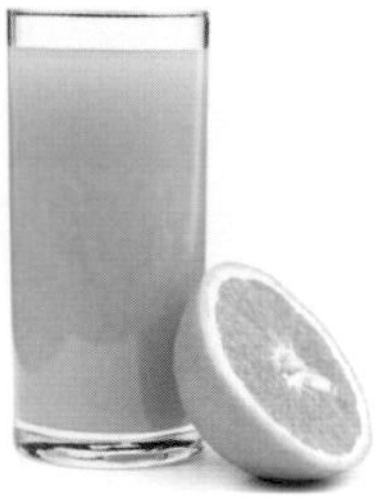

4 عَصِيرُ الْبُرْتُقَال
çaşiiru -l-burtuqaal
orange juice

5 لَبَن
laban
milk

6 قَهْوَة
qahwah
coffee

7 شَاي
shaay
tea

8 شَايٌ مُثَلَّج
shaayun muthal-laj
iced tea

9 حَلِيبُ الصُّويَا
ḥaliibu -ṣ-ṣuuyaa
soy milk

10 مِيَاهٌ غَازِيَّة (كُوكَاكُولَا)
miyaahun ghaaziy-yah (kukaakuulaa)
fuzzy water (coca co

11 مِيَاهُ الصُّنْبُور
miyaahu - ṣ-ṣunbuur
tap water

15 مَشْرُوبَاتُ الْحِمْيَة (الدَّايِتْ)
mashruubaatu -l-ḥimyah (‘ad-daayit)
diet drinks

16 مَشْرُوبَاتُ الطَّاقَة
mashruubaatu - ṭ-ṭaaqah
energy drinks

12 مَاء
maa‘
water

13 يَشْرَب
yashrab
to drink

14 عَطْشَان
çaṭshaan
thirsty

17 مَشْرُوبَاتٌ رِيَاضِيَّة
mashruubaatun riyaaḍiy-yah
sports drinks

18 كُوكْتِيل
kuktiil
cocktails

19 نَبِيذٌ أَحْمَر
nabii*th*zun 'aḥmar
red wine

20 نَبِيذٌ أَبْيَض
nabii*th*zun 'abyaḍ
white wine

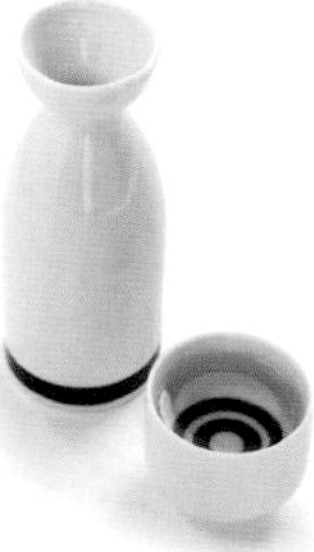

24 نَبِيذٌ أَصْفَر
nabii*th*zun 'aṣfar
yellow wine

21 وِيسْكِي
wiskii
whiskey

22 شَامْبَانِيَا
***sh*aambaaniyah**
champagne

23 كُحُولٌ أَبْيَض
kuḥuulun 'abyaḍ
white spirit

25 جِعَة (بِيرَة)
jiçah (biirah)
beer

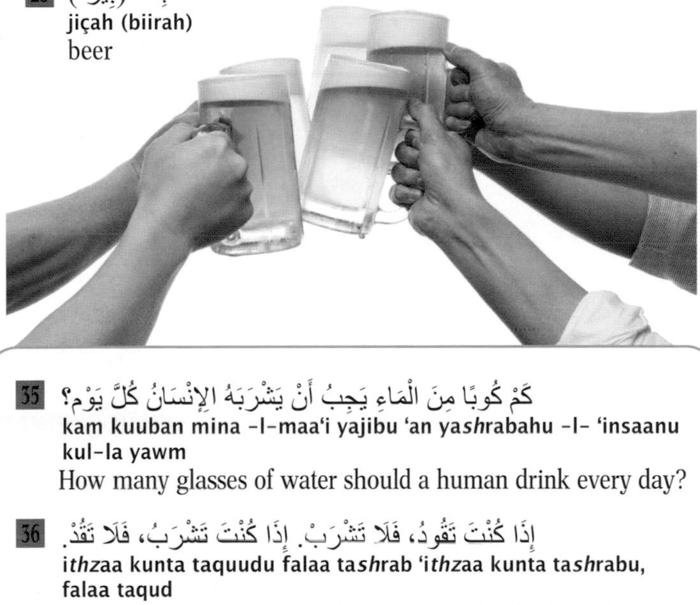

Additional Vocabulary

26 مَشْرُوبَاتٌ غَازِيَّةٌ (صُودَا)
ma*sh*ruubaatun *gh*aaziy-yah (ṣuuda)
sodas

27 مُبَرِّدُ مَاء
mubar-ridu maa'
water dispenser

28 مَاءٌ سَاخِن
maa'un saa*kh*in
hot water

29 مَاءٌ بَارِد
maa'un baarid
cold water

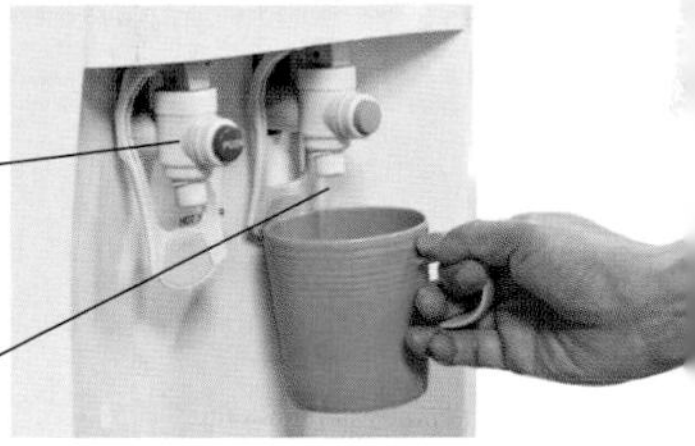

30 مُكَعَّبَاتُ ثَلْج
mukaç-çabaatu *th*alj
ice cubes

31 مَاءٌ مُثَلَّج
maa'un mu*th*al-laj
ice water

32 كُوبٌ زُجَاجِيّ
kuubun zujaajiy-y
glass cup

33 فِنْجَان
finjaan
cup

34 زُجَاجَة
zujaajah
bottle

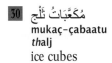

35 كَمْ كُوبًا مِنَ الْمَاءِ يَجِبُ أَنْ يَشْرَبَهُ الإِنْسَانُ كُلَّ يَوْمٍ؟
kam kuuban mina -l-maa'i yajibu 'an ya*sh*rabahu -l- 'insaanu kul-la yawm
How many glasses of water should a human drink every day?

36 إِذَا كُنْتَ تَقُودُ، فَلَا تَشْرَبْ. إِذَا كُنْتَ تَشْرَبُ، فَلَا تَقُدْ.
i*th*zaa kunta taquudu falaa ta*sh*rab 'i*th*zaa kunta ta*sh*rabu, falaa taqud
If you (m) drive, don't drink. If you (m) drink, don't drive.

37 أُرِيدُ شَيْئًا سَاخِنًا لِأَشْرَبَه.
'uriidu *sh*ay'an saa*kh*inan li'a*sh*rabah
I want something hot to drink.

37 اَلْفَوَاكِهُ الطَّازَجَةُ وَالْمُكَسَّرَاتُ وَالْحُبُوب

'alfawakihu -ṭ-ṭaazajatu wa-l-mukas-saraatu wa-l-ḥubuub

Fresh Fruits, Nuts and Grains

1 تُفَّاح
tuf-faaḥ
apple

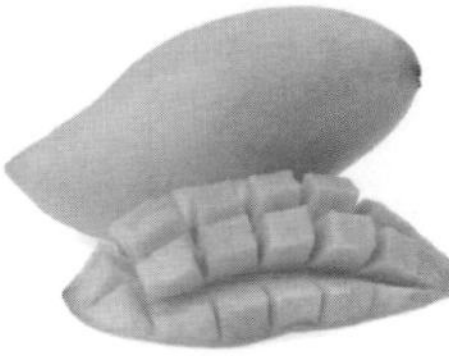

2 مَانْجُو
maanjuu
mango

3 بُرْتُقَال
burtuqaal
orange

4 يُوسُفِيّ
yuusufiy-y
mandarin orange

5 كُمِّثْرَى
kum-mi*th*raa
pear

6 جَوْزُ الْهِنْد
jawzu-l-hind
coconut

7 مَوْز
mawz
banana

8 أَنَانَاس
'anaanaas
pineapple

9 خَوْخ
kh*aw*kh
peach

10 بَابَايَا
baabaayaa
papaya

11 لَيْمُونٌ أَصْفَر
laymuunun 'aṣfar
lemon (yellow)

12 لَيْمُونٌ أَخْضَر
laymuunun 'a*kh*ḍar
lime (green)

13 لِيتْشِي
liit*sh*i
lychee

14 لُونْجَان
luunjaan
longan

15 فَرَاوِلَة
faraawilah
strawberry

16 عِنَب
çinab
grape

17 شَمَّام
***sh*am-maam**
cantaloupe

18 بِرْسِيمُون (كَاكَا)
pirsiimuun (kaakaa)
persimmon

19 بِطِّيخ
biṭ-ṭii*kh*
watermelon

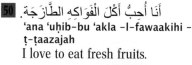

50 أَنَا أُحِبُّ أَكْلَ الْفَوَاكِهِ الطَّازَجَة.
'ana 'uḥib-bu 'akla -l-fawaakihi -ṭ-ṭaazajah
I love to eat fresh fruits.

20 فُولٌ سُودَانِيّ
fuulun suudaaniy-y
peanuts

21 عَيْنُ جَمَلٍ
çaynu jamal
walnuts

22 الْبَقَان
'albaqaan
pecans

23 فُسْتُق
fustuq
pistachios

24 لَوْز
lawz
almonds

29 كَاجُو
kaajuu
cashew nuts

25 الْمُكَسَّرَاتُ الْمَكَادِيمِيَا
'almukas-saraatu -l-makaadiimyaa
macadamia nuts

26 الْكَسْتَنَاء
'alkastanaa'
chestnuts

27 بُنْدُق
bunduq
hazel nuts

28 صُنُوبَر
ṣunuubar
pine nuts

30 بُذُورُ الْيَقْطِين (لُبٌّ أَبْيَض)
buthzuuru -l- yaqṭiin (lub-bun 'abyaḍ)
pumpkin seeds

31 بُذُورُ الْبِطِّيخ
buthzuuru -l-biṭ-ṭiikh
watermelon seeds

32 بُذُورُ زَهْرَةِ عَبَّادِ الشَّمْس
buthzuuru zahrati çab-baadi -sh-shams
sunflower seeds

33 شُوفَان
shuufaan
oats

34 شَعِير
shaçiir
barley

35 الدُّخْن
'ad-dukhn
millet

36 الْحِنْطَةُ السَّوْدَاء
'alḥinṭatu 'as-sawdaa'
buckwheat

37 أُرْز
'urz
rice

38 قَمْح
qamḥ
wheat

39 حُبُوبُ السِّمْسِم
ḥubuubu- s-simsim
sesame seeds

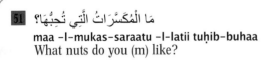

51 مَا الْمُكَسَّرَاتُ الَّتِي تُحِبُّهَا؟
maa -l-mukas-saraatu -l-latii tuḥib-buhaa
What nuts do you (m) like?

52 أَنَا أُحِبُّ الْكَاجُو. مَاذَا عَنْكَ؟
'ana 'uḥib-bu -l-kaajuu mathzaa çank
I like cashew nuts. What about you (m)?

53 أَنَا عِنْدِي حَسَاسِيَّةٌ مِنَ الْمُكَسَّرَات.
'ana çindii ḥasaasiy-yatun mina -l- mukas-saraat
I am allergic to nuts.

54 هَلْ يُمْكِنُنِي الْحُصُولُ عَلَى سَلَطَةٍ أُخْرَى بِدُونِ مُكَسَّرَات؟
hal yumkinuni -l-ḥuṣuulu çalaa salaṭatin 'ukhraa biduuni mukas-saraat
Can I have another salad without nuts?

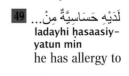

Additional Vocabulary

40 حُبُوب
ḥubuub
grains; cereals

41 مُكَسَّرَات
mukas-saraat
nuts

42 مُقَرْمَشَات
muqarmashaat
crackers

43 دَقِيقُ الشُّوفَان
daqiiqu -sh-shuufaan
oatmeal

44 فَوَاكِهُ مُجَفَّفَة
fawaakihu mujaf-fafah
dried fruits

45 بُقُولِيَّات
buquuliy-yaat
beans

46 ذُرَة
thzurah
corn

47 دَقِيق
daqiiq
flour

48 عَصِيرُ فَوَاكِه
çaṣiiru fawaakih
fruit juice

49 لَدَيْهِ حَسَاسِيَّةٌ مِنْ...
ladayhi ḥasaasiy-yatun min
he has allergy to

38 فِي السُّوق
fi - s-suuk
At the Market

1 لَحْم
laḥm
meat

2 لَحْمٌ بَقَرِيٌّ
laḥmun baqariy-y
beef

3 أَوْرَاقُ الْكُزْبَرَة؛ (الْكُزْبَرَةُ)
'awraaqu -l-kuzbarah; ('alkuzbara
coriander leaves; cilantro

4 بَقْدُونِس
baqduunis
parsley

5 لَحْمُ خِنْزِير
laḥmu khinziir
pork

6 خَرُوف (لَحْمُ الضَّأْنْ)
kharuuf (laḥmu - ḍ- ḍa'n)
lamb (mutton)

7 إِكْلِيلُ الْجَبَل (رُوزْمَارِي)
'ikliilu-l-jabal (ruuzmaary)
rosemary

8 بَطَّة
baṭ-ṭah
duck

9 دَجَاج (فِرَاخ)
dajaaj (firaakh)
chicken

10 لَيْمُون
laymuun
lemon

11 مَأْكُولَاتٌ بَحْرِيَّة
ma'kuulaatun baḥriy-yah
seafood

12 سَمَك
samak
fish

13 أُخْطُبُوط
'ukhṭubuuṭ
octopus

16 بَيْض
bayḍ
eggs

17 خَضْرَاوَات
khaḍraawaat
vegetables

14 شَبَت
shabat
dill

15 جَمْبَرِي (قُرَيْدِس)
jambari (quraydis)
shrimp (prawns)

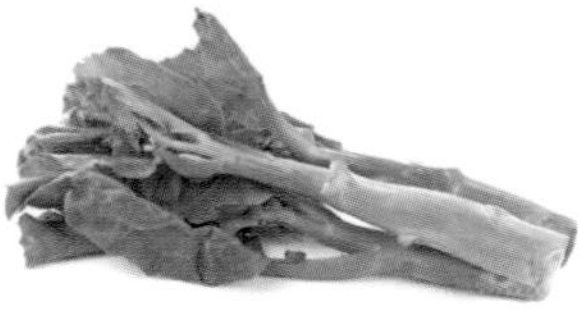

18 اللِّفْتُ الصِّينِيّ
'al-liftu - ṣ- ṣiiniy-y
Chinese kale

19 كُرُنْب صِينِيّ
kurunb ṣiiniy-y
bok choy

20 الْمَلْفُوفُ الصِّينِيُّ الْمُزْهِر
'almalfuufu- ṣ - ṣiiniy-yu -l-muzhir
choy sum; Chinese flowering cabbage

21 سَبَانِخ
sabaanikh
spinach

22 بَرَاعِمُ الْبُقُول
baraaçimu -l- buquul
bean sprouts

60 فِي مِصْرَ نُحِبُّ شِرَاءَ طَعَامِنَا مِنَ الْبَاعَةِ الْمَحَلِّيِّينَ.
fii miṣra nuḥib-bu shiraa'a ṭaçaamina mina lbaaçati lmaḥal-liy-yiin
In Egypt, we like to buy our food at the fresh market.

61 الْخُضَارُ وَاللُّحُومُ طَازَجَةٌ جِدًّا هُنَا. وَهُوَ أَرْخَصُ قَلِيلًا مِنَ السُّوبَرِ مَارْكِتْ.
'alkhuḍaaru wa-l-luḥuumu ṭaazajatun jid-dan hunaa wa huwa 'arkhaṣu qaliilan mina -s-suubar markit
The vegetables and meat are very fresh here. And it is slightly cheaper than the supermarket.

23 الثُّومُ الْمُعَمَّرُ الصِّينِيّ
'ath-thuumu-l muçam-maru-ṣ-ṣiiniy-y
Chinese chives

24 فُلْفُلٌ حُلو
fulfulun ḥulw
bell pepper

25 بَاذِنْجَان
baathzinjaan
eggplant

26 طَمَاطِم
ṭamaaṭim
tomato

27 كَرَفس
karafs
celery

28 بَطَاطِس
baṭaaṭis
potato

29 ثُوم
thuum
garlic

30 زَنْجَبِيل
zanjabiil
ginger

31 خَسّ
khas-s
lettuce

32 فِطْر
fiṭr
mushroom

33 خِيَار
khiyaar
cucumber

34 بُرُوكْلِي
buruuklii
broccoli

35 جَزَر
jazar
carrot

36 بَصَل
baṣal
onions

37 فُلْفُلٌ حَارّ
fulfulun ḥaar-r
chili peppers

38 الْبَصَلُ الأَخْضَر
'albaṣalu -l 'akhḍar
green onions

39 بِطِّيخٌ شِتْوِيّ
biṭ-ṭiikhun shitwiy-y
winter melon

40 الْقَرْعُ الْمُرُّ
'alqarçu -l- mur-r
bitter gourd

41 مَلْفُوفٌ صِينِيٌّ
malfuufun ṣiiniy-y
Chinese cabbage

42 تُوفُو
tuufuu
tofu

Additional Vocabulary

43 سُوق
suuq
market

44 طَرْخُون
ṭarkhuun
tarragon

45 طَازَج
ṭaazaj
fresh

46 قَرْنَبِيط
qarnabiiṭ
cauliflower

47 يَقْطِين
yaqṭiin
pumpkin

48 هِلْيُون
hilyuun
asparagus

49 كُوسَة
kusah
zucchini

50 رَيْحَان
rayḥaan
basil

51 مَرْيَمِيَّة
maryamiy-yah
sage

52 زَعْتَرْ
zaçtar
thyme

53 مَلْفُوف (كُرُنب)
malfuuf (kurunb)
cabbage

54 فَاصُولْيَا خَضْرَاءُ
faaṣuulya khaḍraa'
green beans;
string beans

55 زَعْتَرٌ بَرِّي (أُورْجَانُو)
zaçtarun bar-riy ('urjaanuu)
oregano

56 الْبُرُوكْلِي الصِّينِيّ
'alburuukli - ṣ - ṣiiniy-y
Chinese broccoli

57 أَنْوَاعُ اللُّحُوم
'anwaaçu -l- luḥuum
types of meat

58 لَحْمٌ بَقَرِيٌّ مَفْرُوم
laḥmun baqariy-yun mafruum
ground beef

59 لَحْمُ خِنْزِير مَفْرُوم
laḥmu khinziirin mafruum
ground pork

62 تَوَابِل
tawaabil
seasonings

63 صُوصُ الصُّويَا
ṣuuṣu ṣ-ṣuuyaa
soy sauce

64 صُوصُ الْفُلْفُلِ الْحَارّ
ṣuuṣu -l- fulfuli -l-ḥaar-r
chili sauce

65 زَيْتُ السِّمْسِمِ
zaytu -s-simsim
sesame oil

66 زَيْتُ الزَّيْتُونِ
zaytu -z-zaytuun
olive oil

67 صُوصُ الْمَحَارِ
ṣuuṣu -l- maḥaar
oyster sauce

68 مَسْحُوقُ شَطَّة
masḥuuqu *shaṭaah*
chili powder

69 فُلْفُلٌ مَطْحُونٌ
fulfulun maṭḥuun
ground pepper

70 مِلْح
milḥ
salt

71 قِرْفَة
qirfah
cinnamon

72 يَنْسُون
yansuun
star anise

73 كُرْكُم مَطْحُون
kurkum maṭḥuun
ground turmeric

Additional Vocabulary

74 خَلّ
***kh*al-l**
vinegar

75 سُكَّر
suk-kar
sugar

76 بُودْرَةُ الْكَارِي
buudratu -l-kaarii
curry powder

77 نِشَا
ni*sh*aa
starch

78 زَيْتُ الطَّهْي
zaytu-ṭ-ṭahy
cooking oil

79 حَلْوَى
ḥalwaa
candy

80 سَبْعُ بُهَارَات
sabçu buhaaraat
seven spices

81 زَيْتُ جَوْزِ الْهِنْد
zaytu jawzi -l- hind
coconut oil

82 زَيْتُ النَّخِيل
zaytu -n-na*kh*iil
palm oil

83 نَبِيذُ الطَّبْخ
nabii*thz*u -ṭ-ṭab*kh*
cooking wine

84 زَيْتُ الْفُولِ السُّودَانِيِّ
zaytu -l-fuuli s-suudaaniy-y
peanut oil

85 جُلُوتومَات أُحَادِيَّةُ الصُّودْيُوم
juluutuumaat 'uḥaadiy-yahatu ṣ-ṣuudyuum
monosodium glutamate (MSG)

86 مَعْجُونُ فُولِ الصُّوَيَا
maçjuunu fuuli- ṣ-ṣuuyaa
soybean paste

87 يَسْهُلُ طَهْيُ الطَّعَامِ الْعَرَبِيِّ بِمُجَرَّدِ حُصُولِكَ عَلَى جَمِيعِ الْمُكَوِّنَات.
yas-hulu ṭahyu -ṭ-ṭaçaami -l-çarabiy-yi bimujar-radi ḥuṣuulika çalaa jamiiçi -l-mukaw-winaat
Arabic food is easy to cook once you have all the ingredients.

English-Arabic Index

The following information is included for each entry–the English word, the Arabic word and its transliteration, the theme number and the order in which the word appeared in that theme, followed by the page number where the word appears. For example:

English word	Arabic word/Transliteration		Theme number and order	Page in book
mother	أَمّ	'um-m	[2-14]	13

blog مُدَوَّنَة **mudaw-wanah** [23-38] *55*
blood دَم **dam** [4-42] *17*
blood pressure ضَغْطُ الدَّم **ḍaghṭu-d-dam** [27-9] *62*
blood test اخْتِبَارُ دَم **'ikhtibaaru dam** [27-7] *62*
blood vessels الْأَوْعِيَةُ الدَّمَوِيَّة **'al-'awçiyatu -d-damawiy-yah** [4-43] *17*
blouse (بُلُوزَة) قَمِيصٌ نِسَائِيٌّ **qamiiṣun nisaa'iy-y (buluuzah)** [10-7] *28*
blue أَزْرَق **'azraq** [7-6] *22*
board سَبُّورَة **sab-buurah** [20-2] *48*
boarding pass بِطَاقَةُ صُعُودِ الطَّائِرَة **biṭaaqatu ṣuçuudi - ṭ-ṭaa'irah** [31-9] *70*
bok choy كُرُنْب صِينِيّ **kurunb ṣiiniy-y** [38-19] *84*
bones عَظْم **çaẓm** [4-44] *17*
book كِتَاب **kitaab** [19-7] *46*
book shelf رَفُّ الْكُتُب **raf-fu -l-kutub** [3-35] *15*
boots (بُوطْ) حِذَاءٌ طَوِيلٌ **ḥithzaa'un ṭawiil (buuṭ)** [14-3] *36*
both of كُلٌّ مِنْ **kul-lun min** [5-22] *19*
bottle زُجَاجَة **zujaajah** [36-34] *81*
boutique (مَتْجَر) بُوتِيك **buutiik (matjar)** [10-24] *29*
bowl (وِعَاء) صَحْن **ṣaḥn (wiçaa')** [34-9] *76*
brain مُخّ **mukh-kh** [4-30] *17*
bread خُبْز **khubz** [34-7] *76*
bridge (كُوبْرِي) جِسْر **jisr (kubrii)** [11-27] *31*
broccoli بُرُوكْلِي **buruuklii** [38-34] *85*
brother-in-law نَسِيب **nasiib** [2-32] *12*
brown بُنِّيّ **bun-niy-y** [7-9] *22*
browser مُتَصَفِّح **mutaṣaf-fih** [23-39] *55*
buckwheat الْحِنْطَةُ السَّوْدَاء **'alḥinṭatu 'as-sawdaa'** [37-36] *83*
bus route [12-24] *33*
طَرِيقُ الْحَافِلَة (طَرِيقُ الْأُتُوبِيس \ الْبَاصْ) **ṭariiqu -l-ḥaafilah (ṭariiqu -l-'utubiis \ 'albaaṣ)**
bus stop مَوْقِفُ الْأُتُوبِيس **mawqifu-l 'utu-biis** [12-13] *33*
but وَلَكِنْ **wa laakin** [28-37] *65*
butter زِبْدَة **zibdah** [35-34] *79*
butterfly فَرَاشَة **faraashah** [29-27] *67*
by بِوَاسِطَة **biwaasiṭah** [28-31] *65*

C

CD/DVD [23-12] *54*
قُرْصٌ مَضْغُوط (سِي دِي) دِي فِي دِي **qursun maḍghuuṭ (sii dii) dii vii dii**
cabbage (كُرُنْب) مَلْفُوف **malfuuf (kurunb)** [38-53] *85*
cable network شَبَكَةُ الْكَابِل **shabakatu -l- kaabil** [23-43] *55*
cake (كِيكَة) كَعْكَة **kaçkah (kiikah)** [35-22] *79*
calculator آلَةٌ حَاسِبَة **'aalatun ḥaasibah** [5-16] *19;* [20-11] *48*
calculus حِسَابُ التَّفَاضُلِ وَالتَّكَامُل **ḥisaabu -t-tafaaḍuli wa-t-takaamul** [19-49] *47*
calendar (نَتِيجَة) تَقْوِيم **taqwiim (natiijah)** [16-4] *40*
calligraphy فَنُّ الْخَطّ **fan-nu -l- khaṭ-ṭ** [21-5] *50*
camera (كَامِيرَا) آلَةُ تَصْوِير **'aalatu taṣwiir (kamiraa)** [31-15] *70*
candy حَلْوَى **ḥalwaa** [38-79] *86*
cantaloupe شَمَّام **sham-maam** [37-17] *82*
car سَيَّارَة **say-yaarah** [12-1] *32*
carpet سَجَّادَة **saj-jaadah** [3-12] *14*
carrot جَزَر **jazar** [38-35] *85*
cash نَقْدًا **naqdan** [9-35] *27*
cashew nuts كَاجُو **kaajuu** [37-29] *83*
cashier (كَاشِير) مُحَاسِب **muḥaasib (kashiir)** [10-26] *29*
cat قِطَّة **qiṭ-ṭah** [29-22] *67*
cauliflower قَرْنَبِيط **qarnabiiṭ** [38-46] *85*
ceiling سَقْف **saqf** [3-4] *14*
celery كَرَفْس **karafs** [38-27] *85*
cello تِشِيلُّو **tishiil-luu** [26-8] *60*
Centime (Morocco, Algeria) سِنْتِيم **cintiim** [9-11] *26*
central business district (CBD) مِنْطَقَةُ الْأَعْمَالِ الْمَرْكَزِيَّة **minṭaqatu-l-'açmaali-l-markaziy-yah** [11-21] *31*
Cent (Egypt, Jordan, Syria) قِرْش **qirsh** [9-8] *26*
century (100 years) قَرْن **qarn** [16-43] *41*
cereal (الْكُورْنْ فِلِيكْس\سِيرْيَالْ) حُبُوب **ḥubuub ('alkuurn fliks/siiryaal)** [35-24] *79*
certainly بِكُلِّ تَأْكِيد **bikul-li ta'kiid** [10-33] *29*
chair كُرْسِيّ **kursiy-y** [3-8] *14*
champagne شَامْبَانِيَا **shaambaaniyah** [36-22] *81*
changes تَغْيِيرَات **taghyiiraat** [28-29] *65*
chat room (شَاتْ رُووم) غُرْفَةُ الدَّرْدَشَة **ghurfatu -d-dardashah (shaat ruum)** [23-19] *55*
cheap رَخِيص **rakhiiṣ** [9-27] *27*
check شِيك **shiik** [9-18] *27*
cheek خَدّ **khad-d** [4-4] *16*
cheese جُبْن **jubn** [35-23] *79*
chef (شِيف) طَاهِي **ṭaahii (shiif)** [25-11] *59*
chef (cook) (طَبَّاخ) طَاهِي **ṭaahii (ṭab-baakh)** [34-2] *76*
chemistry كِيمِيَاء **kiimiyaa'** [19-35] *47*
chest صَدْر **ṣadr** [4-25] *17*
chestnuts الْكَسْتَنَاء **'alkastanaa'** [37-26] *83*
chicken دَجَاج **dajaaj** [29-19] *67;* [34-25] *77;* (فِرَاخ) دَجَاج **dajaaj (firaakh)** [38-9] *84*
children أَطْفَال **'aṭfaal** [2-4] *12*
chili peppers فُلْفُلٌ حَارّ **fulfulun ḥaar-r** [38-37] *85*
chili powder مَسْحُوقُ شَطَّة **masḥuuqu shaṭaah** [38-68] *86*
chili sauce صُوصُ الْفُلْفُلِ الْحَارّ **ṣuuṣu -l- fulfuli -l-ḥaar-r** [38-64] *86*
chin ذَقْن **thzaqn** [4-13] *16*
Chinese broccoli الْبُرُوكْلِي الصِّينِيّ **'alburuukli - ṣ - ṣiiniy-y** [38-56] *85*
Chinese cabbage مَلْفُوفٌ صِينِيٌّ **malfuufun ṣiiniy-y** [38-41] *85*
Chinese chives الثُّومُ الْمُعَمَّرُ الصِّينِيّ **'ath-thuumu-l muçam-maru-ṣ-ṣiiniy-y**[38-23] *85*
Chinese kale اللِّفْتُ الصِّينِيّ **'al-liftu - ṣ-ṣiiniy-y** [38-18] *84*
chocolates شُكُولَاتَة **shukulaatah** [18-17] *45*
choice اخْتِيَار **'ikhtiyaar** [34-29] *77*
choy sum; Chinese flowering cabbage الْمَلْفُوفُ الصِّينِيُّ الْمُزْهِر **'almalfuufu- ṣ - ṣiiniy-yu -l-muzhir** [38-20] *84*
Christmas الْكِرِيسْمَاس **'alkriismaas** [18-24] *45*
church كَنِيسَة **kaniisaah** [11-31] *31*
cinema (سِينِمَا) دَارُ عَرْضٍ سِينِمَائِيّ **daaru çarḍin siinimaa'iy-y (siinimaa)** [11-20] *31*
cinnamon قِرْفَة **qirfah** [38-71] *86*
city مَدِينَة **madiinah** [11-12] *30*
classmates زُمَلَاءُ الصَّفّ **zumalaa'u -ṣ-ṣaf-f** [20-13] *48*
classroom فَصْلٌ دِرَاسِيّ **faṣlun diraasiy-y** [20-4] *48*
clean نَظِيف **naẓiif** [28-18] *65*
clean energy طَاقَةٌ نَظِيفَة **ṭaaqatun naẓiifah** [28-21] *65*
clear (sky) صَافِي **ṣaafii** [14-4] *36*
clear day يَوْمٌ صَافِي **yawmun ṣaafii** [14-5] *36*
clever مَاهِر **maahir** [20-17] *49*
clock السَّاعَة **'as-saaçah** [15-6] *38*
close مُغْلَق **mughlaq** [8-12] *25*
clothes ثِيَاب **thiyaab** [10-6] *28*
clothing size حَجْمُ الْمَلَابِس **ḥajmu -l-malaabis** [7-29] *23*
cloud سَحَابَة **saḥaabah** [14-24] *37*
cloudy (غَمَامِيّ) ضَبَابِيّ **ḍabaabiy-y (ghamaamiy-y)** [14-7] *36*
coal فَحْم **faḥm** [28-23] *65*
coat or jacket مِعْطَف **miçṭaf** [14-18] *37*
cocktails كُوكْتِيل **kuktiil** [36-18] *81*
coconut جَوْزُ الْهِنْد **jawzu-l-hind** [37-6] *82*
coconut oil زَيْتُ جَوْزِ الْهِنْد **zaytu jawzi -l- hind** [38-81] *86*
coffee قَهْوَة **qahwah** [35-19] *79;* [36-6] *80*
cold بَارِد **baarid** [14-22] *37*
cold water مَاءٌ بَارِد **maa'un baarid** [36-29] *81*
cold weather طَقْسٌ بَارِد **ṭaqsun baarid** [14-23] *37*
college كُلِّيَّة **kul-liy-yah** [20-34] *49;* [25-23] *59*
colors الْأَلْوَان **'al'alwaan** [7-1] *22*
coffee table طَاوِلَةُ الْقَهْوَة **ṭaawilatu -l-qahwah** [3-11] *14*
coin currency عُمْلَةٌ مَعْدِنِيَّة **çumlatun maçdiniy-yah** [9-2] *26*
company شَرِكَة **sharikah** [25-20] *59*
comparing prices مُقَارَنَةُ الْأَسْعَار **muqaaranatu-l-'asçaar** [10-28] *29*
competition مُنَافَسَة **munaafasah** [30-13] *69*
completed (adj) مُكْتَمِل **muktamil** [28-34] *65*
computer (كُمْبِيُوتَر) حَاسِبٌ آلِيّ **ḥaasibun 'aaliy-y (kumbiyuutar)** [23-1] *54*
computer lab [20-38] *49*
مَعْمَلُ حَاسِبٍ آلِيّ (مَعْمَل كُمْبِيُوتَرْ) **maçmalu ḥaasibin 'aaliy-y (maçmal kumbiyuutar)**
concert حَفْلَةٌ مُوسِيقِيَّة **ḥaflatun musiiqiy-yah** [26-15] *61*
conference center مَرْكَزُ الْمُؤْتَمَرَات **markazu-l-mu'tamaraat** [11-8] *30*
connected to the internet (online) مُتَّصِلٌ بِالْإِنْتَرْنِت (أُونْ لَايِنْ) **mut-taṣilun bil'itarnit ('un layin)** [23-35] *55*
cooked rice أُرْزٌ مَطْبُوخ **'urzun maṭbuukh** [34-10] *76*
cooked vegetable (طَبِيخ) خُضَار مَطْبُوخ **khuḍaar maṭbuukh (ṭabiikh)** [34-24] *77*
cooker hood شَفَّاطُ الْمَطْبَخ **shaf-faaṭu -l-maṭbakh** [3-28] *15*
cooking oil زَيْتُ الطَّهْي **zaytu-ṭ-ṭahy** [38-78] *86*
cooking wine نَبِيذُ الطَّبْخ **nabiithzu -ṭ-ṭabkh** [38-83] *86*
coriander leaves; cilantro أَوْرَاقُ الْكُزْبَرَة؛ (الْكُزْبَرَة) **'awraaqu -l-kuzbarah; ('alkuzbarah)** [38-3] *84*
corn ذُرَة **thzurah** [37-46] *83*
cosmetics مُسْتَحْضَرَاتُ تَجْمِيل **mustaḥḍaraatu tajmiil** [10-17] *29*
country code (رَقْمُ) الْبَلَد رَمْزُ **ramzu (raqmu) lbalad** [24-26] *56*
course; curriculum مُقَرَّرٌ تَعْلِيمِيّ **muqar-rarun taçliimiy-y** [21-35] *51*
cow بَقَرَة **baqarah** [29-13] *67*
crackers مُقَرْمَشَات **muqarmashaat** [37-42] *83*
credit card بِطَاقَةُ ائْتِمَانِيَّة **biṭaaqatuni-'-timaaniy-yah** [9-20] *27;* [10-30] *29* بِطَاقَةُ ائْتِمَانٍ (كرِيدِتْ كَارْدْ) **biṭaaqatu 'timaan (kriidit kaard)**
crops مَحَاصِيل **maḥaaṣiil** [17-17] *43*
cruise center مَرْكَزُ الرِّحْلَاتِ الْبَحْرِيَّة **markazu -r-riḥlaati -l-baḥriy-yah** [31-42] *71*
cucumber خِيَار **khiyaar** [38-33] *85*
culture ثَقَافَة **thaqaafah** [21-18] *51*
cup فِنْجَان **finjaan** [36-33] *81*
currency عُمْلَة **çumlah** [31-22] *71*
currency exchange أَسْعَارُ الصَّرْف **'asçaaru-ṣ-ṣarf** [9-22] *27*
curry powder بُودْرَةُ الْكَارِي **buudratu -l-kaarii** [38-76] *86*
curtain سِتَارَة **sitaarah** [3-17] *14*
customer زَبُون **zabuun** [1-20] *11*
customs جُمْرُك **jumruk** [31-27] *71*
cut قَطْع **qaṭç** [27-26] *63*
cute; adorable لَطِيف **laṭiif** [29-30] *67*

D

dance (performance art) الرَّقْص **'ar-raqṣ** [26-26] *61*
dark color لَوْنٌ غَامِق **lawnun ghaamiq** [7-15] *22*
daughter ابْنَة **'ibnah** [2-5] *12*
daughter-in-law زَوْجَةُ الابْن **zawjatu -libn** [2-28] *12*
day يَوْم **yawm** [16-3] *40*
day of a month يَوْمٌ مِنَ الشَّهْر **yawmun mina -sh-shahr** [16-28] *41*
decade (10 years) عَقْد **çaqd** [16-42] *41*
December دِيسَمْبِر **diisambir** [16-27] *41*
decision قَرَار **qaraar** [10-36] *29*
debt دَيْن **dayn** [9-31] *27*
delivery van شَاحِنَةُ التَّوْصِيل **shaaḥinatu-t-tawṣiil** [12-7] *32*
dentist (f) طَبِيبَةُ الْأَسْنَان (دُكْتُورَةُ الْأَسْنَان) **ṭabiibatu -l- 'asnaan (duktuuratu -l-'asnaan)** [25-14] *59*
dentistry طِبُّ الْأَسْنَان **ṭib-bu -l-'asnaan** [27-40] *63*

department store مَتْجَرٌ مُتَعَدِّدُ الأَقْسَام **matjarun mutaçad-didu-l-'aqsaam** [10-23] *29*

dermatology طِبُّ الأَمْرَاضِ الْجِلْدِيَّة **ṭib-bu -l- 'amraaḍi ljildiy-yah** [27-51] *63*

desk/office مَكْتَب **maktab** [3-36] *15*

desktop computer [23-4] *54* حَاسُوبٌ مَكْتَبِيّ (كُمْبِيُوتَرْ) **ḥaasuubun maktabiy-y (kumbiyuutar)**

diacritics; tone marks عَلَامَاتُ التَّشْكِيل **çalaamaatu -t-tashkiil** [21-38] *51*

dialects (of different Arabic countries) لَهَجَات **lahajaat** [21-37] *51*

diary يَوْمِيَّات (مُذَكَّرَات) **yawmiy-yaat (muthzakiraat)** [16-40] *41*

dictionary قَامُوس **qaamuus** [19-11] *46*

diet drinks مَشْرُوبَاتُ الْحِمْيَة (الدَّايِتْ) **mashruubaatu -l-ḥimyah ('ad-daayit)** [36-15] *80*

difficult صَعْب **ṣaçb** [8-15] *25;* [21-28] *51*

digestive system الْجِهَازُ الْهَضْمِيّ **'al-jihaazu -l- haḍmiy-y** [4-37] *17*

digits أَعْدَاد **'açdaad** [5-29] *19*

dill شَبَت **shabat** [38-14] *84*

Dinar (Jordan, Kuwait Libya, Bahrain, Algeria, Iraq) دِينَار **diinaar** [9-5] *26*

dinosaur دَيْنَاصُور **daynaaṣuur** [29-10] *66*

direction اتِّجَاه **'it-tijaah** [13-36] *35*

Dirham (UAE) دِرْهَم **dirham** [9-6] *26*

discount خَصْم / تَنْزِيل **khaṣm / tanziil** [9-26] *27*

distance مَسَافَة **masaafah** [13-37] *35*

doctor (f) طَبِيبَة (دُكْتُورَة) **ṭabiibah (duktuurah)** [27-5] *62*

doctor's consultation room [27-18] *62* غُرْفَةُ اسْتِشَارَةِ الطَّبِيب **ghurfatu -stishaarati ṭ -ṭabiib**

dog كَلْب **kalb** [29-21] *67*

donuts دُونَات **duunaat** [35-5] *78*

door بَاب **baab** [3-46] *15*

down تَحْت **taḥt** [8-1] *24*

downtown وَسَطُ الْبَلَد **wasaṭu-l-balad** [11-24] *31*

dragon تِنِّين **tin-niin** [29-23] *67*

drawer دُرْج **durj** [3-34] *15*

dried fruits فَوَاكِهُ مُجَفَّفَة **fawaakihu mujaf-fafah** [37-44] *83*

drill (academic) تَدْرِيب **tadriib** [21-29] *51*

driver سَائِق **saa'iq** [12-3] *32*

drums طُبُول **ṭubuul** [26-6] *60*

duck بَطَّة **baṭ-ṭah** [38-8] *84*

E

ear أُذُن **'uthzun** [4-2] *16*

ear, nose and throat أَنْف وَأُذُن وَ حَنْجَرَة **'anf wa 'uthzun wa ḥanjarah** [27-49] *63*

early مُبَكِّرًا **mubak-kiran** [15-24] *39*

early morning الصَّبَاحُ الْبَاكِر **'aṣ-ṣabaaḥu-l-baakir** [15-18] *39*

earbuds سَمَّاعَاتُ الأُذُن **sam-maaçaatu -l- 'uthzun** [26-22] *61*

earth; ground أَرْض **'arḍ** [28-30] *65*

east شَرْق **sharq** [13-10] *34*

Easter Day شَمُّ النَّسِيم **sham-mu -n-nasl-im** [18-21] *45*

easy سَهْل **sahl** [8-15] *25;* [21-27] *51*

economics اقْتِصَاد **'iqtiṣaad** [19-32] *47*

eggplant بَاذِنْجَان **baathzinjaan** [38-25] *85*

eggs بَيْض **bayḍ** [38-16] *84*

Egypt مِصْر **miṣr** [32-2] *72*

Eid Al 'adHa عِيدُ الأَضْحَى **çiidu -l -'aḍḥaa** [18-7] *44*

Eid Al fitr عِيدُ الْفِطْر **çiidu -l-fiṭr** [18-6] *44*

Eid Cookies كَحْكُ الْعِيد **kaḥku -l-çiid** [18-11] *44*

eight ثَمَانِيَة **thamaaniyah** [5-8] *18*

eight pieces of clothing [22-5] *52* ثَمَانِي قِطَعٍ مِنَ الْمَلَابِس **thamaanii qiṭaçin mina -l-malaabis**

elbow مِرْفَق **mirfaq** [4-27] *17*

electric car سَيَّارَةٌ كَهْرُبَائِيَّة **say-yaaratun kahrubaa'iy-yah** [28-6] *64*

electric socket مِقْبَسُ الْكَهْرَبَاء **miqbasu -l-kahrabaa'** [3-56] *14*

elementary school مَدْرَسَةٌ ابْتِدَائِيَّة **madrasatun-ibtidaa'iy-yah** [20-30] *49*

elephant فِيل **fiil** [29-14] *67*

elevator مِصْعَد **miṣçad** [3-45] *15*

email بَرِيدٌ إِلِكْتِرُونِيّ (إِيمِيل) **bariidun 'iliktiruuniy-y ('iimiil)** [23-15] *54*

emergency طَوَارِئ **ṭawaari'** [27-27] *63*

emergency room غُرْفَةُ الطَّوَارِئ **ghurfatu - ṭ-ṭ awaari'** [27-2] *62*

employee مُوَظَّف **muwaẓ-ẓaf** [25-25] *59*

end of the school day انْتِهَاءُ الْيَوْمِ الدِّرَاسِيّ **'intihaa'u -l- yawmi -d-diraasiy-y** [6-37] *20*

end of the school year holiday إِجَازَةُ انْتِهَاءِ السَّنَةِ الدِّرَاسِيَّة **'ijaazatu -ntihaa'i -s-sanati -d-diraasiy-yah** [18-29] *45*

energy drinks مَشْرُوبَاتُ الطَّاقَة **mashruubaatu - ṭ-ṭaaqah** [36-16] *80*

engineer مُهَنْدِس **muhandis** [25-4] *58*

English اللُّغَةُ الإِنْجِلِيزِيَّة **'al-lughatu -l-'injiliiziy-yah** [33-1] *74*

enter دُخُول **dukhuul** [8-6] *24*

enthusiastic مُتَحَمِّس **mutaḥam-mis** [2-42] *12*

entrepreneur رَائِدُ أَعْمَال **raa'idu 'açmaal** [25-21] *59*

environment بِيئَة **bii'ah** [28-27] *65*

equal يُسَاوِي **yusaawii** [5-21] *19*

eraser مِمْحَاة **mimḥaah** [19-14] *47*

essay مَقَالَة **maqaalah** [21-17] *51*

Europe أُورُوبَّا **'urub-baa** [32-20] *73*

even more أَكْثَر وَ أَكْثَر **'akthar wa 'akthar** [10-35] *29*

even numbers أَرْقَامٌ زَوْجِيَّة **'arqaamun zawjiy-yah** [5-25] *19*

Everybody eats together. الْجَمِيعُ يَأْكُلُونَ مَعًا **'aljamiiçu ya'kuluuna maçan** [6-14] *21*

exam (exams) امْتِحَان (امْتِحَانَات) **'imtiḥaan ('imtiḥaanaat)** [19-1] *46*

exercise book كِتَابُ تَدْرِيبَات **kitaabu tadriibaat** [21-24] *51*

exit خُرُوج **khuruug** [8-6] *24*

expensive غَالِي **ghaalii** [9-28] *27*

expressway طَرِيقٌ سَرِيع **ṭariiqun sariiç** [11-18] *31*

extremely لِلْغَايَة **lilghaayah** [29-33] *67*

eye عَيْن **çayn** [4-8] *16*

eyebrow حَاجِب **ḥaajib** [4-7] *16*

F

face وَجْه **wajh** [4-5] *16*

Facebook فِيسْ بُوك **fiis buk** [24-17] *57*

fake مُزَوَّر **muzaw-war** [8-26] *25*

falafel طَعْمِيَّة **ṭaçmiy-yah** [34-16] *77*

family أُسْرَة **'usrah** [2-39] *12*

family name اسْمُ الْعَائِلَة **'ismu -l-çaa'ilah** [1-29] *11*

famous مَشْهُور **mash huur** [26-30] *61*

far بَعِيد **baçiid** [8-24] *25;* [13-43] *35*

farmer مُزَارِع **muzaariç** [25-19] *59*

fast سَرِيع **sariiç** [8-27] *25*

fat سَمِين **samiin** [8-13] *25*

father أَب **'ab** [2-12] *13*

Father's Day عِيدُ الأَب **çiidu -l- 'ab** [18-14] *44*

fava beans فُول **fuul** [34-18] *77*

February فِبْرَايِر **fibraayir** [16-17] *41*

female أُنْثَى **'unthaa** [2-3] *12*

festival مِهْرَجَان **mihrajaan** [18-1] *44*

fever حُمَّى **ḥum-maa** [27-12] *62*

fifteen minutes past six [15-8] *38* السَّاعَةُ السَّادِسَةُ وَخَمْسَ عَشْرَةَ دَقِيقَة / السَّاعَةُ السَّادِسَةُ وَرُبْع **'as-saaçatu - s-saadisatu wa khamsa çashrata daqiiqah / as-saaçatu-s-saadisatu wa rubç**

fifteen minutes to seven [15-10] *38* السَّاعَةُ السَّابِعَةُ إِلَّا خَمْسَ عَشْرَةَ دَقِيقَة (رُبْع) **'as-saaçatu -s-saabiçatu 'il-la khamsa çashrata daqiiqah (rubç)**

file مِلَفّ (فَايِل) **milaf-f (faayil)** [23-27] *54*

finally أَخِيرًا **'akhiiran** [15-36] *39*

financier مُمَوِّل **mumaw-wil** [25-3] *58*

fingers (a finger) أَصَابِع (م.إِصْبَع) **'aṣaabiç (s. 'iṣbaç)** [4-15] *16;* أَصَابِع (إِصْبَع) **'aṣaabiç ('iṣbaç)** [34-8] *76*

finish line خَطُّ النِّهَايَة **khaṭu -n-nihaayah** [30-14] *69*

fire engine سَيَّارَةُ الإِطْفَاء **say-yaaratu -l-'iṭfaa'** [12-16] *33*

firefighter رَجُلُ الإِطْفَاء **rajulu -l- 'iṭfaa'** [25-18] *59*

fireworks أَلْعَابٌ نَارِيَّة **'alçaabun naariy-yah** [18-3] *44*

first aid kit حَقِيبَةُ الإِسْعَافَاتِ الأَوَّلِيَّة **ḥaqiibatu -l-'isçaafaati -l- 'aw-waliy-yahh** [27-54] *63*

fish (pl) سَمَك **samak** [29-28] *67;* [38-12] *84*

five خَمْسَة **khamsah** [5-5] *18*

five minutes past six [15-5] *38* السَّاعَةُ السَّادِسَةُ وَخَمْسُ دَقَائِق **'as-saaçatu - s-saadisatu wa khamsu daqaa'iq**

five minutes to seven السَّاعَةُ السَّابِعَةُ إِلَّا خَمْسَ دَقَائِق **'as-saaçatu -s-saabiçatu 'il-la khamsa daq'iq** [15-11] *38*

five tickets خَمْسُ تَذَاكِر **khamsu tathzaakir** [22-4] *52*

flashcards بِطَاقَاتٌ تَعْلِيمِيَّة **biṭaaqaatun taçliimiy-yah** [21-3] *50*

floor أَرْض **'arḍ** [3-16] *14*

flour دَقِيق **daqiiq** [37-47] *83*

flower زَهْرَة **zahrah** [28-2] *64*

Fls (Bahrain, UAE) فِلْس **fils** [9-9] *26*

flute نَاي **naay** [26-11] *60*

fog ضَبَاب **ḍabaab** [14-25] *37*

foot قَدَم **qadam** [4-22] *17;* [13-41] *35*

for the purpose of (لِـ) لِغَرَضِ **ligharaḍi (li)** [28-33] *65*

forehead جَبْهَة **jabhah** [4-17] *17*

forest غَابَة **ghaabah** [28-14] *65*

fork شَوْكَة **shawkah** [34-13] *76*

former سَابِق **saabiq** [17-19] *43;* [20-43] *49*

four أَرْبَعَة **'arbaçah** [5-4] *18*

four-story building مَبْنًى مِنْ أَرْبَعَةِ طَوَابِق **mabnan min 'arbaçati ṭawaabiq** [22-11] *53*

four seasons الْمَوَاسِمُ الأَرْبَعَةُ (الْفُصُول) **'almawaasimu-l-'arbaçah (alfuṣuul)** [17-18] *43*

fraction (part) جُزْء **juz'** [5-23] *19*

free wifi وَايْ فَايْ مَجَّانِيّ **waay faay maj-jaaniy-y** [31-30] *71*

French اللُّغَةُ الْفَرَنْسِيَّة **'al-lughatu -l-faransiy-yah** [33-2] *74*

french fries بَطَاطِس مَقْلِيَّة **ṭaaṭis maqliy-yah** [35-27] *79*

frequently مِرَارًا وَتَكْرَارًا **miraaran wa takraaran** [15-33] *39*

fresh طَازَج **ṭaazaj** [38-45] *85*

freshman year in college [20-40] *49* السَّنَةُ الأُولَى فِي الْكُلِّيَّة **'as-sanatu-l-'uulaa fi -l-kul-liy-yah**

Friday يَوْمُ الْجُمُعَة **yawmu -l -jumuçah** [16-14] *40*

friends أَصْدِقَاء **'aṣdiqaa'** [1-35] *11*

(eat till) full شَبْعَان **shabçaan** [8-19] *25*

fruit juice عَصِيرُ فَوَاكِه **çaṣiiru fawaakih** [35-18]; *79* [36-3] *80;* [37-48] *83*

future مُسْتَقْبَل **mustaqbal** [8-22] *25*

fuzzy water (coca cola) مِيَاهٌ غَازِيَّة (كُوكَاكُولَا) **miyaahun ghaaziy-yah (kukaakuulaa)** [36-10] *80*

G

garage مِرْآب (جَرَاج) **mir'aab (garaaj)** [3-54] *14*

garbage truck شَاحِنَةُ النُّفَايَات **shaaḥinatu-n-nufaayaat** [12-6] *32*

garden حَدِيقَة **ḥadiiqah** [28-1] *64*

garlic ثُوم **thuum** [38-29] *85*

gas station مَحَطَّةُ وَقُود **maḥaṭ -ṭatu waquud** [11-6] *30*

gathering تَجَمُّع **tajam-muç** [1-19] *11*

general medicine الطِّبُّ الْعَامّ **'aṭ-ṭib-bu -l- çaam-m** [27-41] *63*

general surgery الْجِرَاحَةُ الْعَامَّة **'aljiraaḥatu -l-çaam-mah** [27-42] *63*

generally بِصِفَةٍ عَامَّة **biṣifatin çaam-mah** [10 34] *29*

geography جُغْرَافِيَا **jughraafiyaa** [19-36] *47*

geometry هَنْدَسَة **handasah** [19-30] *47*

German اللُّغَةُ الأَلْمَانِيَّة **'al-lughatu -l-'almaaniy-yah** [33-4] *74*

gift هَدِيَّة **hadiy-yah** [18-23] *45*

ginger زَنْجَبِيل **zanjabiil** [38-30] *85*

giraffe زَرَافَة **zaraafah** [29-3] *66*

glass cup كُوبٌ زُجَاجِيّ **kuubun zujaajiy-y** [36-32] *81*

glasses نَظَّارَة **naẓ-ẓaarah** [10-11] *28*
globe الْكُرَةُ الْأَرْضِيَّة **'alkuratu-l-'arḍiy-yah** [32-32] *73*
gloves (جَوَانْتِي) قُفَّازَات **quf-faazaat (gawaantii)** [14-31] *37*
go straight انْطَلِقْ مُبَاشَرَةً **'inṭaliq mubaasharatan** [12-26] *33*
go straight (imperative) انْطَلِقْ مُبَاشَرَةً **'inṭ-ṭaliq mubaasharatan** [13-31] *35*
goat مَاعِز **maaçiz** [29-11] *67*
gold ذَهَبِيّ **thzahabiy-y** [7-13] *22*
golf جُولْف **julf** [30-15] *69*
good جَيِّد **jay-yid** [8-7] *24*
good weather طَقْسٌ جَيِّد **ṭaqsun jay-yid** [14-34] *37*
Google جُوجَلْ **googal** [24-18] *57*
gorilla غُورِيلَّا **ghuril-la** [29-8] *66*
grade (level at school) صَفٌّ دِرَاسِيٌّ **ṣaf-fun diraasiy-y** [19-45] *47*
grades دَرَجَات **darajaat** [20-19] *49*
grains; cereals حُبُوب **ḥubuub** [37-40] *83*
grammar نَحْو **naḥw** [21-19] *51*
granddaughter حَفِيدَة **ḥafiidah** [2-30] *12*
grandfather جَدّ **jad-d** [2-8] *13*
grandmother جَدَّة **jad-dah** [2-7] *13*
grandson حَفِيد **ḥafiid** [2-29] *12*
grape عِنَب **çinab** [37-16] *82*
grass عُشْب **çushb** [28-5] *64*
gray رَمَادِيّ **ramaadiy-y** [7-10] *22*
Greek اللُّغَةُ الْيُونَانِيَّة **'al-lughatu -l-yuunaaniy-yah** [33-10] *75*
green أَخْضَر **'akhḍar** [7-7] *22*
green beans; string beans فَاصُولْيَا خَضْرَاء **faaṣuulya khaḍraa'** [38-54] *85*
green onions الْبَصَلُ الْأَخْضَر **'albaṣalu -l 'akhḍar** [38-38] *85*
ground beef لَحْمٌ بَقَرِيٌّ مَفْرُوم **laḥmun baqariy-yun mafruum** [38-58] *85*
ground pepper فُلْفُلٌ مَطْحُونٌ **fulfulun maṭḥuun** [38-69] *86*
ground pork لَحْمُ خِنْزِيرٍ مَفْرُوم **laḥmu khinziirin mafruum** [38-59] *85*
ground turmeric كُرْكُم مَطْحُون **kurkum maṭḥuun** [38-73] *86*
guesthouse / lodge دَارُ الضِّيَافَةِ / نُزُل **daaru - ḍ-ḍiyaafah/nuzul** [31-40] *71*
guitar (عِينَار) قِيثَارَة **qiithaarah (ghiitaar)** [26-1] *60*
gym (جِيمْ) صَالَةٌ رِيَاضِيَّةٌ **ṣaalatun riyaaḍiy-yah (jim)** [11-19] *31*
gynecology طِبُّ النِّسَاء **ṭib-bu -n-nisaa'** [27-44] *63*

H

hail (مَطَرٌ كَثِير) وَابِل **waabil (maṭarun kathiir)** [14-29] *37*
hair شَعْر **shaçr** [4-6] *16*
Halala (Saudi) هَلَلَة **halalah** [9-10] *26*
Halloween هَالُووِين **haaluuwiin** [18-20] *45*
half past six السَّاعَةُ السَّادِسَةُ وَنِصْفٌ **'as-saaçatu - s-saadisatu wa nisf** [15-9] *38*
ham لَحْمُ خِنْزِير **laḥmu khinziir** [35-12] *78*
hamburger هَمْبَرْغَر **hamburghar** [35-26] *79*
hand كَف **kaf** [4-19] *17*
hand fan مِرْوَحَةُ يَد **mirwaḥatu yad** [17-14] *43*
happy سَعِيد **saçiid** [1-10] *10;* [8-31] *25*
hat (طَاقِيَّة) قُبَّعَة **qub-baçah (ṭaaqiy-yah)** [10-16] *28;* [14-30] *37*
hazel nuts بُنْدُق **bunduq** [37-27] *83*
he has allergy to ... لَدَيْهِ حَسَاسِيَّةٌ مِنْ **adayhi ḥasaasiy-yatun min** [37-49] *83*
head رَأْس **ra's** [4-1] *16*
health صِحَّة **ṣiḥ-ḥah** [4-47] *17*
healthy صِحِّيّ **siḥ-ḥiy-y** [30-29] *69*
heart قَلْب **qalb** [4-32] *17*
Hebrew اللُّغَةُ الْعِبْرِيَّة **'al-lughatu -l-çibriy-yah** [33-11] *75*
here هُنَا **hunaa** [13-2] *34*
herring رِنْجَة **ringah** [34-17] *77*
high عَالِي **çaalii** [8-28] *25*
high school مَدْرَسَةٌ ثَانَوِيَّةٌ **madrasatun thaanawiy-yah** [20-32] *49*
high speed train قِطَارٌ فَائِقُ السُّرْعَة **qiṭaarun faa'iqu -s-surçah** [12-8] *32*
highlighter (هَايْلَيْتَر) قَلَمُ تَمْيِيز **qalamu tamyiiz (haaylaytar)** [19-19] *47*
Hindi اللُّغَةُ الْهِنْدِيَّة **'al-lughatu -l-hindiy-yah** [33-13] *75*
history تَارِيخ **taariikh** [19-26] *47*
hobby هِوَايَة **hiwaayah** [26-29] *61*
home delivery تَوْصِيلٌ لِلْمَنَازِل **tawṣiilun lilmanaazil** [10-27] *29*
homework (وَاجِب) عَمَلٌ مَنْزِلِيّ **çamalun manziliy-y (waajib)** [19-47] *47*
honeymoon شَهْرُ الْعَسَل **sharu -l- çasal** [18-31] *45*
hope أَمَل **'amal** [27-28] *63*
horse حِصَان **ḥiṣaan** [29-15] *67*
horse carriage عَرَبَةُ الْحِصَان **çarabatu -l- ḥiṣaan** [12-32] *33*
hospital مُسْتَشْفَى **mustashfaa** [27-1] *62*
hot حَارّ **ḥaar-r** [14-20] *37*
hot dog نَقَانِق **naqaaniq** [35-1] *78*
hot water مَاءٌ سَاخِن **maa'un saakhin** [36-28] *81*
hot weather طَقْسٌ حَارّ **ṭaqsun ḥaar-r** [14-21] *37*
hotel فُنْدُق **funduk** [11-1] *30;* [31-1] *70*
hotel reservation حَجْزٌ فُنْدُقِيّ **ḥajzun funduqiy-y** [31-21] *71*
hour سَاعَة **saaçah** [15-1] *38*
house بَيْت **bayt** [3-49] *14;* [11-26] *31*
housefly ذُبَابَة **thzubaabah** [29-25] *67*
How are things? مَا الْأَخْبَار؟ **ma-l-'akhbaar?** [1-33] *11*
how much longer? كَمْ تَبَقَّى مِنَ الْوَقْت؟ **kam tabaq-qaa mina -l- waqt** [13-56] *35*
however وَمَعَ ذَلِك **wa maça thzaalik** [28-38] *65*
hungry جَوْعَان **jawçaan** [8-19] *25*
hurricane إِعْصَار **'içsaar** [14-38] *37*
husband زَوْج **zawj** [2-26] *12*
husband and wife زَوْجٌ وَزَوْجَة **zawjun wa zawjah** [2-13] *13*

I

I أَنَا **ana** [2-20] *13*
I wash my hair أَغْسِلُ شَعْرِي **'aghsilu shaçrii** [6-23] *20*
ice cream (آيِسْ كِرِيم) بُوظَة **buuẓah ('aayis kiriim)** [35-7] *78*
ice cubes مُكَعَّبَاتُ ثَلْج **mukaç-çabaatu thalj** [36-30] *81*
ice-skating التَّزَحْلُقُ عَلَى الْجَلِيد **'at-tazaḥluqu çala -l- jaliid** [30-16] *69*
ice water مَاءٌ مُثَلَّج **maa'un muthal-laj** [36-31] *81*
iced tea شَايٌ مُثَلَّج **shaayun muthal-laj** [36-8] *80*
identical تَطَابُق **taṭaabuk** [29-35] *67*
idiom تَعْبِيرٌ اصْطِلَاحِيّ **taçbiirun i-ṣṭilaaḥiy-y** [21-34] *51*
idle كَسُول **kasuul** [8-8] *24*
if (لَوْ) إِذَا **'ithzaa (law)** [28-40] *65*
illness مَرَض **maraḍ** [4-48] *17*
immediately حَالًا **ḥaalan** [13-57] *35*
important (مُهِمّ) هَامّ **haam-m (muhim-m)** [27-34] *63*
in a moment بَعْدَ لَحْظَة **baçda laḥẓah** [15-34] *39*
in front أَمَام **'amaam** [13-14] *34*
in the afternoon; pm بَعْدَ الظُّهْر **baçda -ẓ-ẓuhr** [15-21] *39*
in the morning; am فِي الصَّبَاح **fi - ṣ-ṣabaaḥ** [15-19] *39*
in the past فِي الْمَاضِي **fi -l-maaḍii** [15-32] *39*
Independence Day عِيدُ الاسْتِقْلَال **açiidu -l- istiqlaal** [18-22] *45*
index مُؤَشِّر **mu'ash-shir** [28-25] *65*
India الْهِنْد **'alhind** [32-29] *73*
Indonesian اللُّغَةُ الإِنْدُونِيسِيَّة **'al-lughatu -l-'induuniisiy-yah** [33-14] *75*
injection حَقْن **ḥaqn** [27-17] *62*
inside بِالدَّاخِل **bid-daakhil** [8-21] *25;* دَاخِل **daakhil** [13-34] *35*
installment قِسْط **qisṭ** [9-36] *27*
intelligent ذَكِيّ **thzakiy-y** [20-20] *49*
interest فَائِدَة **faa'idah** [9-29] *27*
Internet شَبَكَةُ الإِنْتَرْنِت **shabakatu -l-'intarnit** [24-21] *56*
Internet access [23-16] *55* دُخُولٌ إِلَى الإِنْتَرْنِت (أَكْسِيسْ لِلنِّت) **dukhuulun 'ila -l-'intarnit ('aksis lin-nit)**
Internet cafes (كَافِيهِ النِّت) مَقَاهِي الإِنْتَرْنِت **maqaahi -l-'intarnit (kaafiih 'in-nit)** [24-4] *56*
Internet language لُغَةُ الإِنْتَرْنِت **lughatu -l-'intarnit** [24-25] *56*
Internet slang عَامِّيَّةُ الإِنْتَرْنِت **çaam-miy-yatu -l-'intarnit** [24-23] *56*
intestines أَمْعَاء **'amçaa'** [4-34] *17*
introduce yourself عَرِّفْ نَفْسَك **çar-rif nafsaka** [1-14] *10*
Iraq الْعِرَاق **'alçiraaq** [32-8] *72*
is raining تُمْطِر **tumṭir** [14-11] *36*
Islamic Year السَّنَةُ الْهِجْرِيَّة **'as-sanatu -l-hijriy-yah** [18-8] *44*
it هُوَ - هِيَ **huwa (m) - hiya (f)** [29-31] *67*
it hurts يُؤْلِم **yu'lim** [27-21] *63*
Italian اللُّغَةُ الإِيطَالِيَّة **'al-lughatu -l-'iiṭaaliy-yah** [33-5] *74*
Italy إِيطَالِيَا **'iiṭaaliyaa** [32-31] *73*

J

January يَنَايِر **yanaayir** [16-16] *41*
Japanese اللُّغَةُ الْيَابَانِيَّة **'al-lughatu -l-yaabaaniy-yah** [33-8] *74*
jeans (بَنْطَلُون جِينْز) سِرْوَالُ جِينْز **sirwaal jiinz (banṭaluun jiinz)** [10-9] *28*
joyful مَسْرُور **masruur** [1-11] *10*
judge (f) قَاضِيَة **qaaḍiyah** [25-2] *58*
July يُولْيُو **yulyuu** [16-22] *41*
June يُونْيُو **yuunyuu** [16-21] *41*
junior year in college [20-42] *49* السَّنَةُ الثَّالِثَةُ فِي الْكُلِّيَّة **'as-sanatu th-thaalithatu fi -l-kul-liy-yah**

K

kabsa كَبْسَة **kabsah** [34-5] *76*
karaoke كَارْيُوكِي **karyuukii** [26-12] *61*
ketchup كَاتْشَب **kaatshab** [35-36] *79*
kettle (كِيتِل) مِغْلَاة **mighlah (kiitil)** [3-29] *15*
keyboard (كِي بُورْد) لَوْحَةُ مَفَاتِيح **lawuḥatu mafaatiiḥ (kii burd)** [23-5] *54*
kidneys كُلَى **kulaa** [4-33] *17*
kilometer كِيلُومِتْر **kiluu mitr** [13-38] *35*
kitchen مَطْبَخ **maṭbakh** [3-23] *15*
kitchen cabinet خِزَانَةُ الْمَطْبَخ **khizaanatu -l- maṭbakh** [3-25] *15*
keys مَفَاتِيح **mafaatiiḥ** [3-5] *14*
knee رُكْبَة **rukbah** [4-20] *17*
knife سِكِّين **sik-kiin** [34-14] *76*
kofta كُفْتَة **kuftah** [34-22] *77*
Korean اللُّغَةُ الْكُورِيَّة **'al-lughatu -l-kuuriy-yah** [33-16] *75*
kunafa كُنَافَة **kunaafah** [18-13] *44*
kushary كُشَرِي **kusharii** [34-6] *76*
Kuwait كُوَيْت **kuwayt** [32-13] *72*

L

L size مَقَاسُ حَجْمٍ كَبِير **maqaasu ḥajmin kabiir** [7-33] *23*
laboratory مَعْمَل **maçmal** [20-22] *49*
laboratory test فَحْصٌ مَخْبَرِيّ **faḥṣun makhbariy-y** [27-8] *62*
lamb (mutton) (لَحْمُ الضَّأْنْ) خَرُوف **kharuuf (laḥmu - ḍ- ḍa'n)** [38-6] *84*
lamp مِصْبَاح **miṣbaah** [3-7] *14*
laptop (لَابْ تُوبْ) حَاسُوبٌ مَحْمُول **ḥaasuubun maḥmuul (laab tuub)** [23-6] *54*
large size حَجْمٌ كَبِير **ḥajmun kabiir** [7-35] *23*
larger أَكْبَر **'akbar** [7-40] *23*
lasagne لَازَانْيَا **laazaanyaa** [35-9] *78*
last month الشَّهْرُ الْمَاضِي **'ash-shahru -l-maaḍii** [16-33] *41*
last week الْأُسْبُوعُ الْمَاضِي **'al'usbuuçu -l-maaḍii** [16-31] *41*
last year السَّنَةُ الْمَاضِيَة **'as-sanatu -l-maaḍiyah** [16-35] *41*
late مُتَأَخِّرًا **muta'akh-khiran** [15-25] *39*
later (لَاحِقًا) فِيمَا بَعْدُ **fiimaa baçd (laaḥiqan)** [15-27] *39*
laundry room غُرْفَةُ الْغَسِيل **ghurfatu -l- ghasiil** [3-38] *15*
lawyer مُحَامِي **muḥaamii** [25-1] *58*
leap year سَنَةٌ كَبِيسَة **sanatun kabiisah**

[16-41] *41*
Lebanon لُبْنَان **lubnaan** [32-6] *72*
lecture hall قَاعَةُ الْمُحَاضَرَات **qaaçatu -l-muḥaaḍaraat** [20-14] *48*
left side الْجَانِبُ الأَيْسَر **'aljaanibu l'aysar** [13-27] *35*
leg رِجْل **rijl** [4-21] *17*
leisure time وَقْتُ فَرَاغ **waqtu faraagh** [6-26] *20*
lemon (yellow) لَيْمُونٌ أَصْفَر **laymuunun 'aṣfar** [37-11] *82*
lemon لَيْمُون **laymuun** [38-10] *84*
less (a few) قَلِيل **qaliil** [8-3] *24*
lesson دَرْس **dars** [21-22] *51*
letter خِطَاب **khiṭaab** [19-12] *46*
lettuce خَسّ **khas-s** [38-31] *85*
level (of achievement) مُسْتَوى **mustawaa** [19-51] *47*
library مَكْتَبَة **maktabah** [20-3] *48*
Libya لِيبْيَا **liibyaa** [32-12] *72*
light color لَوْنٌ فَاتِح **lawnun faatiḥ** [7-16] *22*
light switch [3-55] *14*
قَابِسُ الضَّوْء (مِفْتَاحُ النُّور) (الْكُبْس) **qaabisu - ḍ-ḍaw' (miftaaḥu -n-nuur) ('alkubs)**
lightning بَرْق **barq** [14-12] *36*
lime (green) لَيْمُونٌ أَخْضَر **laymuunun 'akhḍar** [37-12] *82*
linguistics لُغَوِيَّات **lughawiy-yaat** [21-21] *51*
lion أَسَد **'asad** [29-5] *66*
lips شِفَاه **shifaah** [4-14] *16*
Lira (Syria, Lebanon) لِيرَة **liirah** [9-7] *26*
literature أَدَب **'adab** [19-25] *47*
liver كَبِد **kabid** [4-35] *17*
living room غُرْفَةُ الْمَعِيشَة **ghurfatu -l-maçiishah** [3-1] *14*
loan اقْتِرَاض **'iqtiraaḍ** [9-30] *27*
long طَوِيل **ṭawiil** [8-9] *24*
long-distance running [30-8] *68*
جَرْيٌ لِمَسَافَاتٍ طَوِيلَة **jaryun limasaafaatin ṭawiil-lah**
long distance call (international call)
مُكَالَمَةٌ دَوْلِيَّة **mukaalamatun dawliy-yah)** [24-29] *56*
long vowels حَرَكَاتٌ طَوِيلَة **ḥarakaatun ṭawiilah** [21-41] *51*
longan لُونْجَان **luunjaan** [37-14] *82*
love حُبّ **ḥub-b** [19-29] *47*
low مُنْخَفِض **munkhafiḍ** [8-28] *25*
luggages أَمْتِعَة **'amtiçah** [31-4] *70*
lungs رِئَتَان **ri'ataan** [4-31] *17*
lute عُود **çuud** [26-2] *60*
lychee لِيتْشِي **liitshi** [37-13] *82*

M

M size مَقَاسٍ حَجْمٍ مُتَوَسِّط **maqaasu ḥajmin mutawas-siṭ** [7-30] *23*
macadamia nuts الْمُكَسَّرَاتُ الْمَكَادِيمِيَا **'almukas-saraatu -l-makaadiimyaa** [37-25] *83*
main رَئِيسِيّ **ra'iisiy-y** [27-38] *63*
male ذَكَر **thzakar** [2-2] *12*
magazine مَجَلَّة **majal-lah** [19-10] *46*
manager مُدِير **mudiir** [25-17] *58*
Mandarin Chinese لُغَةُ الْمَانْدِرِينْ الصِّينِيَّة **lughatu-l-maandirii 'aṣ - ṣiiniy-yah** [33-19] *75*
mandarin orange يُوسُفِيّ **yuusufiy-y** [37-4] *82*
mango مَانْجُو **maanjuu** [37-2] *82*
map خَرِيطَة **khariiṭah** [31-2] *70*
marker pen (مَارْكَر) قَلَمُ تَحْدِيد **qalamu taḥdiid (maarkar)** [19-15] *47*
market سُوق **suuq** [38-43] *85*
March مَارِس **maaris** [16-18] *41*
mashed potatoes بَطَاطِس مَهْرُوسَة **baṭaaṭis mahruusah** [35-14] *78*
mask قِنَاع **qinaaç** [28-28] *65*
mathematics رِيَاضِيَّات **riyaaḍiy-yaat** [19-4] *46*
May مَايُو **maayuu** [16-20] *41*
meat لَحْم **laḥm** [38-1] *84*
medicine دَوَاء **dawaa'** [27-15] *62*
medium size حَجْمٌ مُتَوَسِّط **ḥajmun mutawas-siṭ** [7-36] *23*
memorial monument نَصْبٌ تَذْكَارِيّ **naṣbun tathzkariy-y** [31-33] *71*
menu قَائِمَةُ الطَّعَام **qaa'imatu ṭ-ṭaçaam** [34-4] *76*
meter مِتْر **mitr** [13-40] *35*
method / way طَرِيقَة **ṭariiqah** [25-29] *59*
Microsoft مَايِكْرُوسُوفْت **mayikruusuft** [24-20] *57*
microwave مَايْكْرُويف **maykruwiiv** [3-24] *15*
middle; center وَسَط **wasaṭ** [13-28] *35*
middle school مَدْرَسَةٌ مُتَوَسِّطَة **madrasatun mutawas-siṭah** [20-31] *49*
midnight مُنْتَصَفُ اللَّيْل **muntaṣafu - l-layl** [15-22] *39*
mile مِيل **miil** [13-39] *35*
millennium (1000 years) أَلْفِيَّة **'alfiy-yah** [16-44] *41*
millet الدُّخْن **'ad-dukhn** [37-35] *83*
milk لَبَن **laban** [36-5] *80*
mineral water مِيَاهٌ مَعْدِنِيَّة **miyaahun maçdiniy-yah** [36-2] *80*
minute دَقِيقَة **daqiiqah** [15-2] *38*
mobile phone (مُوبَايْل) جَوَّال **jaw-waal (mubaayil)** [24-9] *56*
Monday يَوْمُ الاِثْنَيْن **yawmu -l-ithnayn** [16-10] *40*
Modern Standard Arabic (MSA)
اللُّغَةُ الْعَرَبِيَّةُ الْفُصْحَى الْمُعَاصِرَة **'al-lughatu -l- çarabiy-yatu -l- fuṣḥa -l- muçaaṣirah** [21-36] *51*
money (مَال) نُقُود **nuquud (maal)** [9-24] *27*
monkey قِرْد **qird** [29-7] *66*
month شَهْر **shahr** [16-2] *40*
monosodium glutamate (MSG) [38-85] *86*
جُلُوتُومَات أُحَادِيَّةُ الصُّودْيُوم **juluutuu-maat 'uḥaadiy-yahatu ṣ-ṣuudyuum**
monuments آثَار **'aathaar** [11-30] *31*
moon قَمَر **qamar** [14-27] *37*
more (a lot) كَثِير **kathiir** [8-3] *24;* [10-35] *29*
Morocco الْمَغْرِب **'almaghrib** [32-3] *72;* [32-27] *73*
mosque مَسْجِد **masjid** [11-34] *31*
mosquitoes بَعُوض **baçuuḍ** [29-24] *67*
mother أُمّ **'um-m** [2-14] *13*
Mother's Day عِيدُ الأُمّ **çiidu -l-'um-m** [18-15] *44*
motorcycle دَرَّاجَةٌ بُخَارِيَّةٌ (مُوتُوسِيكِل) **dar-raajatun bukhaariy-yah (mutusiikl)** [12-9] *32*
mountain climbing تَسَلُّقُ الْجِبَال **tasal-luqu -l-jibaal** [30-4] *68*
mouse (مَاوِس) فَأْرَة **fa'rah (maawis)** [23-10] *54*
mousepad وِسَادَةُ الْفَأْرَة (مَاوِسْ بَادْ) **wisaadatu -l- fa'rah (maawis baad)** [23-9] *54*
mouth فَم **fam** [4-10] *16*
multimedia وَسَائِطُ مُتَعَدِّدَة **wasaa'iṭu mutaçad-didah** [23-37] *55*
muscles (s. a muscle) عَضَل (م. عَضَلَة) **çaḍal (s. çaḍalah)** [4-24] *17*
museum (مَتْحَف) مُتْحَف **mutḥaf (matḥaf)** [11-10] *30;* [31-31] *71*
mushroom فِطْر **fiṭr** [38-32] *85*
music مُوسِيقَى **musiiqaa** [26-34] *61*
musical band فِرْقَةٌ مُوسِيقِيَّة **firqatun musiiqiy-yah** [26-20] *61*
musician مُوسِيقِيّ **musiiqiy-y** [25-8] *58*
my big brother أَخِي الْكَبِير **'akhi-l-kabiir** [2-19] *13*
my big sister أُخْتِي الْكَبِيرَة **'ukhti-l-kabiirah** [2-18] *13*
my cousin (f) (maternal side) ابْنَةُ خَالِي **'ibnatu-khaalii** [2-37] *12;* (f) (paternal side) ابْنَةُ عَمِّي **'ibnatu -çam-mii** [2-35] *12;* (m) (maternal side) ابْنُ خَالِي **'ibnu-khaalii** [2-36] *12*
my niece (brother's daughter) بِنْتُ أَخِي **bintu 'akhiii** [2-24] *13*
my nephew (sister's son) ابْنُ أُخْتِي **'ibnu 'ukhtii** [2-23] *13*
my sister-in-law نَسِيبَتِي **nasiibatii** [2-33] *12*
my younger brother أَخِي الصَّغِير **'akhi -ṣ -ṣaghiir** [2-21] *13*
my younger sister أُخْتِي الصَّغِيرَة **'ukhti -ṣ -ṣaghiirah** [2-22] *13*

N

name اسْم **'ism** [1-23] *11*
nationality جِنْسِيَّة **jinsiy-yah** [1-32] *11*
natural gas غَازٌ طَبِيعِيّ **ghaazun ṭabiiçiy-y** [28-16] *65*
near قَرِيب **qariib** [8-24] *25;* [13-42] *35*
nearby مُجَاوِر **mujaawir** [13-50] *35*
neck رَقَبَة **raqabah** [4-3] *16*
necktie رَابِطَةُ عُنُق (كَرَافَتَّة) **raabiṭatu çunuq (karafat-tah)** [10-15] *28*
neighbor جَار **jaar** [2-44] *12;* [11-29] *31*
nervous system الْجِهَازُ الْعَصَبِيّ **'al-jihaazu -l- çaṣabiy-y** [4-39] *17*
network card بِطَاقَةُ الشَّبَكَة **biṭaaqatu -sh-shabakah** [23-36] *55*
network security أَمْنُ الشَّبَكَات **'amnu -sh-shabakaat** [23-40] *55*
networking شَبَكَة (نِيتْ وُرْكِينْج) **shabakah (nit wurking)** [23-22] *55*
neurology طِبُّ الأَعْصَاب **ṭib-bu -l-'açṣaab** [27-47] *63*
new جَدِيد **jadiid** [8-4] *24*
New Year عَامٌ جَدِيد **çaamun jadiid** [18-2] *44*
New Year's Day رَأْسُ السَّنَةِ الْمِيلَادِيَّة **ra'su -s-sanati -l- miilaadiy-yah** [18-4] *44*
New Year's Eve لَيْلَةُ رَأْسِ السَّنَةِ الْمِيلَادِيَّة **laylatu ra'si- s-sanati -l-miilaadiy-ya** [18-5] *44*
newspaper جَرِيدَة **jariidah** [19-9] *46*
next month الشَّهْرُ الْقَادِم **'ash-shahru -l-qaadim** [16-34] *41*
next week الأُسْبُوعُ الْقَادِم **'al'usbuuçu- l-qaadim** [16-32] *41*
next year الْعَامُ الْقَادِمُ **'alçaamu -l-qaadim** [16-38] *41*
night لَيْل **layl** [15-16] *39*
night class صَفٌّ لَيْلِيّ **ṣaf-fun layliy-y** [20-25] *49*
nine تِسْعَة **tisçah** [5-9] *18*
no لا **laa** [8-18] *25*
noon الظُّهْر **'ẓ-ẓuhr** [15-20] *39*
north شَمَال **shamaal** [13-6] *34*
North America أَمْرِيكَا الشَّمَالِيَّة **'amriika -sh-shamaaliy-yah** [32-18] *73*
northeast شَمَال شَرْق **shamaal sharq** [13-8] *34*
northwest شَمَال غَرْب **shamaal gharb** [13-7] *34*
nose أَنْف **'anf** [4-9] *16*
not to own لا يَمْلِك **laa yamlik** [8-16] *25*
notebook دَفْتَر **daftar** [19-18] *47*
noun اسْم **'ism** [21-6] *51*
November نُوفَمْبِر **nuvambir** [16-26] *41*
nuclear energy طَاقَةٌ نَوَوِيَّة **ṭaaqatun nawawiy-yah** [28-17] *65*
numbers أَرْقَام **'arqaam** [5-28] *19*
nurse (f) مُمَرِّضَة **mumar-riḍah** [27-4] *62*
nursery school حَضَانَة **ḥaḍaanah** [20-29] *49*
nuts مُكَسَّرَات **mukas-saraat** [37-41] *83*

O

o'clock سَاعَة **saaçah** [15-26] *39*
oatmeal دَقِيقُ الشُّوفَان **daqiiqu -sh-shuufaan** [35-25] *79;* [37-43] *83*
oats شُوفَان **shuufaan** [37-33] *83*
ocean مُحِيط **muḥiiṭ** [28-7] *64*
October أُكْتُوبَر **'uktuubar** [16-25] *41*
octopus أُخْطُبُوط **'ukhṭubuuṭ** [38-13] *84*
odd numbers أَرْقَامٌ فَرْدِيَّة **'arqaamun fardiy-yah** [5-26] *19*
of course بِالطَّبْع (بِكُلِّ تَأْكِيد) **biṭ-ṭabçi (bikul-li ta'kiid)** [28-39] *65*
off (electricity) مُغْلَق **mughlaq** [8-32] *25*
office مَكْتَب **maktab** [25-15] *58*
oil نَفْط **nafṭ** [28-22] *65*
ointment مَرْهَم (دِهَان) **marham (dihaan)** [27-30] *63*
old قَدِيم **qaadiim** [8-4] *24;* (age) كَبِير **kabiir** [8-10] *25*
olive oil زَيْتُ الزَّيْتُون **zaytu -z-zaytuun** [38-66] *86*
Oman عُمَان **çumaan** [32-16] *72*
on (electricity) مَفْتُوح **maftuuḥ** [8-32] *25*
on a cruise فِي رِحْلَةٍ بَحْرِيَّة **fii riḥlatin baḥriy-yah** [31-12] *70*
on a traveling bus فِي حَافِلَةِ الرِّحْلَات **fii ḥaafilati -r-riḥlaat** [31-13] *70*

oncology طِبُّ الْأَوْرَام **ṭib-bu -l-'awraam** [27-45] *63*
one وَاحِد **waaḥid** [5-1] *18*
one bowl of soup وِعَاءُ حِسَاءٍ وَاحِد **wiçaa'u ḥisaa'in waaḥid** [22-6] *52*
one chair كُرْسِيٌّ وَاحِد **kursiy-yun waaḥid** [22-8] *52*
one group of people [22-9] *53* مَجْمُوعَةٌ وَاحِدَةٌ مِنَ النَّاسِ **majmuuçatun waaḥidatun mina -n-naas**
one half نِصْف **nisf** [5-11] *18*
one pair of shoes زَوْجٌ وَاحِدٌ مِنَ الْأَحْذِيَة **zawjun waaḥidun mina -l-'aḥthziyah** [22-3] *52*
one pound جُنَيْهٌ وَاحِد **gunayhun waaḥid** [9-12] *26*
one quarter رُبْع **rubç** [5-13] *18*
one side جَانِبٌ وَاحِد **jaanibun waaḥid** [13-52] *35*
one third ثُلْث **thuluth** [5-14] *18*
onions بَصَل **baṣal** [38-36] *85*
online chat دَرْدَشَةٌ عَبْرَ الْإِنْتَرْنِت (شَات) **dardashatun çabra -l-'intarnit (shaat)** [23-20] *55*
online friends [24-2] *56* أَصْدِقَاءُ عَبْرَ الإِنْتَرْنِت (أُون لَاين) **'aṣdiqaa'u çabra l'intarnit**
online search بَحْثٌ عَلَى الْإِنْتَرْنِت **baḥthun çala -l-'intarnit** [23-41] *55*
online shopping [10-29] *29* التَّسَوُّقُ عَبْرَ الْإِنْتَرْنِت (التَّسَوُّق أُونْ لَايِنْ) **'at-tasaw-wuqu çabra-l-'intarnit ('attasaw-wuq 'un layin);** التَّسَوُّقُ عَبْرَ الْإِنْتَرْنِت **'at-tasaw-wuqu çabra l-'intarnit** [24-3] *56*
open مَفْتُوح **maftuuḥ** [8-12] *25*
opera أُوبِرَا **'ubiraa** [26-17] *61*
operating system نِظَامُ تَشْغِيل **nithzaamu tashghiil** [23-25] *55*
ophthalmology طِبُّ الرَّمَد (الْعُيُون) **ṭib-bu -r-ramad ('alçuyuun)** [27-50] *63*
opportunity فُرْصَة **furṣah** [25-30] *59*
orange بُرْتُقَالِيّ **burtuqaaliy-y** [7-11] *22;* بُرْتُقَال **burtuqaal** [37-3] *82*
orange juice عَصِيرُ الْبُرْتُقَال **çaṣiiru -l-burtuqaal** [36-4] *80*
orchestra أُورْكِسْتِرَا **'urkistiraa** [26-28] *61*
oregano زَعْتَرٌ بَرِّي (أُورِجَانُو) **zaçtarun bar-riy ('urjaanuu)** [38-55] *85*
organs أَعْضَاء **'açḍaa'** [4-36] *17*
outside بِالْخَارِج **bilkhaarij** [8-21] *25;* خَارِج **khaarij** [13-33] *35*
oven فُرْن **furn** [3-27] *15*
overcast غَائِم **ghaa'im** [14-6] *36*
overtime work عَمَلٌ إِضَافِيّ **çamalun 'iḍaafiy-y** [25-28] *59*
oyster sauce صُوصُ الْمَحَار **ṣuuṣu -l-maḥaar** [38-67] *86*

P

painting لَوْحَة **lawḥah** [3-6] *14*
Palestine فِلَسْطِين **filasṭiin** [32-7] *72*
palm oil زَيْتُ النَّخِيل **zaytu -n-nakhiil** [38-82] *86*
Palm Sunday أَحَدُ الشَّعَانِين (السَّعَف) **'aḥadu sh-shaçaaniin ('as-saçaf)** [18-10] *44*
pancakes فَطِيرَة (بَانْ كِيك) **faṭiirah (baan kiik)** [35-30] *79*
panda بَانْدَا **baandaa** [29-9] *66*
papaya بَابَايَا **baabaayaa** [37-10] *82*
paper currency عُمْلَةٌ وَرَقِيَّة **çumlatun waraqiy-yah** [9-1] *26*
parents وَالِدَان **waalidaan** [2-6] *12*
park مُنْتَزَه **muntazah** [28-3] *64*
parsley بَقْدُونس **baqduunis** [38-4] *84*
passenger مُسَافِر (رَاكِب) **musaafir (raakib)** [12-28] *33*
passport جَوَازُ سَفَر **jawaazu safar** [31-8] *70*
password كَلِمَةُ الْمُرُور (بَاسْوُرْدْ) **kalimatu -l-muruur (baaswurd)** [23-17] *55*
past مَاضِي **maaḍii** [8-22] *25*
pasta; spaghetti مَعْكَرُونَة (مَكَرُونَة) (اسْبَاكِتِي) **maçkaruunah (makaruunah) ('isbaakit-tii)** [35-4] *78*
patient (f) مَرِيضَة **mariiḍah** [27-3] *62*
peach خَوْخ **khawkh** [37-9] *82*
peach blossoms أَزْهَارُ الْخَوْخ **'azhaaru -l-khawkh** [17-7] *42*
peacock طَاوُوس **ṭaawuus** [29-18] *67*
peanut oil زَيْتُ الْفُولِ السُّودَانِيّ **zaytu -l-fuuli s-suudaaniy-y** [38-84] *86*
pear كُمَّثْرَى **kum-mithraa** [37-5] *82*
pecans الْبَقَان **'albaqaan** [37-22] *83*
peanuts فُولٌ سُودَانِيّ **fuulun suudaaniy-y** [37-20] *83*
pedestrian مُشَاة **mushaah** [11-32] *31*
pedestrian crossing عُبُورُ الْمُشَاة **çubuuru-l-mushaah** [11-33] *31*
pediatrics طِبُّ الْأَطْفَال **ṭib-bu -l- 'aṭfaal** [27-43] *63*
pen قَلَم **qalam** [19-13] *47*
pencil قَلَمُ رَصَاص **qalamun raṣaaṣ** [19-20] *47*
pencil sharpener مِبْرَاة (بَرَّايَة) **mibraah (bar-raayah)** [19-16] *47*
percent % نِسْبَةٌ مِئَوِيَّة **nisbatun mi'awiy-yah** [5-24] *19*
persimmon بِرْسِيمُون (كَاكَا) **pirsiimuun (kaakaa)** [37-18] *82*
pertaining to مُتَعَلِّقٌ بِـ **mutaçal-liqun bi** [27-33] *63*
pharmacist صَيْدَلَانِيّ (صَيْدَلِيّ) **ṣaydalaaniy-y (ṣaydaliy-y)** [25-6] *58*
phone cards بِطَاقَاتُ الْجَوَّال (الْهَاتِف) **biṭaaqaatu -l- jaw-waal ('alhaatif)** [24-32] *56*
phone charger شَاحِنُ الْجَوَّال (الْهَاتِف) **shaaḥinu -l- jaw-waal ('alhaatif)** [24-31] *56*
photocopier آلَةُ تَصْوِيرِ مُسْتَنَدَات **'aalatu taṣwiiri mustanadaa** [20-7] *48*
photograph صُورَةٌ فُوتُوغْرَافِيَّة **ṣuratun futughraafiy-yah** [31-16] *70*
photographer مُصَوِّرٌ فُوتُوغْرَافِيّ **muṣawir-run futuughraafiy-y** [25-12] *59*
phrase عِبَارَة **çibaarah** [21-14] *51*
physical education تَرْبِيَةٌ بَدَنِيَّة **tarbiyatun badaniy-yah** [19-5] *46*
physics فِيزِيَاء **fiiziyaa'** [19-34] *47*
physiotherapy عِلَاجٌ طَبِيعِيّ **çilaajun ṭabiiçiy-y** [27-46] *63*
piano بِيَانُو **biyaanuu** [26-9] *60*
pillow وِسَادَة **wisaadah** [3-19] *14*
pills أَقْرَاصُ الدَّوَاء **'aqraaṣu -d-dawaa'** [27-16] *62*
pilot طَيَّار **ṭay-yaar** [25-13] *59*
pine nuts صُنُوبَر **ṣunuubar** [37-28] *83*
pineapple أَنَانَاس **'anaanaas** [37-8] *82*
pink وَرْدِيّ **wardiy-y** [7-12] *22*
pistachios فُسْتُق **fustuq** [37-23] *83*
pizza بِيتْزَا **biitzaa** [35-3] *78*
place مَكَان **makaan** [13-51] *35*
plane ticket تَذْكِرَةُ طَيَرَان **tathzkiratu ṭayaraan** [31-20] *71*
plant نَبَات **nabaat** [28-19] *65*
plate طَبَق **ṭabaq** [34-12] *76*
playing with water اللَّعِبُ بِالْمَاء **'al-laçibu**
poem قَصِيدَة **qaṣiidah** [21-16] *51*
police station قِسْمُ الشُّرْطَة **qismu-sh-shurṭah** [11-17] *31*
pollution تَلَوُّث **talaw-wuth** [28-4] *64*
pop music مُوسِيقَى الْبُوب **musiiqa -l-bub** [26-27] *61*
pork لَحْمُ خِنْزِير **laḥmu khinziir** [38-5] *84*
ports مَنَافِذ (بُورْتِس) **manaafithz (puurtis)** [23-14] *54*
Portuguese اللُّغَةُ الْبُرْتُغَالِيَّة **'al-lughatu -l- burtughaaliy-yah** [33-18] *75*
position مَرْكَزٌ وَظِيفِيّ **markazun waẓifiy-y** [25-35] *59*
post office مَكْتَبُ الْبَرِيد **maktabu-l-bariid** [11-16] *31*
postcard بِطَاقَةٌ بَرِيدِيَّة **biṭaaqatun bariidiy-yah** [31-29] *71*
potato بَطَاطِس **baṭaaṭis** [38-28] *85*
potted plant نَبَاتٌ مَحْفُوظٌ بِوِعَاء (زَرْع) **nabaatun maḥfuuẓun biwiçaa' (zarç)** [3-47] *15*
Pound (Egypt, Sudan) جُنَيْه **gunayh** [9-3] *26*
predicate خَبَر **khabar** [21-32] *51*
preposition حَرْفُ جَرّ **ḥarfu jar-r** [21-10] *51*
prescription وَصْفَةٌ طِبِّيَّة **waṣfatun ṭib-biy-yah** [27-32] *63*
price سِعْر **siçr** [9-25] *27*
principal مُدِير **mudiir** [20-18] *49*
private school مَدْرَسَةٌ خَاصَّة **madrasatun khaaṣ-ṣah** [20-27] *49*
professor(أُسْتَاذ) دُكْتُورٌ جَامِعِيٌّ **duktuurun jaamiçiy-y ('ustaathz)** [20-10] *48*
program بَرْنَامَج **barnaamaj** [26-32] *61*
Prophet Muhamed Birthday celebration لْمَوْلِدُ النَّبَوِيُّ الشَّرِيف **'almawlidu -n-nabawiy-yu -sh-shariif** [18-26] *45*
public bus حَافِلَةٌ عَامَّة (أُتُوبِيس عَام) **ḥaafilatun çaam-mah ('utubiis çaam)** [12-12] *33*
public school مَدْرَسَةٌ عَامَّة **madrasatun çaam-mah** [20-28] *49*
pudding مُهَلَّبِيَّة **muhal-labiy-yah** [35-8] *78*
pullover / sweater سُتْرَة **sutrah** [14-19] *37*
pumpkin يَقْطِين **yaqṭiin** [38-47] *85*
pumpkin seeds بُذُورُ الْيَقْطِين (لُبٌّ أَبْيَض) **buthzuuru -l- yaqṭiin (lub-bun 'abyaḍ)** [37-30] *83*
punctual دَقِيق **daqiiq** [15-23] *39*
purple بَنَفْسَجِيّ **banafsajiy-y** [7-8] *22*
purpose / objective هَدَف **hadaf** [19-43] *47*

Q

Qatar قَطَر **qaṭar** [32-9] *72*
quarter (hour) رُبْع **rubç** [15-7] *38*
question (problem) سُؤَال (مُشْكِلَة) **su'aal (mushkilaah)** [19-46] *47*
quiet هَادِئ **hadi'** [28-10] *64*

R

radiology طِبُّ الْإِشْعَاع **ṭib-bu -l-'ishçaaç** [27-48] *63*
rain مَطَر **maṭar** [14-10] *36*
raincoat مِعْطَفُ مَطَر **miçṭafu maṭar** [14-2] *36*
rainstorm عَاصِفَةٌ مُمْطِرَة **çaaṣifatun mumṭirah** [14-28] *37*
raise your hand ارْفَعْ يَدَك **'rfaç yadak** [20-9] *48*
Ramadan رَمَضَان **ramaḍaan** [18-9] *44*
reading قِرَاءَة **qiraa'ah** [19-2] *46*
real حَقِيقِيّ **ḥaqiiqiy-y** [8-26] *25*
receipt إِيصَال **'iiṣaal** [9-33] *27*
recycling إِعَادَةُ التَّصْنِيع **'içaadatu -t-taṣniiç** [28-20] *65*
red أَحْمَر **'aḥmar** [7-2] *22*
red wine نَبِيذٌ أَحْمَر **nabiithzun 'aḥmar** [36-19] *81*
refrigerator ثَلَّاجَة (بَرَّاد) **thal-laajah (bar-raad)** [3-26] *15*
refund اسْتِرْدَادُ الْمَالِ الْمَدْفُوع **'istirdaadu-l-maali-l-madfuuç** [10-42] *29*
relatives أَقَارِب **'aqaarib** [2-31] *12*
respiratory system الْجِهَازُ التَّنَفُّسِيّ **'al-jihaazu -t-tanaf-fusiy-y** [4-38] *17*
restaurant مَطْعَم **maṭçam** [31-35] *71*
rice أَرُز **'urz** [37-37] *83*
right صَحِيح **ṣaḥiiḥ** [8-25] *25*
right side الْجَانِبُ الْأَيْمَن **'aljaanibu -l 'ayman** [13-29] *35*
river نَهْر **nahr** [28-8] *64*
road طَرِيق **ṭariiq** [11-37] *31*
roof سَطْح **saṭḥ** [3-51] *14*
room غُرْفَة **ghurfah** [3-22] *14*
rosemary إِكْلِيلُ الْجَبَل (رُوزْمَارِي) **'ikliilu-l-jabal (ruuzmaary)** [38-7] *84*
roses وَرْد **ward** [18-18] *45*
rowing تَجْدِيف **tajdiif** [30-18] *69*
rugby الرُّجْبِي **'ar-rujbii** [30-3] *68*
ruler مِسْطَرَة **misṭarah** [19-17] *47*
running جَرْي **jary** [30-10] *68*
Russian اللُّغَةُ الرُّوسِيَّة **'al-lughatu -r-ruusiy-yah** [33-3] *74*
Ryal (Saudi Arabia, Yemen, Oman, Qatar) رِيَال **riyaal** [9-4] *26*

S

S size مَقَاسُ حَجْمٍ صَغِير **maqaasu ḥajmin ṣaghiir** [7-31] *23*
SIM card شَرِيحَةُ الْجَوَّال **shariiḥatu -l- jaw-waal** [24-30] *56*
sad حَزِين **ḥaziin** [8-31] *25*
sage مَرْيَمِيَّة **maryamiy-yah** [38-51] *85*

salad سَلَطَة **salaṭah** [35-13] *78*

salt مِلْح **milḥ** [38-70] *86*

salted fish فَسيخ **fasiikh** [18-12] *44*

same نَفْس **nafs** [29-34] *67*

sand break حَواجِز رَمْلِيَّة **ḥawaajizu ramliy-yah** [28-13] *65*

sandwich سانْدْويتْش **sandwiitsh** [35-2] *78*

Santa Claus سانْتا كُلوز **saanta kuluuz** [18-25] *45*

satisfied راضِي **raaḍii** [1-9] *10*

Saturday يَوْمُ السَّبْت **yawmu -s - sabt** [16-15] *40*

Saudi Arabia [32-14] *72*
اَلْمَمْلَكَةُ الْعَرَبِيَّةُ السُّعودِيَّةُ (السُّعودِيَّة) **'almamlakatu -l-çarabiy-yatu -s-suçuudiy-yah ('as-suçuudiy-yah)**

sausage سُجُق **sujuq** [35-16] *78*

savings مُدَّخَرات (ادِّخار) **mud-dakharaat ('id-dikhaar)** [9-21] *27*

scanner ماسِحٌ ضَوْئِيّ (سْكانَر) **maasiḥun ḍaw'iy-y (scaanar)** [23-11] *54*

scarf وِشاح (شال) **wishaaḥ (shaal)** [10-20] *29*

schedule جَدْوَل **jadwal** [12-30] *33*

school مَدْرَسَة **madrasah** [20-26] *49*

science عُلوم **çuluum** [19-31] *47;* [20-12] *48*

scissors مِقَصّ **miqaṣ-ṣ** [19-21] *47*

screen شاشَة **shaashah** [23-2] *54*

seafood مَأْكولاتٌ بَحْرِيَّة **ma'kuulaatun baḥriy-yah** [38-11] *84*

seasonings تَوابِل **tawaabil** [38-62] *86*

second ثانِيَة **thaaniyah** [15-3] *38*

secretary (f) سِكْرِتيرَة **sikirtiirah** [25-16] *58*

self نَفْس **nafs** [2-40] *12*

selfie سِلْفي **silfii** [24-14] *57*

senior year in college [20-430] *49*
سَنَةُ التَّخَرُّجِ مِنَ الْكُلِّيَّة **sanatu -t-takhar-ruji mina -l-kul-liy-yah**

sentence جُمْلَة **jumlah** [21-13] *51*

September سِبْتَمْبِر **sibtambir** [16-24] *41*

service provider مُزَوِّدُ الْخِدْمَة **muzaw-widu -l-khidmah** [25-34] *59*

sesame oil زَيْتُ السِّمْسِم **zaytu -s-simsim** [38-65] *86*

sesame seeds حُبوبُ السِّمْسِم **ḥubuubu-s-simsim** [37-39] *83*

seven سَبْعَة **sabçah** [5 7] *18*

Seven continents of the world
اَلْقارّاتُ السَّبْعُ فِي الْعالَم **'alqaar-raatu -s-sabçatu fi-l-çaalam** [32-17] *73*

seven spices سَبْعُ بُهارات **sabçu buhaaraat** [38-80] *86*

several times عِدَّةُ مَرّات **çid-datu mar-raat** [27-35] *63*

shape شَكْل **shakl** [7-38] *23*

shawarma شاوِرْما **shaawirmaa** [34-23] *77*

she buys تَشْتَري **tashtarii** [10-1] *28*

she cries تَبْكي **tabkii** [6-1] *20*

she exercises تَتَمَرَّن **tatamar-ran** [30-6] *68*

she looks at تَنْظُرُ إِلى **tanẓuru 'ilaa** [6-4] *20*

she plays basketball تَلْعَبُ كُرَةَ السَّلَّة **talçabu kurata -s-sal-lah** [30-22] *69*

she sits تَجْلِس **tajlis** [6-6] *20*

sheep خَروف **kharuuf** [29-12] *67*

shift work عَمَلٌ بِنِظامِ الْوَرْدِيّات **çamalun biniẓaami -l- wardiy-yaat** [25-33] *59*

ship سَفينَة **safiinah** [12-14] *33*

shirt قَميص **qamiiṣ** [10-14] *28*

shoes أَحْذِيَة **'aḥthziyah** [10-13] *28*

shop دُكّان (مَتْجَر) **duk-kaan (matjar)** [10-22] *29;* مَتْجَر (مَحَلّ) **matjar (maḥal-l)** [11-3] *30*

shop staff مُوَظَّفو الْمَتْجَر **muwaẓ-ẓafu-l-matjar** [10-25] *29*

shopping bag حَقيبَةُ التَّسَوُّق **ḥaqiibatu-t-tasaw-wuq** [10-4] *28*

shopping center; mall مَرْكَزُ تَسَوُّق (مول) **markazu tasaw-wuq (muul)** [11-22] *31*

short قَصير **qaṣiir** [8-5] *24;* [8-9] *24*

short essay مَقالَةٌ قَصيرَة **maqaalatun qaṣiirah** [21-15] *51*

short vowels حَرَكاتٌ قَصيرَة **ḥarakaatun qaṣiirah** [21-40] *51*

shoulder كَتِف **katif** [4-23] *17*

shower دُش **dush** [3-41] *15*

shrimp (prawns) جَمْبَري (قُرَيْدِس) **jambari (quraydis)** [38-15] *84*

siblings إِخْوَة **'ikhwah** [2-38] *12*

side جانِب **jaanib** [13-49] *35*

sidewalk مَمَرٌّ لِلْمُشاة (رَصيف) **mamar-run lilmushaah (raṣiif)** [11-23] *31*

sightseeing مَعالِمُ سِياحِيَّة **maçaalimu siyaaḥiy-yah** [31-28] *71*

silver فِضِّيّ **fiḍ-ḍiy-y** [7-14] *22*

simple بَسيط **basiiṭ** [21-25] *51*

singer مُغَنّي **mughan-nii** [26-14] *61*

sink حَوْض **ḥawḍ** [3-40] *15*

six سِتَّة **sit-tah** [5-6] *18*

six people سِتَّةُ أَشْخاص **sit-tatu 'ashkhaaṣ** [22-10] *53*

size حَجْم (مَقاس) **ḥajm (maqaas)** [7-39] *23*

skeletal system نِظامُ الْهَيْكَلِ الْعَظْمِيّ **niẓaamu -l-haykali -l-çaẓmiy-y** [4-40] *17*

skiing التَّزَلُّج **'at-tazal-luj** [30-17] *69*

skin جِلْد **jild** [4-41] *17*

skinny نَحيف **naḥiif** [8-13] *25*

skirt تَنّورَة (جيبَة) **tan-nuurah (jiibah)** [10-8] *28*

skyscraper ناطِحَةُ سَحاب **naaṭiḥatu saḥaab** [11-11] *30*

slow بَطيء **baṭii'** [8-27] *25*

small حَجْمٌ صَغير **ḥajmun ṣaghiir** [7-37] *23*

small size صَغير **ṣaghiir** [8-11] *25*

small change قِطَعُ نُقودٍ مَعْدِنِيَّةٍ صَغيرَة (فَكَّة) **qiṭaçu nuquudin maçdiniy-yatin ṣaghiirah (fak-kah)** [9-19] *27*

smaller أَصْغَر **'aṣghar** [7-41] *23*

smartphone [24-1] *56*
هاتِفٌ ذَكِيّ (تِليفونٌ ذَكِيٌّ) (سمارْتْ فون) **haatifun thzakiy-y (tiliifuun thzakiy-y) (smaart fuun)**

smartwatch ساعَةٌ ذَكِيَّة **saaçatun thzakiy-yah** [15-14] *39*

snake ثُعْبان **thuçbaan** [29-17] *67*

snow ثَلْج **thalj** [14-15] *36*

snowball fights تَراشُقُ كُرَةِ الثَّلْج **taraashuqu kurati -th-thalj** [17-15] *43*

social studies دِراساتٌ اِجْتِماعِيَّة **diraasaa-tun - ijtimaaçiy-yah** [19-48] *47*

socks جَوارِب (شَرابات) **jawaarib (sharaabaat)** [10-12] *28*

sodas مَشْروباتٌ غازِيَّة (صودا) **mashruubaatun ghaaziy-yah (ṣuuda)** [36-26] *81*

sofa أَريكَة (كَنَبَة) **'ariikah (kanabah)** [3-15] *14*

software بَرْنامَج (سوفْتْ وير) **barnaamaj (suft wiir)** [23-24] *55*

solar energy طاقَةٌ شَمْسِيَّة **ṭaaqatun shamsiy-yah** [28-9] *64*

Some countries in the Middle East
بَعْضُ الدُّوَلِ فِي الشَّرْقِ الْأَوْسَط **baçḍu -d-duwali fi -sh-sharqi -l-'awsaaṭ** [32-1] *72*

son اِبْن **'ibn** [2-1] *12*

son-in-law زَوْجُ الاِبْنَة **zawju -libnah** [2-27] *12*

sophomore year in college [20-41] *49*
اَلسَّنَةُ الثّانِيَةُ فِي الْكُلِّيَّة **'as-sanatu -th-thaaniyatu fi -l-kul-liy-yah**

sound صَوْت **ṣawt** [6-18] *20*

soup حِساء (شوربَة) **ḥisaa' (shurbah)** [34-26] *77*

south جَنوب **januub** [13-13] *34*

South America أَمْريكا الْجَنوبِيَّة **'amriika -l-januubiy-yah** [32-19] *73*

southeast جَنوب شَرْق **januub sharq** [13-12] *33*

southwest جَنوب غَرْب **januub gharb** [13-11] *34*

souvenir shop مَتْجَرُ بَيْعِ تَذْكارات **matjaru bayçi tathzkaaraat** [31-14] *70*

soy milk حَليبُ الصّويا **ḥaliibu -ṣ-ṣuuyaa** [36-9] *80*

soy sauce صوصُ الصّويا **ṣuuṣu ṣ-ṣuuyaa** [38-63] *86*

soybean paste مَعْجونُ فولِ الصّويا **maçjuunu fuuli- ṣ-ṣuuyaa** [38-86] *86*

Spanish اللُّغَةُ الْإِسْبانِيَّة **'al-lughatu -l-'isbaaniy-yah** [33-6] *74*

special خاصّ **khaaṣ-ṣ** [34-30] *77*

spinach سَبانِخ **sabaanikh** [38-21] *84*

spoon مِلْعَقَة **milçaqah** [34-15] *76*

sports رِياضات **riyaaḍaat** [30-25] *69*

sports car سَيّارَةٌ رِياضِيَّة **say-yaaratun riyaaḍiy-yah** [12-10] *32*

sports drinks مَشْروباتٌ رِياضِيَّة **mashruubaatun riyaaḍiy-yah** [36-17] *80*

sports shirt قَميصٌ رِياضِيّ **qamiiṣun riyaaḍiy-y** [30-26] *69*

sports shoes; sneakers حِذاءٌ رِياضِيّ **ḥithzaa'un r-riyaaḍiy-y** [30-27] *69*

spring الرَّبيع **'ar-rabiiç** [17-1] *42*

sprint عَدْو **çadw** [30-9] *68*

stadium إِسْتاد **'istaad** [11-15] *31*

star anise يَنْسون **yansuun** [38-72] *86*

starch نَشا **nishaa** [38-77] *86*

steak شَريحَةُ لَحْم (سْتيك) **shariiḥatu laḥm (stiik)** [35-15] *78*

stomach مَعِدَة **maçidah** [4-49] *17*

stopwatch ساعَةُ الْإيقاف (سْتوبْ واتْش) **saaçatu -l- 'iiqaaf (stup waat**[15-13] *39*

story قِصَّة **qiṣ - ṣah** [19-28] *47*

stove مَوْقِد **mawqid** [3-31] *15*

street شارِع **shaariç** [11-4] *30*

street corner زاوِيَةُ الشّارِع **zaawiyatu -sh-shaariç** [11-28] *31*

strange غَريب **ghariib** [29-39] *67*

strong signal إِشارَةٌ قَوِيَّة **'ishaaratun qawiy-yah** [24-12] *57*

student طالِب **ṭaalib** [20-15] *48*

study room غُرْفَةُ الدِّراسَة **ghurfatu -d-diraasah** [3-32] *15*

study time وَقْتُ الدِّراسَة **waqtu -d-diraasah** [6-27] *20*

subject (in a nominal sentence) مُبْتَدَأ **mubtada'** [21-33] *51*

suburb ضاحِيَة **ḍaaḥiyah** [11-25] *31*

subway مِتْرو الْأَنْفاق **mitru-l-'anfaaq** [12-11] *33*

sudden مُفاجِئ (عاجِل) **mufaaji' (çaajil)** [15-35] *39*

sunflower seeds بُذورُ زَهْرَةِ عَبّادِ الشَّمْس **buthzuuru zahrati çab-baadi-sh-shams** [37-32] *83*

strawberry فَراوِلَة **faraawilah** [37-15] *82*

stuffed cabbage مَلْفوف (مَحْشي كُرُنْب) **malfuuf (maḥshi kurunb)** [34-20] *77*

stuffed grape leaves مَحْشي وَرَقِ عِنَب **maḥshii waraqi çinab** [34-19] *77*

suitcase حَقيبَةُ سَفَر **ḥaqiibatu safar** [31-5] *70*

sugar سُكَّر **suk-kar** [38-75] *86*

summer الصَّيْف **'aṣ-ṣayf** [17-2] *42*

summer vacation إِجازَةُ الصَّيْف **'ijaazatu -ṣ-ṣayf** [18-27] *45*

sun شَمْس **shams** [14-26] *37*

sun shade ظِلُّ الشَّمْس **ẓil-lu-sh- shams** [17-10] *42*

sunblock lotion [17-16] *43*
كِريم (دِهان) حِمايَةٍ مِنْ حُروقِ الشَّمْس **kiriim (dihaan) ḥimaayatin min ḥuruuqi-sh-shams**

Sunday يَوْمُ الْأَحَد **yawmu -l-'aḥad** [16-5] *40;* [16-9] *40*

sunny weather طَقْسٌ مُشْمِس **ṭaqsun mushmis** [14-36] *37*

supermarket سوقٌ مَرْكَزِيّ (سوبَرْمارْكِت) **suuqun markaziy-y (super market)** [11-5] *30*

swimming سِباحَة **sibaaḥah** [30-19] *69*

Syria سوريا **suuriy-yaa** [32-4] *72*

T

table طاوِلَة **ṭaawilah** [3-14] *14*

table lamp مِصْباحُ الطّاوِلَة **miṣbaaḥu -ṭ-ṭaawilah** [3-33] *15*

table tennis تِنِسْ طاوِلَة **tinis ṭaawilah** [30-1] *68*

tablet كُمْبيوتَر لَوْحِيّ (تابْلِت) **kumbiyuutar lawḥiy-y (taablit)** [23-3] *54*

Tagalog اللُّغَةُ التّاغْلوغِيَّة **'al-lughatu -t-taaghluughiy-yah** [33-17] *75*

talent مَوْهِبَة **mawhibah** [19-38] *47*

tall طَويل **ṭawiil** [8-5] *24*

tap صُنْبور (حَنَفِيَّة) **ṣunbuur (ḥanafiy-yah)** [3-39] *15*

tap water مِياهُ الصُّنْبور **miyaahu -ṣ-ṣunbuur** [36-11] *80*

tarragon طَرْخون **ṭarkhuun** [38-44] *85*

tasty (delicious) طَيِّبُ الْمَذَاق (لَذِيْذ) **ṭay-yibu -l- mathzaaq (lathziithz)** [35-29] *79*

tax free مُعْفَاةٌ مِنَ الضَّرَائِب **muçfaatun mina-ḍ-ḍaraa'ib** [10-41] *29*

taxes ضَرَائِب **ḍaraa'ib** [9-34] *27*

taxi (سَيَّارَةُ أُجْرَة (تَاكْسِي **say-yaaratu 'ujrah (taxi)** [12-2] *32*

tea شَاي **shaay** [36-7] *80*

teacher (f) (مُعَلِّمَة (مُدَرِّسَة **muçal-limah (mudar-risah)** [20-6] *48*

teeth (s. a tooth) (أَسْنَان (م. سِنّ **'asnaan (s. sin-n)** [4-12] *16*

telephone number (رَقْمُ الْهَاتِفِ (التِّلِيفُون **raqmu -l- haatif ('at-tilifuun)** [24-28] *56*

telephone operator عَامِلَةُ التِّلِيفُون **çaamilatu -t-tiliifuun (f)** [25-10] *58*

ten عَشْرَة **çashrah** [5-10] *18*

tennis تِنِس **tinis** [30-23] *69*

tennis racket مِضْرَبُ تِنِس **miḍrabu tinis** [30-24] *69*

test اخْتِبَار **'ikhtibaar** [19-37] *47*

textbook كِتَابٌ مَدْرَسِيّ **kitaabun madrasiy-y** [20-24] *49*

texting رَسَائِلُ نَصِّيَّة **rasaa'ilu naṣ-ṣiy-yah** [24-22] *56*

Thai اللُّغَةُ التَّايْلانْدِيَّة **'al-lughatu -t-taaylaandiy-yah** [33-15] *75*

Thanksgiving عِيدُ الشُّكْر **çiidu -sh-shukr** [18-19] *45*

the east الشَّرْق **'sh-sharq** [13-45] *35*

the news الأَخْبَار **'al'akhbaar** [19-8] *46*

the north الشَّمَال **'sh-shamaal** [13-48] *35*

the same thing نَفْسُ الشَّيْء **nafsu-sh-shay'** [10-31] *29*

the south الْجَنُوب **'aljanuub** [13-46] *35*

the west الْغَرْب **'algharb** [13-47] *35*

the year after next الْعَامُ بَعْدَ الْقَادِم **'alçaamu baçda -l-qaadim** [16-39] *41*

the year before الْعَامُ السَّابِقُ **'alçaamu -s-saabiq** [16-36] *41*

there هُنَاك **hunaak** [13-3] *34*

thigh فَخِذ **fakhithz** [4-28] *17*

things أَشْيَاء **'ashyaa'** [10-39] *29*

thirsty عَطْشَان **çaṭshaan** [36-14] *80*

this year هَذَا الْعَامُ **hathza -l-çaam** [16-37] *41*

three ثَلاثَة **thalaathah** [5-3] *18*

three books ثَلاثَةُ كُتُب **thalaathatu kutub** [22-2] *52*

three cars ثَلاثُ سَيَّارَات **thalaathu say-yaaraat** [22-7] *52*

three quarters ثَلاثَةُ أَرْبَاع **thalaathatu 'arbaaç** [5-12] *18*

thunder رَعْد **raçd** [14-13] *36*

thunderstorm عَاصِفَةٌ رَعْدِيَّة **çaaṣifatun raçdiy-yah** [14-14] *36*

Thursday يَوْمُ الْخَمِيس **yawmu -l -khamiis** [16-13] *40*

thyme زَعْتَر **zaçtar** [38-52] *85*

ticket counter شُبَّاكُ التَّذَاكِر **shub-baaku -t-tathzaakir** [12-31] *33*

tiger نَمِر **namir** [29-4] *66*

time وَقْت **waqt** [15-17] *39*

tired مُتْعَب **mutçab** [27-22] *63*

to accomplish (يُحَقِّق (يُنْجِز **yuḥaq-qiq (yunjiz)** [28-35] *65*

to add يُضِيف **yuḍiif** [5-20] *19*

to affect (يُؤَثِّرُ عَلَى (فِي **yu'ath-thiru çalaa (fii)** [28-36] *65*

to answer يُجِيب **yujiib** [6-28] *20;* [19-6] *46*

to agree يُوَافِق **yuwaafiq** [6-31] *20*

to allow يَسْمَح **yasmaḥ** [13-58] *35*

to appear يَظْهَر **yaẓhar** [29-37] *67*

to appreciate (يُقَيِّم (يُقَدِّر **yuqay-yim (yuqad-dir)** [26-21] *61*

to arrive يَصِل **yaṣil** [8-20] *25*

to ask يَسْأَل **yas'al** [6-19] *20*

to attend a birthday party يَحْضُرُ عِيدَ مِيلاد **yaḥḍuru çiida miilaad** [18-33] *45*

to bake يَخْبِز **yakhbiz** [35-33] *79*

to barbecue يَشْوِي **yashwii** [35-32] *79*

to bathe يَسْتَحِمّ **yastaḥim-m** [3-48] *15*

to be afraid لِتَكُونَ خَائِفًا **litakuuna khaa'ifan** [29-29] *67*

to be concerned about يَقْلَقُ بِشَأْن **yaqlaqu bi-sha'n** [27-52] *63*

to begin يَبْدَأ **yabda'** [8-23] *25*

to believe يَعْتَقِد **yaçtaqid** [2-43] *12*

to blossom يُزْهِر **yuzhir** [17-8] *42*

to breathe يَتَنَفَّس **to breathe** [6-24] *20*

to borrow يَقْتَرِض **yaqtariḍ** [8-29] *25*

to bring يَحْضُر **yaḥḍur** [10-38] *29*

to brush teeth يَغْسِلُ الأَسْنَان **yaghsilu -l- 'asnaan** [6-11] *21*

to call يُنَادِي **yunaadii** [1-12] *10*

to call a taxi [12-25] *33* (يَسْتَدْعِي سَيَّارَةَ أُجْرَة (يَتَّصِل بِتَاكْسِي **yastadçii say-yaarata 'ujrah (yat-taṣil bitaaksii)**

to catch a cold يُصَابُ بِنَزْلَةِ بَرْد **yuṣaabu binazlati bard** [27-10] *62*

to chat يُدَرْدِش **yudardish** [1-28] *11*

to clean يُنَظِّف **yunaẓ-ẓif** [3-44] *15*

to click (يَنْقُر (كِلِيك **yanqur (kilik)** [23-32] *55*

to come يَأْتِي **ya'tii** [8-17] *25*

to connect to the internet يَتَّصِلُ بِالإِنْتَرْنِت **yat-taṣilu bil'intarnit** [23-34] *55*

to consider يَعْتَبِر **yaçtabir** [13-61] *35*

to cook يَطْبُخ **yaṭbukh** [6-21] *20*

to cough يَسْعُل **yasçul** [27-11] *62*

to count يَعُدّ / يَحْسِب **yaçud-d / yaḥsib** [5-27] *19*

to cycle يَقُودُ دَرَّاجَة **yaquudu dar-raajah** [30-12] *68*

to dance يَرْقُص **yarqus** [26-5] *60*

to dare يَجْرُؤ **yajru'** [29-38] *67*

to depart/leave يُغَادِر **yughaadir** [8-20] *25*

to discover يَكْتَشِف **yaktashif** [27-37] *63*

to divide يَقْسِم **yaqsim** [5-17] *19*

to do household chores [6-38] *20* يَقُومُ بِالأَعْمَالِ الْمَنْزِلِيَّة **yaquumu bi -l-'açmaali -l-manziliy-yah**

to download (تَحْمِيل (دَاوِنْلُودْ **taḥmiil (daawinluud)** [23-33] *55*

to draw blood يَسْحَبُ الدَّم **yasḥabu -d-dam** [27-6] *62*

to drink يَشْرَب **yashrab** [36-13] *80*

to drive a car يَقُودُ سَيَّارَة **yaquudu say-yaarah** [12-21] *33*

to drizzle تُمْطِرُ رَذَاذًا **tumṭiru rathzaathzan** [17-9] *42*

to end يَنْتَهِي **yantahii** [8-23] *25*

to enjoy يَسْتَمْتِعُ بِـ **yastamtiçu bi** [26-33] *61*

to express يُعَبِّر **yuçab-bir** [26-31] *61*

to fall sick يَمْرَض **yamraḍ** [27-13] *62*

to feel يَشْعُر **yashçur** [27-24] *63*

to feel anxious يَشْعُرُ بِالْقَلَق **yashçuru bilqalaq** [13-63] *35*

to feel reassured يَشْعُرُ بِالطُّمَأْنِينَة **yashçuru biṭ - ṭuma'niinah** [27-53] *63*

to find يَجِد **yajid** [31-36] *71*

to forget يَنْسَى **yansaa** [8-30] *25*

to get angry يَغْضَب **yujiib** [6-29] *20*

to get to know يَتَعَرَّفُ عَلَى **yataçar-raf çalaa** [1-7] *10*

to give يُعْطِي **yuçṭii** [8-2] *24*

to go يَذْهَب **yathzhab** [8-17] *25*

to go faster يُسْرِع **yusriç** [12-29] *33*

to go through يَمُرّ **yamur-r** [13-54] *35*

to go to elementary school [20-39] *49* يَدْرُسُ فِي مَدْرَسَةٍ ابْتِدَائِيَّة **yadrusu fi madrasatin -i-btidaa'iy-yah**

to go to school يَذْهَبُ إِلَى الْمَدْرَسَة **yathzhabu 'ila -l- madrasah** [6-36] *20*

to go to work يَذْهَبُ إِلَى الْعَمَل **yathzhabu 'ilaa lçamal** [25-32] *59*

to graduate يَتَخَرَّج **yatakhar-raj** [20-36] *49*

to greet يُحَيِّي **yuḥay-yii** [1-27] *11*

to harvest يَحْصُد **yaḥṣud** [17-13] *43*

to have breakfast يَتَنَاوَلُ الْفَطُور **yatanaawalu -l- faṭuur** [6-39] *20*

to have dinner يَتَنَاوَلُ الْعَشَاء **yatanaawalu -l- çashaa'** [6-41] *20*

to have lunch يَتَنَاوَلُ الْغَدَاء **yatanaawalu -l- ghadaa'** [6-40] *20*

to help يُسَاعِد **yusaaçid** [6-16] *21;* [13-62] *35*

to hug يَحْضُن **yaḥḍun** [1-26] *11*

to improve يَتَحَسَّن **yataḥas-san** [19-40] *47*

to insist on يُصِرُّ عَلَى **yuṣir-ru çalaa** [6-30] *20*

to inspect يُفَتِّش **yufaat-tish** [25-22] *59*

to intern يَتَدَرَّب **yatadar-rab** [25-27] *59*

to kiss يُقَبِّل **yuqab-bil** [1-24] *11*

to know يَعْرِف **yaçrif** [1-31] *11*

to laugh يَضْحَك **yaḍḥak** [6-2] *20*

to learn يَتَعَلَّم **yataçal-lam** [19-3] *46*

to leave يُغَادِر **yughaadir** [13-55] *35*

to leave work يُغَادِرُ الْعَمَل **yughadiru -l- çamal** [6-35] *20*

to listen to يَسْتَمِعُ إِلَى **yastamiçu 'ilaa** [6-3] *20;* [26-25] *61*

to major in يَتَخَصَّصُ فِي **yatakhaṣ-ṣaṣu fii** [20-35] *49*

to make a phone call يُجْرِي مُكَالَمَةً هَاتِفِيَّة **yujrii mukaalamatan haatifiy-yah** [24-10] *56*

to make a small talk [1-40] *11* يُجْرِي مُحَادَثَةً صَغِيرَة **yujrii muḥaadathatan ṣaghiirah**

to make a snowman يَصْنَعُ رَجُلَ الْجَلِيد **yaṣnaçu rajula -l-jaaliid** [17-12] *43*

to meet يُقَابِل **yuqaabil** [1-3] *10*

to move (from one place to another) يَنْتَقِل **yantaqil** [6-15] *21*

to multiply يُضَاعِف **yuḍaaçif** [5-18] *19*

to order يَطْلُب **yaṭlub** [34-28] *77*

to own يَمْلِك **yamlik** [8-16] *25*

to pat on the shoulder اسْمُ الْعَائِلَة **yurab-bitu çala -l-katif** [1-38] *11*

to perform يُؤَدِّي **yu'ad-dii** [26-35] *61*

to play يَلْعَب **yalçab** [6-20] *20*

to play (a musical instrument) يَعْزِف **yaçzif** [26-23] *61*

to play an instrument يَعْزِفُ آلَةً مُوسِيقِيَّة **yaçzifu 'aalatan musiiqiy-yah** [26-24] *61*

to play soccer يَلْعَبُ كُرَةَ الْقَدَم **yalçabu kurata -l-qadam** [30-2] *68*

to photocopy يُصَوِّرُ مُسْتَنَدَات **yuṣaw-wiru mustanadaat** [20-8] *48*

to practice يُمَارِس **yumaaris** [19-23] *47*

to prepare يُعِدّ **yuçid-d** [21-31] *51*

to put يَضَع **yaḍaç** [8-14] *25*

to receive يَتَسَلَّم **yatasal-lam** [8-2] *24*

to receive a phone call يَتَلَقَّى مُكَالَمَةً هَاتِفِيَّة **yatalaq-qaa mukaalamatan haatifiy-yah** [24-11] *56*

to relax يَسْتَرْخِي **to relax** [6-25] *20*

to remember يَتَذَكَّر **yatathzak-kar** [8-30] *25*

to request يَطْلُب **yaṭlub** [6-32] *20*

to resemble يُشْبِه **yushbih** [29-36] *67*

to return يُرْجِع **yurjiç** [8-29] *25*

to review يُرَاجِع **yuraajiç** [19-24] *47*

to ride a bike يَرْكَبُ دَرَّاجَة **yarkabu dar-raajah** [12-22] *33*

to ride a train (يَسْتَقِلُّ الْقِطَار (يَرْكَبُ الْقِطَار **yastaqil-lu-l-qiṭaar (yarkabu-l-qiṭaar)** [12-20] *33*

to sell يَبِيع **yabiiç** [10-2] *28*

to send email [23-18] *55* (يُرْسِلُ بَرِيدًا إِلِكْتْرُونِيًّا (إِيمِيل **yursilu bariidan 'iliktiruuniy-yan ('iimiil)**

to shake hands يُسَلِّمُ بِالْيَد **yusal-limu bilyad** [1-36] *11*

to shop يَتَسَوَّق **yatasaw-waq** [10-3] *28*

to sign in يُسَجِّلُ الدُّخُول **yusaj-jilu -d-dukhuul** [23-23] *55*

to sing يُغَنِّي **yughan-nii** [26-13] *61*

to sleep يَنَام **yanaam** [6-7] *21*

to slow down يُبْطِئ **yubṭi** [12-27] *33*

to smile يَبْتَسِم **yabtasim** [1-25] *11*

to snow تُثْلِج **tuthlij** [14-16] *36*

to speak to يَتَحَدَّثُ إِلَى **yataḥad-dathu 'ilaa** [6-13] *21*

to stand يَقِف **yaqif** [6-5] *20*

to start a conversation يُدَرْدِش **yabda'u-l-muḥaadathah** [1-39] *11*

to strive يَجْتَهِد **yajtahid** [21-30] *51*

to study يَدْرُس **yadrus** [19-42] *47*

to subtract يَطْرَح **yaṭraḥ** [5-19] *19*

to take يَأْخُذ **ya'khuthz** [8-14] *25;* [31-37] *71*

to take a bus (يَسْتَقِلُّ الْحَافِلَة (يَرْكَبُ الْبَاص **yastaqil-lu -l-ḥaafilah (yarkabu-l-baaṣ)** [12-19] *33*

to take a shower يَسْتَحِمّ **yastaḥim-m** [6-22] *20*

to take medicine يَتَنَاوَلُ الدَّوَاء **yatanaawalu -d-dawaa'** [27-14] *62*
to talk يَتَكَلَّم **yatakal-lam** [6-12] *21*
to teach (يُدَرِّس) يُعَلِّم **yuçal-lim (yudar-ris)** [20-5] *48*
to tell يُخْبِر **yukhbir** [13-53] *35*
to think يُفَكِّر **yufak-kir** [13-60] *35*
to travel يُسَافِر **yusaafir** [31-18] *71*
to turn left (to turn right) [12-23] *33* يَتَّجِهُ يَسَارًا (يَتَّجِهُ يَمِينًا) **yat-tajihu yasaaran (yat-tajihu yamiinan)**
to understand يَفْهَم **yafham** [19-22] *47;* [21-26] *51*
to wake up يَسْتَيْقِظ **yastayqiẓ** [6-10] *21*
to walk the dog يُمَشِّي الْكَلْب **yumash-shi-l-kalb** [6-17] *21*
to watch يُشَاهِد **yushaahid** [6-8] *21*
to wave يُلَوِّحُ بِالْيَد **yulaw-wiḥu bilyad** [1-37] *11*
to wish يَتَمَنَّى **yataman-naa** [1-13] *10*
to withdraw money يَسْحَبُ نُقُودًا **yashabu nuquudan** [9-23] *27*
to write يَكْتُب **yaktub** [6-9] *21*
toast (تُوسْتْ) خُبْزٌ مُحَمَّص **ghubzun muḥam-maṣ (tuust)** [35-21] *79*
toaster (تُوسْتَرْ) آلَةُ التَّحْمِيص **'aalatu -t-taḥmiiṣ (tustar)** [3-30] *15*
today الْيَوْم **'alyawm** [16-7] *40*
toes أَصَابِعُ الْقَدَم **'aṣaabiçu -l-qadam** [4-16] *16*
tofu تُوفُو **tuufuu** [38-42] *85*
toilet seat مِقْعَدُ الْمِرْحَاض **miqçadu -l-mirḥaaḍ** [3-43] *15*
tomato طَمَاطِم **ṭamaaṭim** [38-26] *85*
tomorrow غَدًا **ghadan** [16-8] *40*
tongue لِسَان **lisaan** [4-11] *16*
top (higher) أَعْلَى **'açlaa** [19-41] *47*
topic مَوْضُوع **mawduuç** [20-16] *49*
tour guide مُرْشِدٌ سِيَاحِيّ **murshidun siyaaḥiy-y** [31-6] *70*
tourist information center [31-41] *71* مَرْكَزُ الْمَعْلُومَاتِ السِّيَاحِيَّة **markazu -l-maçluumaati -s-siyaaḥiy-yah**
toys (أَلْعَاب) دُمَى **dumaa ('alçaab)** [10-18] *29*
traffic (الْمُرُور) حَرَكَةُ السَّيْر **ḥarakatu-s-sayr ('almuruur)** [11-36] *31*
traffic lights إِشَارَاتُ الْمُرُورِ الضَّوْئِيَّة **'ishaaraatu-l-muruuri - ḍ-ḍaw'iy-yah** [11-35] *31*
train قِطَار **qiṭaar** [12-15] *33*
train station مَحَطَّةُ الْقِطَار **maḥaṭ -ṭatu -l- qiṭaar** [11-9] *30;* [31-34] *71*
trainee مُتَدَرِّب **mutadar-rib** [25-26] *59*
tram تِرَام **tiraam** [12-17] *33*
translation تَرْجَمَة **tarjamah** [21-20] *51*
travel agency وَكَالَةُ السَّفَر **wakaalatu -s-safar** [31-25] *71*
travel by airplane السَّفَرُ بِالطَّائِرَة **'as-safaru bi-ṭ-ṭaa'irah** [31-10] *70*
travel by rail السَّفَرُ بِالْقِطَار **'as-safaru bilqiṭaar** [31-11] *70*
travel guidebook كِتَابُ دَلِيلِ السَّفَر **kitaabu dalllll -s-safar** [31-24] *71*
traveler (f) مُسَافِرَة **musaafirah** [31-3] *70*
tree شَجَرَة **shajarah** [28-15] *65*
trousers (بَنْطَلُون) سِرْوَال **sirwaal (banṭaluun)** [10-10] *28*
truck شَاحِنَة **shaahinah** [12-5] *32*
trumpet بُوق **buuq** [26-10] *60*
Tuesday يَوْمُ الثُّلاثَاء **yawmu th-thulaathaa'** [16-11] *40*
Tunisia تُونِس **Tuunis** [32-5] *72;* [32-26] *73*
turkey دِيكٌ رُومِيّ **diikun ruumiy-y** [35-10] *78*
Turkish اللُّغَةُ التُّرْكِيَّة **'al-lughatu t-turkiy-yah** [33-7] *74*
turn left (imperative) اتَّجِه يَسَارًا **'it-tajih yasaaran** [13-30] *35*
turn right (imperative) اتَّجِه يَمِينًا **'it-tajih yamiinan** [13-32] *35*
TV تِلْفَاز **tilfaaz** [3-10] *14*
two اثْنَان / اثْنَيْن **'ithnaan/'ithnayn** [5-2] *18*
two brothers أَخَوَان **'akhawaan** [2-11] *13*
two cups of tea كُوبَانِ مِنَ الشَّاي **kuubaani mina -sh-shaay** [22-12] *53*
two bags (packets) of sugar [22-1] *52* كِيسَانِ مِنَ السُّكَّر **kiisaani mina -s-suk-kar**
two sisters أُخْتَان **'ukhtaan** [2-15] *13*
two thirds ثُلُثَان / ثُلُثَيْن **thuluthaan / thuluthayin** [5-15] *18*
types of meat أَنْوَاعُ اللُّحُوم **'anwaaçu -l- luḥuum** [38-57] *85*
typhoon إِعْصَار **içsaar** [14-17] *36*

U

UAE الإِمَارَاتُ الْعَرَبِيَّةُ الْمُتَّحِدَة **'al'imaaratu -l- çarabiy-yatu -l-mut-taḥidah** [32-10] *72*
USB flash drive فِلاشَة يُو إِسْ بِي **filaashah yu 'is bii** [23-13] *54*
umbrella (شَمْسِيَّة) مِظَلَّة **miẓal-lah (shamsiy-yah)** [14-1] *36*
uncle (maternal side) خَال **khaal** [2-17] *13;* (paternal side) عَمّ **çiid-m** [2-10] *13*
university جَامِعَة **jaamiçah** [20-33] *49*
up فَوْق **fawq** [8-1] *24*

V

vacation (إِجَازَة) عُطْلَة **çuṭlah ('ijaazah)** [31-19] *71*
vaccination لِقَاح **liqaaḥ** [31-26] *71*
Valentine's Day عِيدُ الْحُبّ **çiidu l-ḥub-b** [18-16] *45*
vegetables خَضْرَاوَات **khaḍraawaat** [38-17] *84*
vegetarian نَبَاتِيّ **nabaatiy-y** [34-27] *77*
vein وَرِيد **wariid** [4-46] *17*
verb فِعْل **fiçl** [21-7] *51*
very جِدًّا **jid-dan** [29-32] *67*
video فِيدِيُو **vidiyuu** [24-24] *56*
video game (فِيدْيُو جِيمْ) لُعْبَةُ فِيدِيُو **luçbatu vidiyuu (vidiyuu gim)** [23-8] *45*
Vietnamese اللُّغَةُ الْفِيتْنَامِيَّة **'al-lughatu -l- fiitnaamiy-yah** [33-12] *75*
vinegar خَلّ **khal-l** [38-74] *86*
violin كَمَان **kamaan** [26-3] *60*
virus (فَايْرَس) فَيْرُوس **vayruus (vaayras)** [23-26] *55*
visa تَأْشِيرَة **ta'shiirah** [31-23] *71*
vocabulary (كَلِمَات) مُفْرَدَات **mufradaat (kalimaat)** [21-39] *51*
volleyball الْكُرَةُ الطَّائِرَة **'alkuraatu -ṭ-ṭaa'irah** [30-20] *69*

W

waiter (جَرْسُون) نَادِل **naadil (garsuun)** [34-32] *77*
waiting room غُرْفَةُ الانْتِظَار **ghurfatu -lintiẓaar** [27-39] *63*
waitress (جَرْسُونَة) نَادِلَة **naadilah (garsuunah)** [34-3] *76*
wall حَائِط **ḥa'iṭ** [3-9] *14*
walking الْمَشْي **'almashy** [30-21] *69*
walnuts عَيْنُ جَمَل **çaynu jamal** [37-21] *83*
warm دَافِئ **daafi'** [17-5] *42*
watch سَاعَة **saaçah** [10-5] *28*
water مَاء **maa'** [28-26] *65;* [36-12] *80*
water dispenser مُبَرِّدُ مَاء **mubar-ridu maa'** [36-27] *81*
bi-l-maa' [17-11] *42*
watermelon بِطِّيخ **biṭ-ṭiikh** [37-19] *82*
watermelon seeds بُذُورُ الْبِطِّيخ **buthzuuru -l- biṭ-ṭiikh** [37-31] *83*
weather طَقْس **ṭaqs** [14-32] *37*
weather forecast نَشْرَةُ الأَخْبَار **nashratu-l-'akhbaar** [14-33] *37*
web address/URL (URL) عُنْوَانُ الْوِيب **çunwaanu -l-wib (yu ar il)** [23-30] *55*
web design تَصْمِيمُ الْمَوَاقِع **taṣmiimu -l-mawaaqiç** [23-29] *55*
web page صَفْحَةُ الْوِيبْ **ṣafḥatu -l-wib** [23-28] *55*
website (وِيبْ سَايِتْ) مَوْقِعٌ إِلِكْتِرُونِيّ **mawqiçun 'iliktiruuniy-y (wib saayit)** [23-21] *55*
Wednesday يَوْمُ الأَرْبِعَاء **yawmu -l -'arbiçaa'** [16-12] *40*
weak signal إِشَارَةٌ ضَعِيفَة **'ishaaratun ḍaçiifah** [24-13] *57*
week أُسْبُوع **'usbuuç** [16-29] *41*
weekend عُطْلَةُ نِهَايَةِ الأُسْبُوع **çuṭlatu nihaayati -l- 'usbuuç** [6-34] *20*
west غَرْب **gharb** [13-9] *34*
Western breakfast فُطُورٌ غَرْبِيّ **faṭuurun gharbiy-y** [35-17] *79*
Western-style food طَعَامٌ عَلَى النَّمَطِ الْغَرْبِيّ **ṭaçaamun çla -n-nama ṭi -l-gharbiy-y** [35-28] *79*
what? مَاذَا؟ **maathzaa** [1-8] *10*
WhatsApp وَاتْسْ آبْ **waats 'aab** [24-6] *56*
wheat قَمْح **qamḥ** [37-38] *83*
where? أَيْنَ؟ **'ayna** [13-1] *34*
whiskey وِيسْكِي **wiskii** [36-21] *81*
white أَبْيَض **'abyaḍ** [7-3] *22*
White Friday الْجُمُعَةُ الْبَيْضَاء **'aljumuçatu-l-bayḍaa'** [10-21] *29*
white rice أُرْزٌ أَبْيَض **'urzun 'abyaḍ** [34-11] *76*
white spirit كُحُولٌ أَبْيَض **kuḥuulun 'abyaḍ** [36-23] *81*
white wine نَبِيذٌ أَبْيَض **nabiithzun 'abyaḍ** [36-20] *81*
whiteboard سَبُّورَةٌ بَيْضَاء **sab-buuratun bayḍaa'** [20-1] *48*
Why? لِمَاذَا؟ **limaathzaa** [1-34] *11*
wife زَوْجَة **zawjah** [2-25] *12*
wifi وَايْ فَايْ **waay faay** [23-42] *55*
wind رِيَاح **riyaaḥ** [14-8] *36*
wind power طَاقَةُ الرِّيَاح **ṭaaqatu -r-riiaaḥ** [28-12] *64*
window (شُبَّاك) نَافِذَة **naafithzah (shub-baak)** [3-18] *14*
windy عَاصِف **çaaṣif** [14-9] *36*
winter الشِّتَاء **'ash-shitaa'** [17-4] *42*
winter melon بِطِّيخٌ شِتْوِيّ **biṭ-ṭiikhun shitwiy-y** [38-39] *85*
winter vacation إِجَازَةُ الشِّتَاءِ **'ijaazatu -sh-shitaa'** [18-28] *45*
wolf ذِئْب **thzi'b** [29-16] *67*
word كَلِمَة **kalimah** [19-27] *47;* [21-12] *51*
work عَمَل **çamal** [25-24] *59*
workbook دَفْتَرُ التَّدْرِيبَات **daftaru-t-tadriibaat** [20-23] *49*
working day يَوْمُ عَمَل **yawmu çamal** [6-33] *20*
world الْعَالَم **'alçaalam** [32-33] *73*
worn out (exhausted) مُنْهَك **munhak** [27-23] *63*
wound جُرْح **jurḥ** [27-25] *63*
wrist watch سَاعَةُ يَد **saaçatu yad** [15-15] *39*
wrong خَطَأ **khaṭa'** [8-25] *25*

X

X إِكْس **'iks** [24-5] *56*
XL size مَقَاسُ حَجْمٍ كَبِيرٍ جِدًّا **maqaasu ḥajmin kabiirin jid-dan** [7-34] *23*
XS size مَقَاسُ حَجْمٍ صَغِيرٍ جِدًّا **maqaasu ḥajmin ṣaghiirin jid-dan** [7-32] *23*

Y

Yahoo يَاهُو **yaahuu** [24-16] *57*
year (سَنَة) عَام **çaam (sanah)** [16-1] *40*
years of life سَنَوَاتُ الْعُمْر **sanawaatu -l-çumr** [16-30] *41*
yellow أَصْفَر **'aṣfar** [7-5] *22*
yellow wine نَبِيذٌ أَصْفَر **nabiithzun 'aṣfar** [36-24] *81*
Yemen الْيَمَن **'alyaman** [32-15] *72*
yes نَعَم **naçam** [8-18] *25*
yesterday أَمْس **'ams** [16-6] *40*
yogurt زَبَادِي **zabaadii** [35-35] *79*
you (f) polite حَضْرَتُكِ **ḥaḍratuki** [1-30] *11;* (m) polite حَضْرَتُكَ **ḥaḍratuka** [1-30] *11*
young (age) صَغِير **ṣaghiir** [8-10] *25;* (small) صَغِير **ṣaghiir** [2-41] *12*
youth hostel (بُيُوتُ الشَّبَاب) نُزُلُ الشَّبَاب **nuzulu -sh-shabaab (buyuutu-sh-shabaab)** [31-39] *71*

Z

zebra حِمَارٌ وَحْشِيّ **ḥimaarun waḥshiy-y** [29-2] *66*
zills صَاجَات **ṣaajaat** [26-7] *60*
zither قَانُون **qaanuun** [26-4] *60*
zoo حَدِيقَةُ الْحَيَوَان **ḥadiiqatu -l-ḥayawaan** [29-1] *66*
zucchini كُوسَة **kusah** [38-49] *85*

Published by Tuttle Publishing, an imprint of Periplus Editions (HK) Ltd

www.tuttlepublishing.com

ISBN: 978-0-8048-5609-6

27 26 25 24 10 9 8 7 6 5 4 3 2 1
Printed in China 2406EP

"Books to Span the East and West"

Tuttle Publishing was founded in 1832 in the small New England town of Rutland, Vermont [USA]. Our core values remain as strong today as they were then—to publish best-in-class books which bring people together one page at a time. In 1948, we established a publishing outpost in Japan—and Tuttle is now a leader in publishing English-language books about the arts, languages and cultures of Asia. The world has become a much smaller place today and Asia's economic and cultural influence has grown. Yet the need for meaningful dialogue and information about this diverse region has never been greater. Over the past seven decades, Tuttle has published thousands of books on subjects ranging from martial arts and paper crafts to language learning and literature—and our talented authors, illustrators, designers and photographers have won many prestigious awards. We welcome you to explore the wealth of information available on Asia at **www.tuttlepublishing.com.**

Distributed by

North America, Latin America & Europe
Tuttle Publishing
364 Innovation Drive
North Clarendon,
VT 05759-9436 U.S.A.
Tel: 1 (802) 773-8930
Fax: 1 (802) 773-6993
info@tuttlepublishing.com
www.tuttlepublishing.com

Asia Pacific
Berkeley Books Pte. Ltd.
3 Kallang Sector #04-01/02
Singapore 349278
Tel: (65) 67412178
Fax: (65) 67412179
inquiries@periplus.com.sg
www.tuttlepublishing.com

The free online audio recordings for pronunciation practice may be accessed as follows:

Type the following URL below into your web browser.

https://www.tuttlepublishing.com/arabic-picture-dictionary

For support, email us at info@tuttlepublishing.com

Photo Credits

istockphoto.com: ***Endpapers*** xavierarnau; Mohamad Kaddoura / ***page 11*** PeopleImages / ***page 12*** xavierarnau; rahhal / ***page 13*** KatarzynaBialasiewicz; Juanmonino / ***page 48*** FatCamera / ***page 49*** ARudolf / ***page 50*** Photographer / ***page 62*** ljubaphoto

dreamstime.com: ***Page 19*** Hou Guima / ***page 25*** Ieva Zigg / ***page 37*** Vchalup / ***page 44*** Oksana Slepko / Mohamad Kaddoura / ***page 45*** Splank / ***page 60*** Sofiia Shunkina

Shuttlestock.com: ***Front cover*** Lotus_studio; AlexAnton; Nataly Studio; AM-Studioo; FoodTurkey; Zurijeta; Pawel Szczepanski / ***Front flap*** OlgaBombologna / ***Back cover*** tunart; Prostock-studio / ***Spine*** from my point of view / ***Endpapers*** Orhan Cam; Prostock-studio; Photo craze; RODWORKS; Ebtikar; Firdaus Mahadi; Syda Productions; Rasto SK; Benny Marty / ***page 2*** rahhal; Basicdog; diplomedia; Rido; Luis Molinero; BearFotos; Dmitry Kalinovsky; Orhan Cam; Sun_Shine; ArtTim / ***page 3*** Hayati Kayhan; Levent Konuk; Parilov / ***page 10*** Rawpixel.com; Kamenetskiy Konstantin; Kues; FS Stock; DisobeyArt; oneinchpunch; michaeljung; Cookie Studio; Roquillo Tebar / ***page 11*** Ground Picture; dotshock; Inside Creative House / ***page 12*** ESB Professional; Prostock-studio; Manop Boonpeng / ***page 13*** Rawpixel.com; rafik beshay; Ahmad A Atwah; donikz; Ebtikar; CEXM; ZouZou / ***page 14*** martinho Smart; Det-anan; Monkey Business Images / ***page 15*** vipman; Photographee.eu; Dimasik_sh; Image Factory; Macrovector; DenisNata; FamVeld / ***page 16*** Vorontsova Katy; iko; aslysun; Sinseeho; Annette Shaff; Butterfly Hunter / ***page 17*** Ebtikar; MSSA; Teguh Mujiono / ***page 18*** Francesco83 / ***page 19*** Vitaly Korovin / ***page 20*** Tutatamafilm; Zurijeta; Asier Romero; Roquillo Tebar; Prostock-studio; Ebtikar / ***page 21*** Zurijeta; Andrey_Popov; Kate Aedon; Prostock-studio; diplomedia; oneinchpunch/ ***page 22*** Frank Fiedler; sociologas; Dmitrij Skorobogatov; Sonya illustration; Solomatina Julia; Shumo4ka; Shumo4ka; George Dolgikh; Nikki Zalewski / ***page 23*** Alhovik; Marcos Mesa Sam Wordley; ESB Professional; Caftor / ***page 24*** visivastudio; wavebreakmedia; ifong; antpkr; Africa Studio; Ivan Demyanov; bright; Elnur; mathom; HomeStudio / ***page 25*** chanut iamnoy; Eric Isselee; akr11_ss; / ***page 26*** RODWORKS; MyCreativeAds; elqusy; Tamer Adel Soliman; Dianzie Mania; D.serra1; hemro; Andrey Lobachev; Wirestock Creators; Prachaya Roekdeethaweesab; vkilikov / ***page 27*** Pixel Embargo; SRStudio; Cozine; Fluid Shutter; pryzmat; lakov Filimonov; Ebtikar; Mega Pixel / ***page 28*** RossHelen; ArtTim; NYS; Vlad Teodor; gogoiso; ARZTSAMUI; Dragan Milovanovic; Konstantin Zubarev; kedrov; Elnur / ***page 29*** Africa Studio; irin-k; vandycan; Konstantin Zubarev / ***page 30*** ibrar.kunri; Rob Wilson; zhu difeng; Sorbis; stockphoto mania; aleks333; ZinaidaSopina; Rasto SK / ***page 31*** Anton_Ivanov; ESB Professional; Tamer Adel Soliman; ovbelov; beibaoke; Prostock-studio; Nikita Rogul; Visaro / ***page 32*** Rawpixel.com; New Africa; ifong; I'm Friday; Chubarov Alexandr; Ministr-84; 3d_man; Veronica Louro / ***page 33*** Sun_Shine; Nerthuz; joyfull; risteski goce; DoublePHOTO studio; stockphoto-graf / ***page 34*** pathdoc; Vadym Pastukh; Freeograph; Jihan Nafiaa Zahri; swissmacky; shopplaywood; Piyawat Nandeenopparit; ArtOfPhotos; lakov Filimonov / ***page 35*** ArtFamily; feelplus; ESB Professional / ***page 36*** ViDI Studio; vhpfoto; Valdis Skudre; Hallgerd; Lonely; Dark Moon Pictures; GCapture; Kazuki Nakagawa; Pop Paul-Catalin / ***page 37*** Karkas; ESB Professional; Ollinka; AlinaMD; Zacarias Pereira da Mata; Stone36; Ryszard Stelmachowicz; Gnilenkov Aleksey; ratmaner / ***page 38*** RTimages; Bluehatpictures; Naufal MQ; Nikolas_jkd / ***page 39*** G. Tbov; KPG Ivary; charnsitr; livingpitty; Benny Marty; Inside Creative House / ***page 40*** Sean Locke Photography; Odua Images / ***page 41*** Ayoub kayor / ***page 42*** Smileus; taveesak srisomthavil; Green Jo; Leonid Ikan; angelo lano, fotohunter; odd-add; Fototaras; skyfish; Ayoub kayor / ***page 43*** ProfStocker; inbevel; kazoka; New Africa; Bestseller Vector; John Bill; Oze stock / ***page 44*** Pressmaster; Bychykhin Olexandr; maximmmmum; Petar Chernaev; apfDesign; vectorsama; Creative-Touch; Svetolk; Memedozaslan; Prostock-studio; Ann_Zhuravleva / ***page 45*** Prostock-studio; topseller; Lotus Images; zelikodan; YanLev; IrisImages; Photo craze; Milles Studio / ***page 46*** JohnnyGreig; FatCamera; Ground Picture; spiber.de; jianbing Lee; Monkey Business Images; Preto Perola; Oleksiy Mark; Bohbeh; AlexLMX; M.Stasy / ***page 47*** 89studio; photka; VINCENT GIORDANO PHOTO; Pavel_Kostenko / ***page 48*** HelloRF Zcool; hxdbzxy; Chutima Chaochaiya; Africa Studio; ESB Professional; stockfour / ***page 49*** Tom Wang / ***page 50*** Yuriy Golub; Billion Photos; Bobby Syahronanda; Firdaus Mahadi / ***page 52*** 54613; HGalina; Customdesigner; Fazakas Mihaly; crystalfoto; sergo1972; Rawpixel.com; AV_photo / ***page 53*** OPOLJA; withGod; eAlisa / ***page 54*** Den Rozhnovsky; Oleksandr_Delyk; Prostock-studio; Bloomicon; Athapet Piruksa; Duda Vasilii; ALEXEY FILATOV; IB Photography; Michalakis Ppalis; Dacian G / ***page 55*** Natasa Adzic; Oleksandr Yuhlichek; Prostock-studio / ***page 56*** Sylvie Bouchard; Stanisic Vladimir; OHishiapply; solomon7; AdriaVidal; tanuha2001; Bojan Milinkov / ***page 57*** fear1ess; bbernard; Sundry Photography; Piotr Swat; Jane0606; nui7711; humphery / ***page 58*** wavebreakmedia; Rido; Basicdog; Viktoriia Hnatiuk; Stuart Jenner; Monkey Business Images; Andrey_Popov; worawit_j; Krakenimages.com; Silvia Radan; diplomedia / ***page 59*** Dmitry Kalinovsky; diplomedia; Luis Molinero; BearFotos; Flashon Studio; puhhha / ***page 60*** Ebtikar; daphnusia images; Africa Studio; Levent Konuk; Dario Sabljak; Baishev; mphot; OZaiachin; furtseff / ***page 61*** wavebreakmedia; Ferenc Szelepcsenyi; Igor Bulgariin; Dereje; Nagy-Bagoly Arpad / ***page 62*** Spotmatik Ltd; Santibhavank P; Bangkok Click Studio; AppleEyesStudio; Romaset; BaLL LunLa; Dragana Gordic; Andrey_Popov; Elena Vasilchenko; Peakstock / ***page 63*** Zerbor; Atstock Productions / ***page 64*** Dashu Xinganling; Nerthuz; OSTILL is Franck Camhi; ssuaphotos; Ase; Kaveex; aphotostory; Goodmorning3am; Ahmet Cigsar; Odua Images; WDG Photo / ***page 65*** dugdax; sezer66; Lev Kropotov; TTstudio; Syda Productions; Ljupco Smokovski / ***page 66*** Vladimir Wrangel; jaroslava V; defpicture; Eric Isselee; Coffeemill; Linda Bucklin / ***page 67*** Natalia D.; Inna Astakhova; photomaster; Grobler du Preez; Eric Isselee; LazyFocus; photosync; Guan jiangchi; Natalya Aksenova; oksana2010; Kirill Vorobyev; Algol; Kletr; S-F; irin-k; BOONCHUAY PROMJIAM; Alex Staroseltsev / ***page 68*** dwphotos; Pressmaster; Paolo Bona; Lunghammer; OSTILL is Franck Camhi; Hassel Stock; Eugene Onischenko; Kamenetskiy Konstantin / ***page 69*** Hurst Photo; Beto Chagas; BlueSkyImage; Maxim Tupikov; Ivan Smuk; pio3; oliveromg; Bojan Milinkov; Syda Productions; FotoAndalucia / ***page 70*** Brian A Jackson; 6/hyotographics; Antonio Guillem; Vitatraveller; Parilov; Sashkin; Matej Kastelic; Rawpixel.com; michaeljung; Syda Productions; Solarisys; Khomulo Anna / ***page 71*** Dean Drobot / ***page 72*** sculpies; idris esen; Aleksandra Tokarz; HasanZaidi; Sanoop.cp; Anson Fernandez Dionisio; MicroStockHub; MhmdArt; Matyas Rehak / ***page 73*** Peter Hermes Furian; Anton Ivanov; Valery Bareta; Ivan Soto Cobos; byvalet; Nicole Kwiatkowski; Guzel Studio; Olga Kashubin / ***page 74*** Phovoir; Dmitriy Bryndin; Stanislav Khokholkov; Alexander Raths; Lifetime Stock; IndigoLT; Elnur; number-one; michaeljung / ***page 75*** Elina-Lava; Howard Sandler; Praisaeng; szefei; CatwalkPhotos; TENGLAO; Kim JinKwon; Tony Magdaraog; mountainpix; leolintang / ***page 76*** Tatiana Bralnina; fizkes; Dmitry Kalinovsky; iamrdm; Natalia Hanin; actistudio; 06photo; Eliane Haykal; Patrick Krabeepetcharat; Rido; AlenKadr / ***page 77*** Viktor Kochetkov; Dina Saeed; Veliavik; Lydia Vero; Esin Deniz; Hayati Kayhan; from my point of view; Ali_Gr; Tatiana Volgutova; Han-Lin; Bo 1982; Dean Drobot / ***page 78*** Valentina Razumova; margouillat photo; iaodesign; Food1.it; George Dolgikh; spaxiax; M. Unal Ozmen; diogoppr; Anatolii Riepin; Tanya Sid; Kokhanchikov; Monticello; Sathit; Valentyn Volkov / ***page 79*** Oleksandra Naumenko; gresei; ScriptX; Monticello; GMEVIPHOTO; pinunpa / ***page 80*** Elena Elisseeva; Igor Sh; Wallenrock; Mariusz Szczygiel; tanuha2001; Picsfive; Africa Studio; Belka10; gowithstock; Oleksiy Mark; Yuri Samsonov; Chones; Shift Drive; Ekkamai Chaikanta / ***page 81*** stockphoto-graf; George Dolgikh; steamroller_blues; Artem_Graf; bonchan; zcw; jazz3311; Thanit Weerawan / ***page 82*** Valentyn Volkov; panda3800; Maks Narodenko; Christian Jung; Lim Yong Hian; Picsfive; ntstudio; FeellFree; Egor Rodynchenko; amasterphotographer; saiko3p; azure1; Chuanthit Kunlayanamitre; Tropper2000; MidoSemsem; Myibean; onair; Elena Schweitzer; rangizzz; szefei / ***page 83*** Hong Vo; Tim UR; timquo; Vladislav S; KITSANANAN; AmyLv; Maks Narodenko; Silvy78; Brent Hofacker; akepong srichaichana; Chalermchai Chamnanyon; Madlen; vitals; Okasana Mizina / ***page 84*** Rudchenko Liliia; Tobik; JIANG HONGYAN; Africa Studio; Igors Rusakovs; Chuanthit Kunlayanamitre; anat chant; Tang Yan Song; Binh Thanh Bui; SOMMAI / ***page 85*** Evgenyi; Zush; Lotus Images; JIANG HONGYAN; jiangdi; bergamont; NIPAPORN PANYACHAROEn / ***page 86*** Jiri Hera; Studio KIWI; Volosina; showcake; phive; Nattika; Kenishirotie

مُتْحَف (مَتْحَف)
muthaf (mathaf)
museum

عِيدُ الْحُبّ
çiidu -l-hub-b
Valentine's Day

كُنَافَة
kunaafah
kunafa

عُمْلَةٌ وَرَقِيَّة
çumlatun waraqiy-yah
paper currency

نَاطِحَةُ سَحَاب
naatihatu sahaab
skyscraper

مَدِينَة
madiinah
city

مَبْنًى سَكَنِيّ
mabnan sakaniy-y
apartment building